1959

Stress and Your Child

A Parent's Guide to Symptoms, Strategies and Benefits

Ruth P. Arent, M.A., M.S.W.

Prentice-Hall, Inc.   Englewood Cliffs, New Jersey

Prentice-Hall International, Inc., *London*
Prentice-Hall of Australia, Pty. Ltd., *Sydney*
Prentice-Hall Canada Inc., *Toronto*
Prentice-Hall of India Private Ltd., *New Delhi*
Prentice-Hall of Japan, Inc., *Tokyo*
Prentice-Hall of Southeast Asia Pte. Ltd., *Singapore*
Whitehall Books, Ltd., *Wellington, New Zealand*
Editora Prentice-Hall do Brasil, Ltda., *Rio de Janeiro*

©1984 by
Prentice-Hall, Inc.
Englewood Cliffs, N.J.

Fourth Printing . . . . . December 1987

Illustrations by
Sally Arent McCain

Library of Congress Cataloging in Publication Data

Arent, Ruth P.
Stress and your child.

Bibliography
Includes index.
1. Stress in children.   2. Family.   3. Child
rearing.   I. Title.
BF723.S75A74.   1984   155.4   84-13373

ISBN 0-13-852708-3

ISBN 0-13-852666-4 {PBK}

Printed in the United States of America

Introduction

Growing up isn't easy. Being a parent isn't a piece of cake. It takes a lot of love to help your children in these complicated times—and adolescents are considered children, too. There are too many lessons to learn and too many teachers. Every adult is a teacher, and the TV set and movie screen are, too. The lessons are contradictory and inconsistent. The children get confused. They are faced with all kinds of expectations to which they cannot always measure up. They are in stress. They need a lot of help. Parents welcome suggestions in order to give the help that their children must have.

A WORKABLE DEFINITION OF STRESS: AN EMOTIONAL CONDITION

The word *stress* is part of the working vocabulary of the structural engineer. It can mean how much strain there is in a structural part of a building. Our body chemistry responds to stress as we adapt to everyday life. In this book, I use an easy-to-understand, workable definition of stress.

Good stress is the pressure or emotional condition that inspires children to finish a lesson, do well in sports, or learn to play a musical instrument. It motivates people to be active, to maintain a positive attitude, to work hard, and to benefit from happy relationships and successes.

Painful stress is the emotional condition that one feels when it is necessary to cope with unsettling, frustrating or harmful situations. It is a disturbing sense of helplessness, perhaps futility, that one feels when there are a number of problems to solve. It is uncomfortable. It can create uncertainty and self-doubt. The situations, called stressors, may or may not be overwhelming. Even stress that is painful may have benefits. Those benefits play an important part in this book.

Stress is a normal part of growing up. There are (1) common or predictable, and (2) unpredictable stressors. I have grouped or classified these as (1) non-traumatic and (2) traumatic.

The common or non-traumatic stressors come from family relationships, school, friendships, teenage acne, physical handicaps, and chronic illnesses. Also included are stressors resulting from poverty, personal problems, religion, and others.

The unpredictable or traumatic stressors are sudden or severe. These include divorce, death, violence or abuse, and accidents.

Many stressors are compounded by a second or a third. A family may have to move because Dad loses his job. The damage to Dad's self-esteem may affect his relationship with all the members of the family. He becomes irritable—even brutal. Mother becomes over-protective of the children. The children pick up on ways to survive. They are adaptable and they care. They will make amazing adjustments if they are certain that they are loved and if you allow them to be children.

The adjustments that the children make demonstrate a coping style. A successful coping style is a way of behaving that reduces painful stress or enhances good stress. An unsuccessful coping style leaves the person feeling incompetent, uncomfortable, frustrated, or disappointed. This book is intended to support parents as their children learn to cope with stress—not to point a finger at parents in a scolding way.

Symptoms of Stress

Indicators of stress are called symptoms. They include both the emotional response to the stressor and the behavior that follows. Symptoms will vary from child to child and from situation to situation. If the symptoms are exaggerated, prolonged, or debilitating, they will not just disappear, nor will the child grow out of them. The more observant you are, the more readily you will be able to identify the symptoms of stress. This book describes signals to look for that denote stress.

In everyday life, there is no way to measure the level of adrenalin that is produced by the body as a child goes from one situation to another. Riding the school bus may be fun and relatively stress free, but entering the class to deal with an angry teacher, or facing the fact that the homework never got done, may bring on noticeable or even vivid stress reactions. Emotions and behaviors rather than the physiology of stress reactions are the concerns of this book.

There is no stress test to determine the stress level of the reader or the children. Rather, the suggestions are geared to helping parents help their children cope with situations that are stressful to them, regardless of how others might react in the same circumstances. Parental divorce may be a major source of stress to some children, while for others it may be such a relief that the stress level drops considerably.

Build a Strong Foundation

A strong foundation provides parents with much-needed confidence. The foundation starts with parental self-acceptance, an understanding of stress, and strategies to make good things happen. The suggestions herein can be useful if you select and improvise from them effectively.
Everyone needs to be reminded to:

• Accept the fact that no one is perfect.

- Remember that first babies are the practice kids!
- Get in touch with your common sense!
- Let go of constant self-criticism.
- Enjoy your children most of the time!
- Feel confident that most kids will get along fine even though they may annoy you or may not come through as good students, steady workers, or beauty queens.
- Accept the tough times along with the easy ones—the kids have to and so do you.
- Express love—it helps to prevent stress.

Every day cannot be Mother's Day or Father's Day with an assortment of nice messages to you, but now and then your kids will tell you how much they love you or how special you are. Welcome those spontaneous expressions! They tell you that all's well in your relationship. This is their way of saying, "Thanks for all your help!"

Ruth P. Arent

Acknowledgments

The love and efforts of many persons are woven into the fabric of this book. I am grateful to all of them—my family, friends, colleagues, teachers, students, and clients. Each of them, knowingly or unknowingly, shared a thought, experience, or question that fostered my momentum to continue the task.

All four of my children—Peggy, Sally, Bonnie, and Doug—have given me an endless supply of faith and encouragement. My husband, Merton Anderson, has been ever so patient.

I am particularly indebted to three persons—to Berniece Antonio who typed the manuscript with such good humor despite the primitive quality of early drafts, to Donald L. Lorenz for his support and endless hours of invaluable help with the detailed organizational work, and to Barbara D. Aiton who provided so many good ideas along with her editing talents and contagious optimism. Thank you all. You have been wonderful associates.

This book is written so that children like my granddaughter, Alexandra, may find love and listen to love—wherever they may be.

Contents

PART III   THE TRAUMATIC SOURCES OF STRESS

PART IV   STRESS TAKES ITS TOLL

PART I

Parents Can Help

What Parents Want For Their Children

Parents are happy when their kids are happy. When the children seem unhappy, parents react quickly. "What's the matter, son?" "What's happened, Ellen?" The questions could be "Why are you under stress?"

Parents want only good stress for the family and that's not possible. But four universal desires for children are obtainable: (1) joy of life, (2) the ability to trust, (3) self-esteem, and (4) the ability to cope successfully.

JOY OF LIFE

The joy of life is something children learn from you. It is a spirit of adventure, a spontaneous outburst of happiness, and instant reaching out to others—"Gee, you look nice today," or "I like the color of your hair!" or "You were thoughtful to hold the door for that lady who was pushing a stroller." The joy of life includes a love of learning and excitement from many different experiences.

TRUST

Children learn trust at home. Trust requires that parents be discreet—that they do not tell the children's carefully shared secrets, or report details of the children's sayings or actions which might be embarrassing. Trust tells the child his folks are humane and respectful. Trust builds from secure bonds. Babies and little ones feel safe when they are totally dependent. Older children feel safe as they struggle to become independent. They trust that their parents will understand when they make mistakes or misbehave. Without trust, every experience is rife with stress.

SELF-ESTEEM

Self-esteem is a major goal. It is the base from which the child's ability to cope with stress will grow. The person with a healthy sense of self-esteem realizes that no one is loved and approved by everybody. He or she will be able to have ideals, interests, enthusiasms, and likes or dislikes without looking to others for commendation. The person with healthy self-esteem is not afraid of failure and finds happiness in many relationships or activities. The child will develop a tolerance for frustration and learn to accept that every person does some things well and others less successfully. They like themselves, like being different from others, and do not find it necessary to be competitive all of the time. The person with healthy self-esteem expresses emotions and shows concern for others.

We will take a closer look at what children need in order to build and maintain healthy self-esteem in Section II, #4. Suggestions for parents are included. In brief, close bonds, flexibility, and an understanding of differences are among the most important elements.

THE ABILITY TO COPE SUCCESSFULLY

The ability to cope successfully is a major goal. Successful coping styles are ways of handling situations, stressful or not, without undue discomfort. They are successful when they reduce painful stress.

Self-esteem greatly affects one's coping style. Each person has his or her own way to deal with pressures and problems. An individual coping style denotes attitudes such as:

- "I can do it."
- "No, I can't."
- "It's their fault, let them fix it."
- "They always want me to do the hard stuff and I'm no good at it."
- "I don't like being around people, they make me nervous."
- "Please help me."
- "Leave me alone."

The child with healthy self-esteem handles situations with confidence. The better a child copes, the more self-confident he or she will become.

Erik Erickson maintains that a child's response to events or circumstances cannot reach beyond his or her stage of development. This provides parents with a fundamental guideline: Don't expect your child to act like an adult in response to stress.

A coping style is not planned. It develops from many experiences and interactions with other people. Without thinking about it, we learn what works for us and what doesn't work, what leaves us feeling happy and successful, and what leaves us feeling frustrated, cheated, and disrespected. Someone may say, "I automatically shut up when my father expresses an opinion!" The message behind this coping style is, "If I argue with him, it will end up in a quarrel, and I will feel guilty and angry. That is not what I want."

Children don't dissect their feelings. They are impulsive, direct, and spontaneous. They learn to be selective in how they handle situations. Parents need to help them see what selections they make and reinforce the ones which have worked to help the child feel happy and competent. (Details on how to do this are found in Section II, #4.)

Young Barney, age eleven, is an angry boy. He has always thought he was an unwanted kid. He displays his anger in many ways. When playing dodge ball on the playground, he intends to hurt others. When teachers question his tardiness, he is rude and sullen. He copes in a self-defeating way. He has no friends and no sense of pride.

Young Fred, who has healthy self-esteem, is bright and cheerful. He occasionally teases the other kids, shows off, talks a lot, but his cheerfulness is contagious. When confronted with a stressful situation, he seems confident. He recently broke his hand but coped by riding his bike one-handed and holding his cast as high as possible.

Jenny is walking along and sees a snake. She's afraid. She can cope by running away, screaming, calling for help, picking up a rock and throwing it at the snake, or standing still. Although Jenny is class president and a student leader, she still hates snakes. In this situation, she copes by running away. Her self-esteem is not endangered. Jenny's encounter with the snake was mighty stressful to her! She doesn't usually avoid stressors. Children cope more successfully in some situations than in others.

It is all very well to read that when the going gets tough, the tough get going, but it takes years to get tough. All the strategies in this book are bent on helping you find ways to guide your children through stressful situations so that each will develop responses that provide feelings of success.

What Parents Need to Do: Parenting Skills that Work

Your purpose as a parent is to help your children achieve a healthy self-esteem and a successful coping style.

1. TAKE CARE OF YOURSELF

You must first take care of yourself. This requires that you

* Become self-aware.
* Be assertive.
* Accept the rights and privileges of parents.

Each of these requirements is defined in this section and the appropriate and necessary strategies to employ with your children are described.

Become Self-Aware

Self-awareness does not require Freudian analysis. It is a practical description, a sketch of you that establishes your individuality. Your children take you as their models. They reflect your emotions. They learn to relate as you show them how to. That is why your self-awareness is so important. When you demonstrate that you like yourself, you show your children a model of healthy self-esteem. As you confront stressors, the children will observe your successful coping style. Your self-inventory might answer questions such as

* Do I find it difficult to express my feelings and emotions?
* Do I show that I don't like to be touched?
* Am I inconsistent, too rigid or demanding with myself or the children?
* Do I begin things which I fail to finish?

- Do I enjoy life? Do I smile, laugh, and giggle?
- Am I frequently disappointed by what the children do or fail to do? How do I show it?
- Am I as assertive as I would like to be? Do I let people walk all over me or do I get too bossy? When I am bossy, do I tend to be sarcastic or very critical?
- Am I creative or am I inordinately the same in the way I run my home, wear my hair, fix meals, answer the telephone?
- Do the children complain that I don't care how they work out their fights with their friends?
- Do people call me loving or do they see me as cold?
- Do I take time to watch a sunset or enjoy music?
- Do I give praise? How?
- Am I very patient or do I have a short temper? Do I feel or show anger a lot?

After taking your personal inventory, you may feel relaxed and satisfied that you measure up quite well to your ideal of a person and a parent. The answers with which you do not feel comfortable may cause stress for yourself and for your children as well. You may be telling yourself, "I should be more expressive," or "I guess I really expect too much from my two year old!"

You may feel tension if you don't measure up to your ideal, so here are some suggestions which you may find useful.

Take the first example: "Do I find it difficult to express my feelings and emotions?" You recognize that an essential part of helping children deal with stress is to urge them to express their emotions. This aspect of stress management in your family needs a lot of hard work on everyone's part.

Consider This List of Emotions or Feelings

Love	Bitterness	Concern
Jealousy	Fear	Uninvolvement
Forgiveness	Unhappiness	Depression
Frustration	Pleasure	Guilt
Loneliness	Anger	Relief
Impatience	Enthusiasm	Uneasiness
Happiness	Compassion	Joy
Worry	Disappointment	Restlessness
Excitement	Delight	

Picture yourself expressing any of these emotions or feelings. Watch yourself in the mirror. Listen to your voice on a tape. Notice how people react to what you say. Listen when your child says, "Mom, when you're worried, you don't talk to anybody. I don't know if you are mad at me or worried about something." Ask a friend to describe how you express your feelings. "Helen, I have never seen you show enthusiasm. You smile briefly when I give you good news. You smile briefly if the children bring home good grades. You never say 'That's great' or 'I'm proud of you.' I wish you could show excitement—give a big hug or use different words!"

It takes practice to

- Accept a description of yourself.
- Read or ask for suggestions from someone close to you.
- Figure out how to change.
- Implement the change.

Choose only one or two feelings to work on at a time. Take disappointment and pleasure, for example. You will begin to feel comfortable when you can express your true feelings in these areas. If you choose to concentrate on anger, describe the ways that you express it. Look at such habits as making belittling remarks or sarcastic comments, clamming up, slapping, scowling, hitting furniture, or walking away. The children get the picture that you are angry. They want to know what made you angry. Your anger results in many unanswered questions and this adds to stress. Discussing the issues alleviates stress.

Feelings can be seen but not heard! Feelings can be heard but not seen! Your kids will sparkle when you sparkle! Practice talking about feelings with your children.

Consider a happy, positive example from your self-inventory, such as, "I am very patient." What a nice way to describe yourself! Suppose your little girl spills flour all over the kitchen floor. You may want to bark at her, but instead you say, "Why, it looks like snow and winter is my favorite season!" You clean up the mess together. You are aware that the child feels guilty—she didn't spill the flour to make you mad. Are you aware that the impatient mom or dad might have spanked, yelled, or sent the child to bed?

Be assertive

From your self-awareness inventory, perhaps you have been reminded that assertiveness is a problem for you. Assertiveness is essential. Again, children will take you as their model.

There are four characteristics of an assertive person.

(1) You are your own best friend. You do what you want to do because you want to do it—as long as no one else will be hurt. You don't do what you do not want to do and you feel comfortable about this. It is okay to like yourself.

(2) You are a good communicator with family friends or strangers. You tell the truth, express feelings, and are a good listener. You give others the freedom to be themselves. This lets you be yourself and still communicate love, caring, concern, and respect.

(3) You go after what is important to you. You don't sit back and just hope that you will get a new job; you pursue it. You don't just hope that your new acquaintance will become a friend or lover; you take the initiative, extend a welcome to the relationship, and follow up on it.

(4) You are able to consider the needs of others but do not let their needs run your life. You make your wishes known. You feel comfortable with the decisions and choices that you make and realize that you cannot always get what you want.

Many books provide the how-to steps for achieving assertiveness, including *Don't Say Yes When You Want To Say No* by Herbert Fensterheim, Ph.D., and Jean Baer; *Your Perfect Right* and *Stand Up, Speak Out and Talk Back* by Robert E. Alberti, Ph.D. and Michael L. Emmons, Ph.D.

Assertiveness extends to the way you manage your children. *Take charge.* Children must have this protection although it is hard for some parents to be in charge graciously.

The assertive parent is not reluctant to express opinions, give directions, set limits, or make decisions on his own behalf and on behalf of the family. The intent is to foster respect and provide meaningful guidelines without being overbearing and repressive.

The assertive parent makes certain that the consequences of inappropriate behavior are understood and carried out. This teaches the child to hold back before striking out or even saying things which may require discipline. This pattern gives the child the message that certain behaviors are not acceptable to you and there is a price to pay. It puts the responsibility on the child. *However, the parent is the teacher, the one who establishes the consequences and carries them out.* Certain consequences can be negotiated with older children ahead of time, but the parent must follow them through by cutting the allowance, or making sure the child doesn't watch TV, for example.

When a parent does not take an in-charge position, everyone experiences stress. By being in charge, you are taking care of you.

Let's look at what happened last week at the Murphy residence. Susie took a small cup and threw it at her brother, Sam. Sam wasn't hurt, but he could have been. Susie has to learn that this kind of behavior has consequences, that mother won't ignore it. Susie is sent to her room. Mother uses parental power and takes charge of the tense situation. Mother does not make excuses for Susie. She doesn't say, "Susie is tired today," or, "I'm sorry that she is jealous of her brother."

The in-charge position involves teaching the concept of options or choices. This is useful after age six. David threw a snowball at Billy and hit him in the face. Mother carries out the consequences. David has to come in the house. She introduces options or choices. "Why did you throw the snowball at Billy?" she asks.

"I hate him, he calls me names," David replies. Mother suggests,

- "You could have come to me and *told* me that you hate Billy."
- "You could have thrown a snowball at the fence."
- "You could have gone off and played by yourself."
- "You could have come in the house to watch TV or read."

"But throwing a snowball at him was not okay."

David may say, "I never thought of that—I was mad!" Encouraging self-control is part of Mother's job and the system of repeating the options or choices many times and in many situations, can help David.

Eventually, David will be able to tell his mom, "Guess what? Today when I got mad at Mary, I called her a dumbbell. I wanted to grab her ponytail, but I remembered about *choosing!*" He will learn to choose a behavior, to use self-control.

Options and choices are important. In junior high school years, when some friendships seem quite fragile, the use of options and choices can help prevent some peaks and valleys.

Children learn from your self-control and from your leadership. You would not want them to be compliant 100 percent of the time—and you know that they won't be! They will appreciate that you took charge when they needed you, and that you taught them that parents are strong people.

Accept the Rights and Privileges of Parents

Parents are people, too. You have rights and privileges. You are adults and do not have to justify or defend to your children your every action and decision. When parents are self-accepting, everyone benefits. You have:

- The right to be yourself, with your strengths and weaknesses.
- The right to be spontaneous, to come out with unrehearsed remarks and suggestions.
- The right to know where the kids are going, with whom they will be riding, and when they will be home.
- The right to enjoy the children, baby the babies, and let kids be kids.
- The right to set limits for the good of everyone.
- The right to make decisions without the approval of others. as long as no one is being hurt.

- The right to break promises when necessary.
- The right to change your mind.
- The right to be wrong.
- The right to be taken care of at times.
- The right to realize there are stages in which child-parent anger is to be expected.
- The right to privacy.
- The right to ask for help, without being criticized, when you feel you need it.
- The right to have fun with the kids.
- The right to get involved in the schools that your children attend.

When you maintain your rights, your children can and do learn respect. Respect diminishes stress. You establish the family and the family life. You can feel reasonably confident as you meet the predictable stressors that any family faces.

2. BOND TO THE CHILDREN

After refreshing your memory by reading the self-awareness checklist, it is essential to consider the matter of parent-child *bonding*. Bonds are ties that denote safety. You create bonds by your attentiveness, availability, and emotional responsiveness.

How to Bond to Infants and Toddlers

You can bond to infants and toddlers by

- Affectionate handling.
- Expressions of delight.
- Introduction of limits.
- Verbalizations such as, "I love you," or "You are so important to me."
- Consistency in your attitudes and in the management of the children.
- *Listening* to what children share.
- Observing, and anticipating wants and needs so that the child can *depend* on you.

Parent-child bonds prepare children for intimacy and trust. The child who has suffered impaired bonding has immeasurable stress. Self-esteem is minimal or damaged. This child displays insecurity and a hunger for approval and closeness.

Suppose that you perceive that your children feel detached from you. You may have heard one of them say, "I feel like a piece of furniture around here." You describe family relationships as distant. There are many ways to improve such a situation.

You can start to overcome detachment with affection. Affection builds bonds. Babies thrive on lots of holding and rocking. Older youngsters may want to sit on your lap or cuddle as you read to them.

Not all parents enjoy holding their babies or cuddling. Perhaps touching is a problem for you. You may enjoy the children but remain emotionally aloof. Nevertheless, nonverbal messages communicated through touching must not be overlooked. For older children, you may want to explain why you are not an openly affectionate person, and how you can be very loving without it. "I come from a no-touch family. I never saw my mother and father touch each other." Verbal communication in this situation is *most* important.

Reaffirm your feelings of love with words and availability. Be ready to go over homework problems, mend favorite jeans, prepare cookies for a birthday party, or fix up a doll for show and tell.

How to Bond to Older Children

Offer

(1) A willingness to be unselfish, such as giving up a meeting.

(2) Repeated acknowledgment that the child is genuinely important to you.

(3) A display of habits that support your commitment. You should be on time, go to school, move away from the TV set, and answer the child's questions thoughtfully.

Ties can be started and strengthened at any time. This can be difficult, but the rewards are meaningful. The stronger the bonds, the weaker the stress.

In Section III, there is a further discussion of the relationship between bonds and mutual respect.

3. RECOGNIZE AND ACCEPT YOUR STYLE OF PARENTING

Parenting is complex. Your style of parenting is formed from a combination of beliefs, preferences, aptitudes, experiences, decisions, goals and personalities that have colored your life over the years. There is no magic moment designated as the point at which one can say, "I'm prepared to be a parent now." Inasmuch as self-acceptance plays an important part in how a parent parents, it is worth noting that some people find that they are not as self-accepting as they would like to be. Perhaps this is due to unhealed wounds from childhood. Perhaps this is so for you. You may have known few moments free of stress. However much you may vow not to treat your kids as you were treated, you find that you inevitably repeat the familiar lessons learned from your folks.

Parenting styles may be:

Authoritarian—harsh and rigid, with physical punishment, prolonged isolation, humiliation, strict rules, repressive demands.

Permissive—lots of explanations, excuses, philosophizing and negotiating, few regulations and standards, many freedoms.

Inconsistent—a mixture of harsh and permissive, without predictable pattern, impulsive, impromptu.

Passive—a laissez-faire approach that assumes, "Children will grow out of it," and "Boys will be boys," unexpressive, condescending.

Interfering—exaggerated monitoring of children's behaviors, friendships, school performance.

Overindulgent—parental needs and wishes subjugated to children's demands, few limits, child dominates family.

If love and respect are understood, any style of parenting may be successful.

Let us picture the particular style that Timmy, a five year old, has become accustomed to. Presently he is screaming and throwing things. He is tearful, won't let himself be touched, and is out of control. What will his parents do? Maybe they will be calm. Maybe they will scream, too. Maybe they will talk and talk and talk. Predictably, for this family, the parenting style will be to spank Tim and send him to his room with no TV for a week. Children almost always adjust to their parents' ways of handling them. Timmy's parents, while they are quite strict, still give him a lot of love. He understands that they are strict. He knows he is loved. He feels secure although he displays his temper.

Karlie, aged ten, describes her parents as "laid back." They are loving but can't seem to find the energy to get involved in her activities. At times they seem disinterested. They may not even express an opinion about how she looks, her friends, her teachers, or her school projects. Karlie has no adjustment problems, does not exhibit any symptoms of stress. The style of parenting is accepted even if the child occasionally protests, begging for more vivid interactions.

You may have some concern about your style of parenting. It is best to remember that

(1) A child's self-esteem is determined by an accumulation of life experiences and relationships.

(2) Children will react differently to their parents according to their individual personalities, ages, perceptions of what they think is loving or unloving, feelings about their brothers and sisters, and so forth. Some children are far more flexible and understanding than others. They react differently to parenting styles and to stressors as well.

(3) Children adapt to a predictable way of life. Little ones do not sit in judgment of their parents. If, for example, going to the sitter is their daily routine, they can be most accepting and secure. Older children may complain but still feel secure because their continuous relationship with a mothering person is not in jeopardy.

Give yourself permission to be pleased at how you accept yourself and manage your children!

There are four issues that relate to parental concerns about a style of parenting.

(1) Children's progress towards independence.
(2) Generational differences.
(3) Changes in your style of parenting.
(4) What to do when parents disagree.

Independence

Parents want their children to prepare to leave the nest. Each child will pull away in his or her own way. You may be worried that your style of parenting will push the child out of the nest prematurely or you may feel that you have a tendency to hold a child back. For example, you insist on giving money even though the child wants to earn it. It is natural to be overprotective once in a while. Your style of parenting will determine, in part, how the children progress toward independence. Ties are a two-way connection; you are responsible for the grasp at your end, but the children must hold on or loosen up according to their individual needs. Age has a lot to do with this. The ebb and flow of independence is determined by stress at home. Children may be reluctant to become independent if they feel they are needed or if your style of parenting denotes that you wish or require closeness.

Generational Differences

Don't chide yourself when you do something deliberately different from what your parents might have done. They were people too, living at a different time with different stressors. You may feel critical of them. Remember, most parents do not want to hurt their children. Appreciate today's more candid and open communication. It wasn't the norm when you were younger.

Changes in Your Style of Parenting

Your parenting style may change during times of great stress for you.

In order to protect the family from misunderstanding your changes, get in the habit of sharing facts and explaining feelings. If you are worried because your mother is ill, share this with the children so that if you react by being snappy, they will understand the reason. Otherwise, they may blame themselves or be needlessly unpleasant to you, thus compounding your problem. Don't overreact to your own inconsistencies. Let the children watch your changes as the lion cubs observe their mother become ferocious as she protects the den.

Changes in parenting style may occur as:

- You get older and your needs and values change.
- The children's needs and demands develop.
- Life circumstances dictate, such as a spouse's illness, death, and increased or decreased income.
- You decide to handle things differently by being assertive, less directive, or more sharing, for example.
- You gain insights.
- You become more patient.

No one style of parenting works for all kids all the time. I have four children. I believe that there were times when I had four different styles of parenting depending on the age and needs of the kids. Peggy's needs as a teenager required more direction than her toddler brother required at that time.

What to Do When Parents Disagree

If parents do not agree on what is the best way to handle children, if one is a commando and the other far more reasonable, *children will be aware of the differences and accept them.* Sharply different parenting styles between a mother and a father will not cause the children to experience stress as long as they perceive each parent as loving and consistent in his or her own way. Stress comes when one parent is working against the other. This opens the way to disrespect, disharmony, and manipulation.

Regardless of how you may describe your way of managing kids, please pose these two questions again and again:

"How do I treat the people whom I love?"
and
"Is this a loving way to handle a young person who is dependent on me?"

Certainly there are times when you are frantic, or tired, or mad, and you may say or do something that you regret. That's how it is in most close relationships. *Parents don't have to add to their own stress by picking apart every interaction, every comment, every decision, gesture, or reaction they make.* Accept that your children will often challenge your style of parenting.

Appreciate that nobody is perfect—an old but ever timely truism. All relationships are contaminated by ambivalence at one time or another.

4. BUILD A PLAN

As a parent, you can establish a plan to help your children build and maintain healthy self-esteem and a successful coping style.

Build and Maintain Healthy Self-Esteem

A plan provides guidelines for parent-child interactions that help the children to feel secure and successful. You are encouraged to:

- Express love.
- Be optimistic.
- Help children learn to accept new situations. Help them feel open to meeting new people and seeing new places.
- Help children understand there is no way to be a carbon copy of somebody else. Help your child accept his or her own freckles, smile, talents, interest, personality, temper, likes, and dislikes.
- *Help children handle separations.* Help them understand the difference between separations and rejection. "I love you, but I have to go to work!"
- Help children learn to handle *delays*. Instant gratification is for babies only. If they are going to solve problems and control themselves, they must take time to think through what's best to do.
- Help children accept their own limitations.
- Help children learn to enjoy noncompetitive situations. The self-esteem of a child who has learned to do something because of his or her own efforts is fun to watch. The first time a child can make a tricycle go forward is a real event!
- Help children be aware of what they have learned to do. This includes not only school lessons but sharing, helping others, expressing love, and self-control.
- Help children enjoy winning. Help them learn the attitude "I am a winner!"
- Help children understand that adults have fears, too. Most everyone is shy sometimes, perhaps afraid to speak in front of a group or to demonstrate how to make a toy.
- Provide opportunities for the child to feel successful, without words. When children can climb to the top of the jungle gym or handle the video tape recorder correctly, they internalize such

accomplishments. The older child discovers he can write a computer program or play the guitar.

- Be affectionate. "If my mom kisses me, then I am special to her." Even a fourteen-year-old boy, who outwardly wants no kisses, may announce, "I think I need a back rub." Touching is important.
- Help kids handle a failure as a failure and not as an indication that "I'm no good." Everyone has failed at something. Babe Ruth hit 714 homeruns but he struck out 1330 times as well.
- Remind children that everyone is capable of changing—even their parents!

Build and Maintain a Successful Coping Style

Research psychologists report that a positive personality, a warm, supportive family, and important friends determine how a child copes with stress. I would add age, the impact of past experiences, and any unusual problems. Your role as a supportive parent may be easier if you follow these guidelines:

(1) Remember that children are spontaneous. They are impulsive and unpredictable. By trial and error, they find out which behaviors are acceptable and which don't work for them. They discover that certain behaviors result in stress for everyone.

(2) Children learn that there are many ways to cope. At some time, parents must explain that some stressors will go away: "You won't have the chicken pox forever!" Some will change: "You'll have a new teacher next year." And some won't change: "Mom and Dad will not be living together anymore."

(3) Help children accept that sometimes they will feel babyish and sometimes very grown up. They can accept that in some stressful situations one loses confidence, and in other situations one feels brave and confident. The purpose of a coping style is to eliminate or relieve present anxiety and to prevent the child from adhering to self-defeating or nonproductive responses to stress.

(4) Changing a coping style is not like changing your clothes. It changes as children mature. Changes occur due to circumstances. Children will change as they emulate someone they admire—a parent, teacher, friend or sibling. Also, changes occur when over a period of time the child realizes that he or she is unhappy and wants to do something about it. Lisa has no friends. She can't cope with teasing without making matters worse. She swears, calls out dirty names, and cries. She needs an adult to help her understand about teasing. Together Mom and Lisa can rehearse all kinds of responses. Lisa can change her coping style.

(5) Children need to be dependent. They need to know what you believe and how you handle your anxiety. They want to admire you and the way you cope.

(6) Tolerate changes, they are part of growing up. As a child copes in various ways self-esteem shifts. Show your love to the child. This will enhance self-esteem and help him or her to formulate a personal, workable coping style.

Because some children are more vulnerable to certain stressors than others, it is not possible to pinpoint what strategy a parent should use in a particular situation. You might use any of the following parental strategies.

- Ignore the child's behavior if the child copes with stressors by whining, cajoling, manipulating.
- Confront the child by saying, "I don't like what you are doing."
- Applaud. "You really handled that well! I'm proud that you didn't give in."
- Verbalize. Explain, talk over, and review the source of the stress and the implications. "That is a useless way for you to deal with the problem. Why not try this...?"
- Emote. Show your feelings. Laugh, cry, hug, stroke, pat.
- Reinforce by your actions. Make changes in your attitude, behavior, or the decisions you make. If a teenager has acne, for instance, mother might change menus and available foods to support the child's efforts.

Above all, parents must:

- *Listen*. Don't interrupt.
- *Understand*. Recognize the uniqueness of the situation.
- *Respect* the child's right to do things differently from the way you might.
- *Remember* the times you didn't cope very well! You had a temper tantrum or quit a task!
- *Participate* in the child's decision making.
- *Recognize* your own tolerance level.
- *Describe* your own coping style.

Above all—watch!! Watch how successfully your child relates to people, learns, and shows delight.

Parents as Caretakers: The Art of Child Management

5. THE NEED FOR MUTUAL RESPECT

Mutual respect is the cornerstone of relationships and directly affects the stress level in the family. Parents feel successful when they hear someone comment, "The kids and parents in that family really respect each other!"

Children respect parents when the bonds between parents and children are close and when parents set reasonable limits, and effectively use both discipline and negotiation. Respect begins with the natural awe that children have for adult, parental power. The young child does not understand the word *respect* but knows the concept or feeling. As a small person, the child intuitively defers to the big people. He knows he must listen and obey. Teenagers may rebel against parental authority and still respect their parents. At this stage, they also need to feel *self*-respect, as they develop moral values and act on them. At this point, fear, if it was ever there, may have abated.

Parents, in turn, need to respect children. Parents demonstrate respect for their young when they acknowledge: (1) a child's need to be his or her own person, and (2) a child's right to opinions which differ from his or her parents'.

Mutual respect follows when children and parents accept and acknowledge similar attitudes. Children learn that parents, too, have the right to hold their own opinions and express them, and to set limits for the children—limits that must be respected whether they are, in the kids' judgment, fair or unfair, lenient or harsh.

Mutual respect may prevent or reduce stress. For example, it enhances problem solving. Disrespect creates stress and produces disharmony. Children perceive a lack of respect in many ways. Myra says, "It's like they don't even know *me*," or, "My feelings never count." Don comments, "We're treated like a flock of chickens—give 'em feed and water and put them on the roost." They see a lack of respect when their parents do not get involved in school affairs, homework, and church activities, for instance. Sensitive children may overreact to lack of respect by becoming angry or pulling away.

Children want to respect their parents but sometimes problems get in the way. Among those problems we may see:

- Parents who are unable or unwilling to let the kids be kids. Children learn to ignore demands and commands that they consider outrageous when parents expect them to act like adults.
- Parents who don't like themselves. When children realize this, they feel pity mixed with disrespect. "My dad really puts himself down. I can't believe it when I hear him complain that he doesn't make as much money as a private in the Army and that he has no friends. I feel sorry for him, but I really can't respect his poor-me stuff. He ought to do something about it."
- Parents who have difficulty making decisions. This baffles the kids. "My mom just can't make up her mind and stay with it. I feel sorry for her but I can't respect her. She doesn't know what she wants or how to get it. Last week she hated her job. I don't know where she's coming from. How can you respect somebody like that?"
- Parents who are not assertive. "I can't stand the way my dad just sits there and takes it when my mom is screaming at him about money. I don't respect anybody who is so passive. I just want to shout 'Hey, Dad, stick up for yourself!'" Children admire assertiveness and they learn from it. (See Section II, #1.)
- Parents who are disrespectful to one another and insist on pointing out weaknesses and faults in order to influence the children. "When my mother belittles my dad and then wants me to agree with her I lose respect for her. She'll ask, 'Did you notice that he .... ?' and I'm supposed to put him down, too."

How To Enhance a Child's Respect For His Parents

You can take steps to increase a child's respect for the parents.

- Help children understand the difference between respect and obedience. Define mutual respect so they will understand it. Admit that a lack of respect creates stress for everybody—parents and kids. "Nobody makes me feel important and nobody is important to me." A child must have an adult to respect.
- Teach the child to tolerate personality differences without feeling disrespectful. (If Mom is too aggressive, help the child learn to

accept her as she is, even though she is hard to get along with or embarrasses him in front of his friends. If she is too passive, this, too, must be accepted.)
- Point out admirable qualities of each parent, such as honesty and cleanliness.
- Build respect in one specific area, if not in all areas—for example, in money management or integrity.
- Be optimistic. Learning to feel respectful may take a long time and may be difficult. If a child is critical, remind the child that parents can and do make changes.
- Help teenagers understand that they may learn to respect parent(s) whom they have not respected before. They can let go of the judgments they held against their parents. "I never really liked my dad when I was younger. He was drunk a lot and I couldn't stand the way he yelled at everybody. Now that I'm older, I really respect him. Now he has stopped drinking, controls his temper, and has a much better job. He is quite a guy."
- Above all, set a good example. Show respect for your spouse, other adults and children.

6.   BONDS SUPPORT MUTUAL RESPECT

Meaningful bonds contribute to mutual respect. Parents as caretakers create chains of emotional links with each member of the family. These links can be strong, binding, and supportive or they can be casual, light, and unreliable. Strong links build from being available and from showing you understand and accept a child's emotions. Kids feel unimportant when their feelings seem to fall on deaf ears. Intellectual explanations interfere with accepting emotions. Shared emotions strengthen bonds. Strong links also build from consistency. Inconsistency damages a chain. Weak links undermine mutual respect and create stress.

Parents as caretakers may not want to be close to the children. They may feel managerial without choosing to be a part of all the normal emotional swings that children have. The children feel detached; they experience profound stress. They perceive their parents as observers, not participants. All of their behaviors may be frantic attempts to create strong bonds. They discover that whether they are loving or hateful, their parents respond in the same way. Patients in primal therapy have recalled strong feelings of loneliness dating back to their stroller and high-chair days. Bonding may become a lifelong struggle. Even within the same family, some children feel close to parents while others feel a weak link or insecure bond.

"My parents have never really been there for me," Carolyn, age fourteen, complains to Chris. "It's kinda like I had to bring myself up." Although she has never been abused, Carolyn feels disconnected from her parents, as if she is unimportant. She has learned to cope with her parents and she shows signs of stress. Carolyn craves attachment. She lies. She makes biting and unnecessary remarks. She is a hyped-up kid, always seeking attention. Her posture is dramatic, her words spoken with an air of sophistication and her clothes "punk." She always seems to be on a mad dash to nowhere. It's as if she makes certain that no one will get too close. Carolyn's parents, unavailable emotionally, show no emotions other than anger. They discourage emotional scenes by giving her impersonal intellectual explanations. Carolyn cannot find an emotional rope to hang on to.

Parental detachment is not the child's fault, but some children believe that they created the distance and blame themselves for disharmony and parental callousness. The pattern may be almost identical to the casual, unemotional family life that the parent knew as a child. It is difficult for a child to break through a parental facade. The detachment itself signifies that the adults may have deep-seated problems that prevent closeness and emotional interdependency.

Even though parent-child links may be weak, children can develop strong bonds among themselves. Children learn about "connectedness" from each other and can relate well to friends, and later, lovers and spouses. They may be demanding, seeking nonstop approval and affection, yet they may learn to give emotional support and express themselves effectively.

What the Child Needs

Can Carolyn be helped? If so, by whom? She needs:

- One person who can tolerate her dramatics and whom she can trust to accept her. This trust may take years to build because Carolyn believes that she is unworthy of parental love. She doesn't realize that she is a victim of adult problems.
- To understand what is acceptable and what is not acceptable behavior, and why she turns to lying, attention-getting and provocation.
- To be helped by a professional so that she can *stop* seeking a closeness with her parents. Occasionally, peer confrontations can also be helpful. When she hears repeatedly, "Come off it! We all have to put up with lousy parents," she may be less frantic. She can overcome self-pity. She can learn the painful lesson that her parents are not going to build strong bonds with her and yet

appreciate that they do care for her. More important, she needs to know that she is a worthwhile person. It may take her years to internalize this.

Can Carolyn's mother and father help? They may not help at all. The reasons for the lack of connectedness are complex, and perhaps beyond her parents' comprehension. When she tries to talk to them about it, they get defensive. "Why, Carolyn, how can you say such a thing? We have always taken good care of you!" Carolyn's parents may feel these are adequate bonds and that nothing more is needed. These parents equate "bonding" with "taking care of," not realizing that their style of caretaking is business like, almost formal. Carolyn's stress level will come down when she realizes that:

- She may have to be more independent than she wants to be, but that this may benefit her in many ways.
- Her parents may not change.
- She can be happy. She can overcome this source of stress.
- Her behavior has been dictated by the weak emotional links. Children of parents in an addiction experience similar problems (See Section IX).
- If she wants more affection from her parents, she may have to take the initiative repeatedly, though the response may be unsatisfactory.

In my experience, children who feel "detached" from their parents try to compensate. Some become very close to other adults. Many teenagers become sexually promiscuous. Others become overly concerned with looks and money. They may be high achievers in school in the hopes of getting parental approval and stronger bonds. Without strong bonds, mutual respect is in jeopardy.

You may discover that you tend to explain away every interaction by remarking, "He's too demanding," or, "She can't seem to wait for anything," or, "Justin has an empty bucket. No matter how much love and attention he gets, he's ready for more!" These may be very accurate descriptions. Each, however, may indicate that the child needs more evidence that he or she is important to you. From the child's point of view, your style of parenting has precluded strong links. The child may show respect but does not feel respected.

May I suggest that you take note and answer these questions:

- Do I routinely explain my child's actions or requests to the child before I respond?
- Do I tend to hold back affection?
- Do I tend to control my emotions and even inhibit displays of enthusiasm causing the children to feel discounted?

Most Families Have Strong Bonds

Unlike Carolyn's, most families have strong bonds. With strong bonds, children experience:

- Predictability.
- Trust.
- A sense of solidarity that carries them through stressful as well as the good times.
- A two-way road whereby the adults listen and respond to the feelings of the children and the children listen and respond to the feelings of their parents.

Children in healthy bonding situations can feel:

- Compassion for others who do not have such support.
- A loyalty that is not undermined even in times of stress.
- Emotional links that can survive even if the parental relationship is torn apart.
- Security to be their own persons, with the freedom to express their individuality.
- A willingness to take risks, a lesson learned from their parents.

7. LIMITS CONTRIBUTE TO MUTUAL RESPECT

Limits are an important part of caretaking. They enhance and stabilize relationships. A child feels your lack of respect when you set limits that aren't adequately explained and thus seem unfair.

Quality of Limits

These questions are clues to the quality of the limits that you set.

- Do your kids complain that you say "No" to an endless number of requests?
- Do you consider yourself a very strict parent?
- Do you take the time to explain your limits (except during a crisis)?
- Do your children have a chance to complain, protest, and ask for more consideration?
- Do your children push until you change your mind?
- Are you ever unfair?
- What kind of comments do you hear from the other kids, or their parents, about the limits that you set?
- Do you use words such as "appropriate," "mannerly," "polite," "mature," "immature," "considerate," "inconsiderate," and assume

that these words make the limits acceptable to the kids? (These words are not likely to comfort the kids when they feel your lack of respect.)
- Are you reluctant to set different limits for each child, adjusted to age?
- Do you tend to be more lenient with one of the children?
- Do you and your spouse agree on limits?
- What happens if you don't agree?
- Do the children try to play one of you against the other?
- Do you frequently feel that you are at the end of your rope and (impulsively) impose a limit that you regret later on?
- What happens then?
- Are you comfortable with apologies?

Your answers to these questions set the stage for changes, necessary in order to build respect. An honest analysis of your answers can help you establish a sense of fairness and still support your take-charge style of management. Without fairness, mutual respect will not grow or survive. Fairness keeps relationships harmonious and stressors to a minimum.

Consider Elaine's case. Elaine is nine and has a problem. Her mother comes home tired and wants a few minutes alone to read the mail, change her clothes, talk on the phone, or perhaps have a glass of wine. This is the routine in the home for fifteen to twenty minutes each afternoon. Mother wants quiet time. She sets this limit. Still, day after day, Elaine rebels. She has so much to tell about school and her Brownie troop. Elaine has learning disabilities and is impulsive. She is unable to respond to words like "fair" and "unfair" as many children do. When she hears her mother say "It's only fair that I have my alone time," she doesn't grasp the intention. She sees the limits her mother sets as mean and rejecting. She does not understand the need for structure and privacy. However, if she continues to misconstrue her mother's need for a short time alone—and to interfere with it—she will be confused about limits and may have problems with all authority persons. Her disrespect is a direct result of her confusion. Still, mother must be consistent. Elaine will learn.

Gary wants to go see a *Star Wars* movie for the third time. His mother says, "You've already seen it twice. Why do you have to see it again? It is expensive and I don't have the time to drive you back and forth." Gary could pay for half of it with Christmas money from his grandparents. His mother still insists that twice is enough. Gary says his friend has seen it six times and thinks his mom is unreasonable and arbitrary. He calls her all kinds of unpleasant names and is openly disrespectful. Mrs. Blake wants Gary's respect. She begins to doubt her position. If she backs down, she demonstrates that she can be manipulated. If she doesn't back down, she knows Gary will be sulky and insulting for days. She is concerned that Mr. Blake, when he gets home, will side with Gary and criticize her in front of her son, who will then become even more disrespectful.

Matters That Need To Be Considered

In this situation, there are several factors to take into account.

- Gary's mother has the right to say "No" in this situation. The child is not going to be seriously deprived if he doesn't get to see the movie a third time. He won't lose friends over it. Very simply, Gary just isn't going to get his own way.
- Mrs. Blake has explained about money and the transportation problem.
- The limit is not one of safety but one of consideration for the parent and possibly the family's financial concerns. These are valid limits that carry important lessons. Gary may protest, but his only concern is his pleasure. At other times, this may sway Mrs. Blake to make alternate arrangements or decide to spend the money.
- Mrs. Blake dreads what will happen when her husband comes home and scolds her for being unfair. He models disrespect. This Mom-against-Dad conflict interferes with most limits she sets. Gary takes advantage of it as frequently as possible. The parents' differences negate respect on everyone's part.
- Mrs. Blake may get depressed because she swims in uncertainty. She questions the limit that she has set.

Mrs. Blake ends up feeling guilty only because she did not bend on a limit that she had set.

Gary may be angry today. He is showing that he is selfish, critical and unfeeling. But later, as Mrs. Blake continues to uphold limits, Gary will become appreciative and respectful.

Both of these examples are commonplace. Lists of limits are endless. They add up to what children are and are not permitted to do. Limits can be very specific, such as, "You may watch this program on TV and *only* this one," and might involve food selection, time spent on the phone, clothes that can be worn, vocabulary that is or is not acceptable. Some families abound in limits. Others leave more of the choices and decisions up to the children. Children do adapt to the parents' style of parenting, of which limit-setting is an important characteristic. Young children usually obey. As children mature, they can accept limits without undue stress or find ways to encourage parents to change.

Limits Go Beyond a Contribution to Mutual Respect

Limits are safety zones. Limits show that parents care. This reduces stress. Announce your limits carefully! Assess how the limits you set effect mutual respect among all the members of the family.

8. BE COMFORTABLE AS A DISCIPLINARIAN

Discipline is important when a child oversteps or violates a limit, and is absolutely essential when children are too young to understand words. It helps the child learn self-control. Self-control, in turn, provides two important things—self-assurance and self-respect. The child learns to appreciate and respect the parent for being a disciplinarian. Fair discipline is something children recognize. They talk about it to their friends. "My mom wouldn't let me get away with that!" or "Dad thinks it's best for me to get home by nine. When I'm late, I know that he won't let me go next time."

Discipline spells out: We mean what we say, and we care. It enhances the Parent-in-Charge position that children need. *It can always be changed, revised, or improved.*

Discipline becomes a source of stress if: (1) it becomes harsh, demeaning punishment which the child cannot understand or considers blatantly unfair; or (2) it is weak, inconsistent, or even nonexistent. Unless a child learns to anticipate discipline or management, he or she will feel stress. A child cannot figure out all the "yes" and "no" answers of the world alone. Without guidance, which encompasses discipline, the child has no one to respect and consequently may feel unloved. Severely emotionally-disturbed children show that they have not had to learn and live by limits or were unable to do so. They are impulsive. Almost without exception, they feel cheated and unloved.

In order to build respect through discipline, a parent must bear in mind that:

- The age, understanding and personality of the child will determine what works and what does not work.
- Words, scolding, may be useful as discipline for one child and not useful for another. Some kids must experience other consequences such as removal from the room, loss of allowance, or reduced play or TV time. "Making the punishment fit the crime" is hard to apply in this day of many options. Let us suppose that Hank was watching TV and started a fight with his brother. His mother tries to reason with him, tells him that they could take turns choosing which channel to watch. Hank snaps "Butt out, Mom, it's none of your business!" No kid should talk to his mom like that! What

discipline would make sense in this situation? Hank is a big fourteen-year old; his mother is not going to wash his mouth out with soap! She will probably choose to send him to his room.

- Consistency builds respect. If misbehavior warrants discipline one time, it warrants it again and again. When a child can predict the discipline, this provides security and respect and serves to inhibit forbidden behaviors.
- The expression, "I can love you and at the same time disapprove of what you do," suggests a valid approach. The parents' love is unconditional and is not withdrawn when a child misbehaves. If a toddler violates a rule and jeopardizes his safety—running into a busy street, for example—spanking may be the only thing he can understand. Administer it lightly. He'll get the message.
- Consider common problems of name-calling. Don't get mad and swear at the child or explode with, "You stupid, thoughtless, no-good kid." Such explosions can sting for a long time, sometimes for a lifetime. Sarcasm has the same effect. They do not build respect.
- Some impulsive physical punishments—slaps, spanks, or pushing—may be forgotten and forgiven more readily than put-downs and insulting names. Discipline is used to build respect as well as character, but it is not an appropriate avenue for adults to vent their disappointments and frustrations.
- Avoid embarrassing your child in front of his friends. I recall when I was a child and would invite my friends to stay overnight. Again and again, in front of my friends, I would be sent to my room because I had been sassy or annoying. I learned not to invite anyone because I was not willing to take the chance of being humiliated. Humiliation does not enhance respect.
- After an incident, provide a chance for the child to talk over with you whether he or she thought you were fair or unfair. Discipline must point the way to improvements. That is one of its most important benefits. If discipline prevents improvements, or creates resentment and fear, don't look for respect.

If discipline is too severe,* these may be the symptoms of stress:

- The child seems very angry a lot of the time.
- The child becomes sneaky in order to avoid getting punished.
- The child cowers or cringes, reminding you of a dog with his tail between his legs.

---

* This is not to be confused with beatings and abuse. It is discipline that is humiliating and consistently out of proportion to the wrongdoing, such as grounding for six months for telling a lie or no TV for a week because the child was five minutes late.

- The child becomes very passive, almost listless, ultracompliant.
- The child threatens to run away from home—or worse, does so.
- The child acts as if you are a dangerous person, someone to be feared.

Discipline to support mutual respect is necessary. If your child does overreact, showing symptoms of stress, you may want to discuss the problem with a professional. Your realization of your child's perceptions and your understanding of his or her needs may encourage you to make changes. Discipline is just one aspect of your relationship with your child and is one of the easiest to assess and remodel.

9. NEGOTIATION BUILDS MUTUAL RESPECT

Some disciplinary patterns can be negotiated with your children. Together, you can decide appropriate consequences for various misdeeds. It takes time to develop the art of negotiating with children. Negotiations are important not only because they can repair problems, but because they can also prevent them. Negotiation builds and maintains mutual respect. *The message behind negotiation is: you are important to me!* It is particularly important to try to anticipate what will need to be negotiated.

How to Negotiate With Your Children

(1) Present the problem to be solved or the need for a plan. "We are arguing too much about feeding the dog. What do you think we can do about this?" or "I need to be away next weekend. I want to decide with you which sitter to hire or what arrangements would be best."

(2) Allow the children to make suggestions. Listen with an open mind. Then share your thoughts or ideas.

(3) Together discuss the pros and cons and together decide what to do. If the plan is a rubber stamp of your ideas and excludes all the suggestions that the children made, be sure that you let them express their feelings. If you are only giving lip service to the children's input, the children will sense that the negotiations are fraudulent. This undermines respect. Use negotiations only when you are open to ideas or suggestions which may not agree with yours. When children have input and then experience the plan or witness improvement in the problem, respect is enhanced and stress is prevented or reduced.

(4) Specify the areas in which you are *not* willing to negotiate, such as disciplinary consequences for some misbehaviors.

Items to Negotiate

Bedtimes	Smoking
TV	Allowances—amount and how spent
Household chores	Babysitting
Tidiness	Grades at school
Bathing	Boundaries in the neighborhood
	Number of dates

Remind the children that situations will come up for which no one is prepared. That's part of living together. Children can be enormously forgiving.

Benefits of Negotiations

The main benefit of negotiation is that it provides a way for kids to ask for changes and for parents to ask for changes, too.

As a parent, insist on your rights: the right to be arbitrary sometimes; the right to be human; the right to make mistakes; the right to be in charge.

PART II

Stress Enters the Picture: Non-Traumatic Sources of Stress

Some children are more affected by stress than others. Some are more vulnerable and fragile. Others seem strong and flamboyant. Nevertheless, every child must handle stress.

This part of the book is concerned with the common or predictable stressors. I have called them non-traumatic. This is an arbitrary label because what may be non-traumatic for one person may be traumatic for another. The stressors in Part II are differentiated from the stressors in Part III (traumatic) because they are not sudden and severe. Most of the stressors in Part II are chronic or universal.

Ages and Stages: Generic Sources of Stress

10. WELCOMING THE NEWBORN: STRESS AND DEVELOPMENT TO AGE FIVE

There is a group of psychologists today whose work demonstrates that children experience stress in the uterus. More important, the time of delivery can be perceived as responsible for significant personality problems and anxiety. These ideas, expressed by primal therapists, build from the thinking of Carl Jung. He believed that the initial separation from the mother drives the child from birth on to seek that original comfort, reassurance, and sense of closeness. Called the search for the safety of the womb, it becomes an important cause of stress. These theories may be true to a point, yet people still find happiness and develop loving relationships without intensive therapy. It is as if we are endowed from birth with an ability to absorb some pain and some tensions.

I have observed many newborns in hospital nurseries. Some were born with the benefit of modern methods—minimal or no anaesthetic for the mother, father's participation, warm blankets, head covers, delayed placental severance. Some of the babies were hyperactive and cried a lot. Some were placid. So it was, too, with babies born in the more traditional methods. Among newborns in rooms with their mothers, there was a range of activity, both restless and relaxed. *Each baby seemed to display his or her own personality right from the start*. Stress, defined in this book as undue pressure or frustration from internal or external causes, could make newborns cry a lot and seem unduly irritable or jumpy. Internal sensitivity, due to immaturity, may account for their difficulties in adjusting to the world outside the uterus. A few may have suffered because of maternal illnesses such as malnutrition or fetal alcohol syndrome.

Pregnancy and the early months of a baby's life may have had a special meaning for you and your partner. Perhaps the most remarkable adjustment you had to make was realizing that you would never be childless again! During the pregnancy, the father-to-be may have felt left out while the pregnant mother-to-be had the advantage of experiencing many changes in herself, and the physical togetherness with the baby. At the same time, parental bonds were building through joint anticipation, planning, worrying, and dreaming. Although research about prenatal emotions is underway, as yet it is not clear that parental relationships result in newborn stress.

New moms and dads are excited and edgy. Generally both experience an intense desire to nurture even though some relate to tiny infants better than others.

Both parents need support. Here are some things you can do to minimize your stress:

- Remember that babies have individual personalities. Some may be more responsive than others. Don't put yourself down because the baby cries. Babies cry from internal stress. Infants are hard to please for any number of reasons.

- If you are well organized, you may feel stress because there is no way to predict when your baby will be awake and demanding or for how long. You may experiment with feeding schedules and feel frustrated when you discover that they work only when a baby is old enough for them to work!

- Take care of yourself. Let some tasks and chores go! It is okay for the dust to settle on the furniture. Dishes can wait for tomorrow morning. Frozen dinners can be delicious.

- Get as much help as you can from grandparents, paid helpers, friends, and neighbors. Let Grandma rock the baby. Welcome those casseroles!

- Sharing baby care is rewarding. Don't overlook your needs and the needs of your spouse. This can be a good time to enrich your marriage.

- Do take time to fondle, rock, sing, and talk to the baby! Remember that infant care is a loving process, properly flavored with delicacies.

- Try to maintain your friendships, especially with other couples who were in a Lamaze class with you or who have young children. Your feelings of, "This is more than I can handle," will diminish when others are reassuring. Stress-free parents tend to have stress-free infants.

11. PARENTING THE YOUNG CHILD—INFANCY TO AGE FIVE

Healthy babies have good days and bad days. Some are more temperamental than others. Some get the colic and some don't. Some are more alert and ready to learn than others.

Between 4½ months and 2 years, all babies will cut teeth, handle spoons, strive for independence, become demanding, etc. Mother will have become a love object, someone indispensable. Surrounded by interest and protectiveness, your child begins to feel secure as a member of the family. While restrictions may provoke a temper tantrum, your child is in love with the world and works hard to develop a sense of self.

Even though there may be episodes of kicking, screaming, sulking, and wailing, children continue to thrive. The screaming might be considered a symptom of momentary stress but should not be considered a sign of maladjustment or emotional trouble. Little folks react vividly to frustrations. A child facing insurmountable stressors, on the other hand, will display significant, repeated, profound, or debilitating symptoms. Perhaps the most significant symptom is the failure to thrive—seen primarily when a child is abused or neglected, or seriously ill physically.

The Era of Experimentation: Benchmarks of Child Development*

Infants and toddlers rarely show profound stress if they are well and if their needs are met. They may fuss when cutting teeth or be impossibly demanding for a day or so after getting a shot, but they are not constantly upset. They may discover that if they protest about settling down for a nap, someone will rescue them, but this is not to be construed as a significant symptom of stress. As a parent, it is reassuring to know that children go through ages and stages and at any one time may display mature and immature behaviors.

Understand that fears, too, are a natural part of the world of the preschool child. We hear about their imaginary playmates—bears under the bed, the "Wicked Witch," and other creatures. These are honest fears. They serve a useful purpose as they help children to distinguish between reality and fantasy. The imaginary bear may haunt the bedroom although no other fears are displayed. What should the parent do? Trust that the make-believe character will eventually fade away. In order to help, leave a night light on, or rearrange the furniture, or allow the child to sleep in a different room for a while. If sleeping patterns are seriously disturbed, you may want to look for other stressors and consult the pediatrician or family doctor. There will seldom be a need for this.

Bathroom routines become important as a child develops. They do

---

*For more detail regarding developments, needs or problems, refer to Gesell and Ilg *Your Child from One to 5 Years* (1946); B. Spock *Baby and Child Care* (1957).

not have to be a source of stress causing the child to have undue fear of the rushing water or such problems as severe constipation. Developmentally, children enjoy feeling competent. They feel competent when they use the toilet. Parents need to have patience. Some youngsters are ready to try this control as young as fourteen months. Others will lumber along until almost four years. You may get tired of diapers and soiled pants, but a child can become potty-trained without unnecessary stress for anyone.

A Child Without Symptoms of Stress: Well-Baby Behaviors

This checklist can help reassure you that your child has progressed through normal developmental stages without unusual symptoms of stress.

Routines

Eating—The child eats most foods, tries to be tidy, has likes and dislikes.

Naps and bedtimes—The child seldom protests, has only occasional nightmares, is comfortable with favorite toys or blankets, and after infancy usually sleeps through the night.

Toilet and bath—There are no problems here, no fears or resistance. Occasional bedwetting may still occur.

Nervous habits—While the child may suck his thumb or chew nails or fingers when upset, there are no ticks, cringing, or soiling.

Social behaviors—Your boy or girl has worked through stages of clinging, is independent, curious, friendly, somewhat affectionate. He or she understands about taking turns, sharing, being friendly. The child accepts changes easily and enjoys grandparents, teachers, other people and places. The child is outgoing and playful, assertive but not overly aggressive. The child may be selective about playmates.

Intellectual development—He registers excitement in new things, explores, questions, remembers well, understands about feelings and that people are sometimes happy and sometimes sad, sometimes afraid and sometimes angry.

Self-control—There are few, if any, temper outbursts. The child accepts limits or recovers rapidly from protests. The child uses words rather than hands or fists in order to express anger.

Most important, you see your child as responsive and happy. You would not describe your Billy or Becky as a child in stress!

I like the statement that Dr. Spock* wrote about your baby's development. "He's repeating the whole history of the human race." He

---

*Spock, Dr. B., *Baby and Child Care*, 1957, page 223-224.

also wrote, "Every baby's face is different from every other's. In the same way, every baby's pattern of development is different. Love and enjoy your child for what he or she is, for what he looks like, for what he does, and forget about the qualities that he doesn't have .... The child who is appreciated for what he is, even if he is homely, or clumsy, or slow, will grow up with confidence in himself, and be happy. He will have a spirit that will make the best of what he has and of all the opportunities that come his way. He will make light of any 'handicaps.'" Such eloquent support is intended to encourage you to enjoy your child without undue stress or anxiety.

Strategies for Support

Let's suppose, however, that there have been some problems, and Billy or Becky show certain symptoms of stress. The child may seem unhappy most of the time or have difficulties sleeping, or display nervous habits or marked signs of anxiety. These strategies may help.

- Remember that children are resilient. They can also be forgiving. Affection from you, lots of it, can rescue a stressful situation, especially if there has been a shortage of attention because of your personal turmoil.
- Keep in mind that you can change. I have great faith that people can change. That is why I am a therapist. You may want to ask for help or read up on a subject to help you find a direction to follow. No matter what changes may be needed, remember that the child's stress level will diminish when you consistently display that "You are important to me."
- Ask yourself if you take the time to keep your child informed of your plans. If you move too rapidly from one obligation to another or bounce into a spontaneous social engagement without taking time to brief your child, the youngster may feel discarded and unimportant. Even little ones must have attention and honesty.
- If you are concerned about a symptom that you see, make certain, before you decide that he or she is in stress, that the child does not have some medical problem. Remember that most young children do not experience tumult. They are always learning ways to express themselves and fend for themselves. One strength builds on another. Maturation and development combine to produce successful coping patterns. Maintain a positive attitude.

These early ages and stages may be called the Era of Experimentation. You are experimenting to develop a workable formula for parenting and the children are experimenting with life.

12. PARENTING THE SCHOOL-AGED CHILD— FIVE TO TWELVE YEARS OF AGE

As your child zooms into school-aged years together you will face new ups and downs. Express your interest in daily activities and be certain to learn the names of their friends and their teachers. (See Section IX, #43, where school problems are described in detail.)

Childhood Friendships

Childhood friendships are major sources of stress which need parental wisdom and love. When peer relationships are happy, all is well. When they are not happy, the world is coming to an end. To a child, it is a mini-tragedy when he or she is not invited to a birthday party or when no one will sit next to him or her on the school bus.

Parents can teach their kids how to get and keep friends

Even first graders can understand some of the concepts. Older youngsters have no difficulty at all.

Ask your children: Can you keep a secret? Encourage your child to respect a friend's plea to "Please don't tell anybody." Too many times, spreading stories or telling secrets leads to a fight and the end of a friendship. Trust is a word a youngster can learn.

Ask your children: Do you share your feelings as well as your toys? Do your children and their friends tell each other when something makes them happy, sad, disappointed, or angry? Remind them that everyone has good days and bad days, in and out of school. Understanding that, they won't let someone else's bad day cause them stress. Help them find ways to be loving and understanding with their friends. Teach them to express their thanks when their friends give them support.

Ask your children: Must everybody like you? Help them understand that they don't have to like everybody and everybody doesn't have to like them. People are different; some will enjoy each other and some won't. It's best to avoid people you dislike. There is no need to be nasty. (See indicators of healthy self-esteem, Section I.)

Ask your children: Do you try to be just like your friend? You may notice that Sarah and Sue daily wear the same color sweaters, and identical socks. This may remind you of when you did the same thing! You may want to say something about being an individual, but dressing alike is a badge of friendship, seldom a symptom of stress.

Ask your children: Do you worry that your best friend won't be your best friend anymore? Why? Because he walked off the playground with somebody else? This may be unnecessary stress. Help your children learn to share their friends. No one owns anybody else and most kids have lots of friends.

Ask your children: Does being popular mean giving in to peer pressure? Explain that even though someone may try to talk you into doing something you don't want to do, you don't have to do it! Everybody wants to be popular but that doesn't require you to give up your opinions or to act like all the others. It may be hard not to go along with what kids tell you to do. Your best friends will understand. If your child is very popular others may expect or ask too much. It can feel scary to have so much power over other kids. Help your child to use power to keep relationships harmonious and communications open.

Ask your children: What do you do when you get into a fight with your friends? Be prepared for an assortment of answers. Remind them that relationships have their ups and downs. Most friendships, even in elementary school, can withstand fights. Young children generally recover from an episode more rapidly than their parents do. It depends on the personality of the child; a few bear grudges for a long time. Suppose Dudley and John had a fight. John called Dudley a punk and said he was stupid and a rotten friend. Dudley's feelings were hurt for days. If he habitually complains about the treatment he gets from others, he is playing a role called "victim." Is this important to him? Is being alone and angry what he really enjoys? Is this his way of getting special attention from you? These may be symptoms of stress. Dudley may not be self-accepting; he retreats from any name calling, disharmony, or rejection. Dudley may need special encouragement, even help, if he bears a grudge for weeks. Fights between friends are part of growing up.

Ask your children: Are there gangs in your class? Are you a member of a gang? During elementary school years, many children are introduced to cliques and even gangs. When they are part of a gang, they feel protected and secure. Still, gangs create stress. Gang membership changes because children are fickle. A kid pushed out may feel destroyed. Outsiders find it hard to handle rejection. Louie may announce, "I wouldn't hang around with those kids for *anything*," and Laurie may say, "They're snobs," but each feels unwanted.

In mixed neighborhoods, gangs may form on the basis of racial or ethnic backgrounds. The issues are complex. For some children, the gang is family. Parents are away; without the gang they would be lonely and afraid. Groups form alliances against other groups; the intensity of threats and fights, even among little people, create stress. The problems are hard to handle. Parents, teachers, and kids need to work together to try to set and enforce rules so that no one gets hurt. It may help if teachers mix groups in the classrooms. Yet, no one can actually choose another's friends.

At the elementary school level, adults can influence some of the gang practices and occasionally persuade the leaders to invite certain outsiders to join. Adolescent or street gangs seldom respect adult interference.

Are gangs or cliques a source of stress for your child? Is it primarily a group of giggly girls who hang out together to talk about boys? Is the group together in a lot of classes as high achievers, reluctant learners, or some such? How do members decide who is in and who is out? Does he or she have a best friend or any friends outside the group? *You have a right to know and to express your opinion.* You may want to demand that your child pull away, but it is virtually impossible to monitor who your child spends time with at school. Remember that most cliques come and go; they usually change as the kids mature.

A best friend is a child's best resource in his social world. The gang or clique they choose to be in may not be too influential because they have each other. This provides leverage if you want to encourage the twosome to pull away from the clique for reasons you have discussed. Parents need to teach the care and feeding of friendships.

Sources of stress facing the child five to twelve years of age:

- The influence of older kids is imposed on young ones. The sixth-grade-girl insists on high heels, makeup and values such as being thin and being cool. The result may be stress for all. Little girls are not mature enough to cope with sexual come-ons that may be expected from provocative makeup and clothing. Parents are caught in a bind. If you say "No," there may be clashes at home. If you say "Yes," you may give your blessing to a situation which may foster problems at school or on the street.
- The influence of affluence. Children of wealthy parents become confused about what is important and what is not important. Some have never had to take responsibility for anything. Some have learned to care more about things than people. Some may try to buy friendships and experience immeasurable stress and uncertainty in their relationships. (See Section X, #44.)
- Girls are maturing at an earlier age. Puberty starts earlier accompanied by pre-adolescent emotional swings. Some girls begin menstruation at nine years of age. They may be self-conscious because they have larger breasts than the other girls in the class. Many girls in the fifth grade might be labeled "adolescents" because of their physical development. Yet they are treated like little fifth-grade kids by teachers and older children, and this causes a great deal of stress. Their self-images may become uncertain; they may become depressed and defensive. They want

to go unnoticed, hate to be different, but their bodies and emotions *are* more mature and this causes stress. Parents must take time to visit school and observe the other kids in order to give support at home.

- The child begins to use logic; parental magic diminishes. The child under seven, even when he is testy or rebellious, has an underlying confidence that parents are right. This faith in parents prevents a lot of stress. At the same time, the child may believe that a family tragedy happened because he had been naughty or done something his parents did not want him to do. Around age twelve, the child may be expected to question parental magic. Without realizing it, the child begins to question the faith in his parents that has been so all-important. He or she begins to use logic. It is as if, in the developmental process itself, a bit of the secure foundation has been chipped away. It amounts to an invisible source of stress, an artifact of a stage of growth.

- Television creates turmoil. TV contributes to stressful parent-child confrontations. Children may easily become addicted to TV and parents struggle to control how much they watch and the shows that they select. Children need help to understand that commercials intend to *sell*, not necessarily to present facts with any objectivity. Kids want the merchandise—a lot of it. They can't have it all, and this causes misunderstandings between children and their parents. When the children emulate weird decisions that heroes or heroines make, there is relatively little a parent can do. This may result in crude gestures, words, and behaviors. Parent-child stress is, in effect, *imposed* on the family. (See Section IX, #42.)

- Children become more perceptive, more inquisitive, and more aware of family and social problems. They begin to experience anxiety from uncertainties that they were never mature enough to understand before. They confront issues about job changes, separation, divorce, death, violence or illness. They watch the news and hear about race riots, the problems of American Indians, rapes, murders, kidnappings, and they want reassurance. Children become fearful. In helping your child manage stress that stems from family or social issues, make certain that you do not make guarantees that you cannot back up. Provide very specific cautions, limits, and guidelines to establish as safe a lifestyle as possible—what streets to go on, when to be home, not to talk to strangers. Social and family problems can be confronted with honesty and definitiveness accompanied by love and affection. It is best to be explicit as you take time to let the children ask many questions and express their fears.

The Child Without Symptoms of Stress: Well-Child Behaviors

This checklist can help reassure you that your child has progressed through normal developmental stages without unusual symptoms of stress (five- to twelve-year-old).*

Routines

Eating—appetite varies, sometimes disinterested in food, not obsessed with weight or size, mostly enjoys eating.

Bedtime—no significant problems, no more bedwetting accidents, may still want favorite toys or blankets, occasionally wants to be in bed with parents or siblings.

Toilet and bath—no problems, wants to be very independent, modesty begins.

Nervous habits—has learned to handle worries by asking questions, as attention span has lengthened seems more patient and composed.

Social behaviors—friends have become very important, some teachers very important also. Less demanding home, willing to share with siblings more readily, strong sense of fairness and unfairness.

Intellectual development—many special interests. Uses explanations and reasoning to avoid or recover from some emotional scenes, such as "I couldn't help it" or "At least I didn't get mad" as examples. Wants to know a lot about his parents when they went to school, reads a lot, watches a lot of TV, likes school.

Self-control—very individual profile; some children passive, others very explosive. Most require very little discipline, want to be liked by parents.

There is an all-pervasive attitude of, "I'm proud of my family." The children have learned to accept their family lifestyle and its various rules and regulations. At our house, we had a trampoline with strict rules for its use. Children in this age range seldom questioned the rules.

Children with problems, barring extreme circumstances, improve rapidly if given warm help. They learn to utilize their maturing ability to conceptualize, understand cause and effect, and to take responsibility for what they say and do.

---

*You are encouraged to refer to Gesell and Ilg, *The Child from Five to Ten*.

13.   PARENTING THE ADOLESCENT

Adolescence As a Source of Stress

Adolescents tell the truth. Just give them a chance to ask and answer questions and express their feelings. They will tell you about the things they like and the things they hate. They have great wisdom and sensitivity. They may be impulsive and dramatic. They want to be happy. They want relationships that count. They want to feel free to make their own mistakes and want to know that you are behind them, no matter what.

Adolescents' search for self-awareness goes on twenty-four hours a day. They want to face their own problems. They want help only when they ask for it.

Why should it be difficult to live with a person with such a purpose in life? What causes so much misunderstanding and stress? Why do adolescents have so many difficulties adjusting to self-imposed demands and demands from you, from friends, school, and from the mixed-up society in which we live? Why... or better yet, why not?

Adolescents are still kids though commonly cheated of childhood.

They are bombarded by confused values and the raw material of relationships and human weaknesses which were not splattered in front of teenagers twenty or twenty-five years ago. They are not protected from painful situations and issues which were sanctified and kept away from kids. They act out in order to discover who they are, what works in society, and what doesn't work. They do not act out to hurt you. They may get mad at you and call you filthy words, which is their vivid way of showing, "This is what I think. This is how I feel, and I am not proud of *me* right now."

These actions create stress for all because relationships abound in uncertainty, anger, and inconsistencies, but this boy or girl wants limits, restrictions, management, discipline, and occasional punishment. When the adolescent feels awkward or unattractive, he or she wants reassurance. He or she wants secretiveness to be respected. Stress results from contradictions, emotional ups and downs, confused or unformulated values, and physical tensions.

Adolescence as a developmental stage is, in itself, a *source* of stress. Stress is a way of life for most parents and teenage kids; no one is at fault. These are times of ambivalence in the parent-child relationship. The parent must be the steady fulcrum that keeps the see-saw of ambivalence from falling over.

For some teenagers, these also are the happiest years of their lives. They love school, friends, the band, babysitting, their new clothes, and the family lifestyle. They have a sense of self that smooths rough times.

They have developed a coping style that works.

Developmental struggles of adolescents can be classified as personal, interpersonal, and societal.

The Adolescent's Personal Concerns as Sources of Stress

(1) Growing at a different rate from classmates causes stress. If development is more rapid than others, he or she may be physically ready to associate with older persons, yet emotionally and socially still too young. That youngster is like a fish out of water. The fourteen-year-old boy who is six feet tall does not feel welcome with high school juniors of his size. Adolescents whose development is slower than average feel alienated. Most of their classmates are interested in the opposite sex, dating, talking about going steady, and sex, while they may not be interested at all. At the same time, they may not enjoy the company of younger children. Isolation may result. The late bloomers feel abnormal and stress results.

(2) The belief that he or she is unattractive causes stress. Adolescents overreact to every pimple. They become addicted to the bathroom scale. Suggestions for skin care or diet may start arguments, some of which may escalate to threats to run away from home. They can become socially immobilized, convinced that they will never attract a mate. Some serious problems may result in socialization and eating disorders, or impaired school achievement.

(3) Peer pressure is a source of stress. At times, teenagers do not want to emulate their friends, but are afraid to stand up for their own ideas. This results in stress.

If the group lifestyle is described as "living in the fast lane" with drugs, booze, kinky sex, disrespect for any authority, and minimal interest in school, it may be hard to break away. At the same time, if the person is too rigid, too nice, too reliable, too studious, this may lead to isolation, limited friendships or lack of spontaneity. Standing apart from friends or changing friends compounds stress. Moving from a familiar lifestyle to an unfamiliar pattern is not easy at all, especially at this age.

(4) Searching for values is a source of stress. This encompasses the issues of smoking pot, using drugs, sexual activities, and jobs, as well as the desire to be both independent and dependent at the same time. Two major questions cause considerable stress: "Why am I doing (not doing) this?" and, "Who am I anyway?" The few years prior to adolescence are usually harmonious. The boy or girl may become idealistic. Now, the pull away from parents may result in strong feelings of anger and disgust which create pain and anxiety. The adolescent examines his or her decisions from the perspective of, "What would my mom or dad think

about this?" As the teenager attempts to become free of parental influence and adjust to personal values, impulses, and desires, stress will become a way of life.

(5) Fears about sexuality cause stress. Fears about one's adequacy as a sexual partner and all the complexities that supposedly will have to be faced may be overwhelming for some teenagers. Today's trend to open discussion about sex, plus pornography, sex role options and the confusion about gay/lesbian issues present questions that the adolescent is intent on answering. Early experimentation may add to stress.

The Adolescent's Interpersonal Concerns as Sources of Stress

(1) Peer acceptance causes stressful situations. The teenager feels inadequate and unrehearsed about how to get in and out of relationships. He or she is trying to determine whether a problem is his or her own or belongs to somebody else. Let's suppose that Mary makes a spiteful or biting remark to Diana. Diana's feelings are hurt. Rather than think "Oh, Mary, she always makes unkind remarks," Diana asks herself, "What did I do? What did I not do?" Then Diana may talk to others about what happened. She tries to decide, "What do I do now?" This problem with Mary interferes with studying and sleeping. Diana is under a lot of stress even though Mary's anger is Mary's problem. Since both Diana and Mary are teenagers, moments and incidents of scrapping or discomfort are to be expected. The ups and downs of relationships cause stress because peer acceptance is a must.

(2) Teacher-student relationships cause stress. Because teachers in high schools may be impersonal, students feel unimportant and for many this causes stress. They wonder whether they, the teacher, or the system is to blame. It is particularly difficult for students who have moved from a relatively small middle school or junior high school to a large, consolidated high school. Many adjust smoothly, but for some there is a considerable period of stress while trying to adjust to instructors who teach subjects, not kids. Most students do not become close to a member of the faculty. (See Section IX, #43 about school.)

(3) Parental attitudes cause stress. A teenager is vulnerable to a parent's criticism, such as, "Oh, grow up!" If the child has been free to make a lot of decisions, this remark is heard as a censure. The implication is that previous behaviors are no longer acceptable, but the criticism doesn't tell how to change. If the teenager has been in a strict home, the "Oh, grow up!" comment is heard as a command. The implication is that parents are no longer willing to permit the child to be so dependent. In both instances, the adolescent is heading down an unfamiliar path strewn with new expectations and rules. This creates stress.

The Adolescent's Societal Concerns as Sources of Stress

(1) School is a societal concern because it involves many people, rules, regulations, requirements, and relationships. (See Section IX, #43.) Stress from school may build or destroy a teenager's self-esteem; this is a high price to pay for a diploma. Handling failure, disrespect, or rejection by dropping out, is a self-defeating way to cope with stress.

Those who handle stress from school in a constructive way are the motivated students who get good grades, become leaders, and are outstanding in athletics and school activities. How the student copes depends on the individual, the school environment, the involvement of the parents, and the learning skills and habits of the child.

School used to be seen as a dress rehearsal for the real world, although the environment was geared to teenagers and their needs. Today, the outside world neglects and discounts the youth. The people in positions of authority in the high school want to prepare students for productive lives, and it is frustrating for all that today it is impossible to come up with any guarantees. This affects a student's attitude toward high school and causes stress.

School may be a haven for some middle-school-aged teenagers, especially if there are serious problems at home. They may thrive in the less personal school climate, enjoying the freedom that comes with promotion from the elementary classrooms. Nevertheless, school is a proving ground and a battle ground rife with possibilities; it often falls short of its potential as a place where students can grow and mature.

Teachers, counselors and administrators can help students deal with stress. Many are dedicated, loving and supportive. However, students tend to short-change themselves by failing to relate to these people because they transfer their pull-away from parents to school personnel. This, in turn, affects their learning and exacerbates stress.

(2) The lack of jobs is a major source of stress. Statistics show that black and Hispanic youths have the most difficulty securing employment. College students across the country have the same complaints. Teenagers who plan to enter the professions face years of training and internships on their way to becoming financially independent. For many this necessitates postponement of having a family, and creates other problems. Self-esteem suffers with economic insecurity or forced dependency.

(3) Military service is presented as a secure place to be. The prospect of leaving home and facing possible active duty appeals to some and frightens others. While a voluntary program is less stressful than conscription or a mandatory draft, the unknowns of military life create stress for all members of the family.

(4) Social problems are sources of stress. Alcoholism, violence,

poverty, pollution, or starvation are examples of causes which commonly produce adolescent anxiety. Drinking, for instance, is not just a personal problem. Each year over half of all auto deaths, two-thirds of all murders, countless other acts of violence, and acute family problems are alcohol related. An estimated 500,000 teenagers are alcoholics. Issues such as poverty and unemployment are more pressing than ever, especially if it is the adolescent's mother or father who is feeling destroyed because no job is available. When your son or daughter dwells on societal problems, hear the stress behind the questions, "What is ahead for me?" or, "What chance have I got?" Hear their pleas for you to make suggestions. Help them to make a commitment to self-improvement or involvement on behalf of society. Teenagers frequently become excellent volunteers in many agencies or settings. Such service denotes a reasonable way to cope with certain stressors.

Symptoms of Stress Teenagers Display

While some teenagers are more vulnerable to stress than others, when symptoms begin to show they are apt to be dramatic and persistent. Often, they are the culmination of years of undiscernible stress.

Routines:

Eating—overeats, starves self, vomits compulsively.

Bedtimes—sleeps too much (missing school, escaping social life), screams, has nightmares, refuses to sleep except in short naps, or under duress; needs sedatives, pills, or alcohol to relax; afraid of quiet—insists on TV, radio or stereo.

Toilet or bath (shower)—is compulsively clean or dirty, severely constipated, or has problem diarrhea.

Nervous habits—has ticks, pulls hair, bites nails, handles parts of the body compulsively, cries very, very easily.

Social behavior—is extremely withdrawn or extremely aggressive, out of control, talks about hating people, wants to be violent, defiant to the point of breaking the law, steals, destroys property, runs away (or threatens to), feels unwanted, can't be alone, feels extreme self-pity or suspiciousness.

Intellectual—quits school, turns off to learning or is obsessed with academic success, refuses to read, watches TV indiscriminately.

Self-control—is unusually controlled or uncontrolled; demonstrates exaggerated or sporadic behavior, perhaps drug or alcohol induced; has temper tantrums; self-destructive behaviors—cuts, pills, unusual accidents.

Activities—is totally disinterested or totally absorbed.

Others—makes self-derogatory remarks such as "I'm ugly," or "My nose is too big," or "I hate red hair;" has a persistent "I can't do it" attitude; needs to blame others for all problems.

As a parent, you may observe symptoms and pass them off as transitory teenage problems. Be conservative, discuss your observations with your child and propose changes or improvements.

If societal issues such as jobs are the stressors, be honest, if not unrealistically encouraging. Point out his or her strengths and help picture how to benefit from them.

Strategies For Support

Routines:

Eating—Parental lectures usually do not help. Many teenagers with weight problems today want counsel from a doctor. Many—especially those with anorexia or bulimia—are secretive. Tell the child that you know what is going on. Offer to get help. Avoid buying some foods, such as sweets. Teenagers resent monitoring. Assume an in-charge attitude when necessary. You may have to take your teenager to the doctor against his or her will if you can't get cooperation.

Sleep—Spend time with your son or daughter before bedtime and talk over problems, gossip, make plans, help with school work. This closeness can offset some stress which causes sleep problems. Often, anxiety about sexuality disturbs sleep. Keep discussions about sex open, reassuring, and confidential.

Toilet or bath—Most teenagers are very private about these matters. Girls may be particularly reluctant to discuss personal hygiene. If the teenage girl is tense at night, suggest that a bubble bath may be a great place to read or study.

Nervous habits—Unless severe, ignore them. Adolescent girls may cry easily.

Social behaviors—These are the most vivid symptoms of stress, with the exception of self-destructive behaviors. They may be the most difficult for a parent to work with. If discipline is indicated, remember that it must be programmed to the individual. Grounding may be of little avail. Taking away allowances usually doesn't help—friends help out and some adolescents may steal. For the middle-school-aged (under fourteen), sometimes moving to a new school is a worthwhile change.

The unhappy teenager with low self-esteem needs parental love and encouragement. Avoid making comparisons with other children. Comparisons only make the fragile teenager feel more fragile and do not inspire a child to change his or her ways. Be open to finding someone to counsel your child.

Intellectual—The teenager in stress may put learning in school at the *bottom* of the list. Talking will not turn this around; he or she has heard your ideas many times before. Parents should insist that the student go to school. By being there, your child is showing some responsibility, which is important, and teacher and peer influence may improve your child's attitude. Ask yourself why your child is disinterested in learning. Is this being confused with not wanting to go to school because of social problems? You need to be both supportive and good-natured about it. A sense of humor can provide momentary release. If the pattern is an escape from social contacts, then that is the issue with which to deal. Most teenagers want to learn, even though some work hard to hide it.

Self-control—It is impossible to regulate someone else's behavior no matter how much you care. Whether prone to temper tantrums, drinking, swearing, or arrogance, self-control is the key. *Be sure that your child understands consequences.* Be assertive in talking about problems. *Your behavior and consistency may help the high school student to manage his or her behavior.* Junior-high teenagers may be more reasonable and more respectful of parental wishes and authority. Set a good example. Keep your temper under control. When your child keeps his cool and doesn't blow up, acknowledge and commend repeatedly.

Regarding self-destructive behavior, remember that these are indicators of *extreme stress*. Take charge. You must be involved, not a bystander waiting to see what will happen next, or if this particular episode is just some silly performance. *Explore* what precipitated the act. Perhaps it was fury over an unfair grade, or impending parental separation. Whatever it was, it was important to your child. Do not embarrass. Do not belittle. Plan the next steps together—talking to a teacher, taking more time to explore feelings about home problems, or lack of friends. If necessary, seek help, the healthy way to confront painful, complicated situations. (See Section XV, #68.)

Activities—Younger teenagers sometimes just want time out from piano lessons or soccer. Find out if this is the case with your child. Often they threaten to quit an activity as a way of checking out how interested you are in what they are doing. Sometimes it is for financial considerations which they have never mentioned to you. They always have a reason, even to the point of saying "Well, Lisa doesn't have to take ballet anymore so I decided to quit, too." Try to insist that children stay with the activity, especially music lessons, because they may be most grateful as adults. It may mean some quarrels, but it reflects your mature judgment. How many of your adult friends have said, "I wish my folks had made me stay with the piano"?

Summary: the strategies for helping adolescents handle stress echo the themes you have read throughout this book.

- Stand firm for what you believe. Children need guidelines, even though they may not comply in some cases.
- Negotiate where meaningful.
- Be available to share facts and feelings.
- Get involved at school—know the teachers, for instance. Be your child's advocate. Recommend schedule changes, classes to take, extra-curricula activities.
- Respect your child's need to be independent and his or her right to make mistakes.
- Be forgiving when necessary, and humble when appropriate.

Three statements provide the foundation for helping your teenagers:

(1) "I love you."
(2) "I realize that you are in stress. I am not going to pretend that I didn't notice."
(3) "I'm sure you will be able to manage your own stress. I'm here to help in any way I can."

Three statements should be avoided:

(1) "You'll get over it."
(2) "When I was your age, I..."
(3) "It's not as bad as you think it is."

Look for changes you need to make. Your teenager may point out that you do need to be more flexible or consistent. Maybe the adolescent needs medical attention. Maybe *you* need to consider a more generous allowance or liberal use of the car.

Ages and stages are the paths that your child must follow to establish his or her own sense of self. Each age and stage will have problems and progressions; they are the generic sources of stress. The changes you make and the improvements your children display in how they cope with stress, are indeed benefits.

The Family as a Source of Stress

14. BASIC CHANGES IN FAMILIES WHICH CREATE STRESS

There is no perfect family constellation. There is no singular right way to be a parent. Neither is it possible for the family of today to emulate the idealized family of the past.

An almost unlimited number of stressors affect family life. Although each child is urged to be his own person, children crave a stable family situation. Even though they hear about many kinds of families, they may cling to the fantasy of the more traditional family constellation. They know about the changes that are taking place—such as divorces, homosexual parents, live-in arrangements—and discover that these changes are not readily accepted and understood by everyone. It is as if they want to know about them, but do not want to be a part of them.

Changes in the middle-class American family reflect pressures from society. The emphasis on material goods and an improved standard of living have usurped the emphasis on interdependent ties and family enterprise. Changes and contemporary contradictions are difficult to manage, and these factors create stress for many. The youngsters are "too old to be so young and too young to be so old." Their childhood is abbreviated. As they contend with adult-like problems, they feel ill-prepared and afraid. Many react with anger to an unstable family life. They feel pushed aside, unnecessary, or overwhelmed.

There are other fundamental changes: (1) Children are considered to be an economic "burden"; (2) Multiple caretakers raise the kids; and (3) The knowledge explosion undermines parents' self-confidence.

An Economic Burden

Children today are often considered an economic "burden" in contrast to being considered the "extra pair of hands" they were in the past.

As family survival shifted from home industry and self-sufficiency to a dependence on others for jobs, income, and economic security, children became considered an expense. One analysis in 1982 concluded that a child born in 1980 will cost $226,000 to feed, clothe, and educate from birth to age eighteen. And that has nothing to do with costs of prenatal and delivery care or special medical needs. For those who can afford them, add music lessons, sports equipment, vacations, then a car and a college education. The decision to have children requires a couple to consider the real issue of expense, where the money will come from, or whether there will be enough money available. Both the parents and the child suffer if there is insufficient money.

When children are considered an economic burden, stress results. Tensions, guilt, anger, and confused values build around the issue of money. "We can't afford that!" "Why are you always asking for something?" "Don't you know that Daddy is worried about money?" "Mom had to go to work or we couldn't buy the new car." Children hear their parents quarreling about expenses. Young children experience stress because they do not understand all the implications and feel helpless to ease the situation.

The single-parent family may be even more stressed about money considerations and the necessity of spending money only on essentials.

Symptoms of Stress

What symptoms of stress may the children show when they perceive themselves as burdens?

- Children may refuse to eat because food is so expensive.
- Youngsters may become obsessed with the idea that they are a burden and may consider self-destruction, thinking, "If I'm not around, that's one less mouth to feed."
- Teenagers may decide that helping with the family income is more important than school. Pre-teenage kids may beg to shovel snow, babysit, or work wherever they can. No matter how much they contribute, they continue to feel guilty and ashamed. At the same time, sophisticated teenagers know that if they earn too much, there may be tax disadvantages which may penalize the family.
- Chronic depression and self-degradation may also show up. Where parents are unemployed (See Section X, #44) the situation is frightening for all. When an affluent family has to shift to a more

moderate lifestyle, the home may abound in misunderstandings and angry relationships.

- Threats to run away may become common.
- Children may reject all gifts and new clothing, demanding hand-me-downs and second-hand items.

Strategies for Support

- Reaffirm that children are loved as people even though economic factors affect family decisions.
- Be discreet about money discussions in front of the children.
- Appreciate children's efforts to ease the situation. Encourage their willingness to wear hand-me-downs and go without extras. Compare your situation with conditions of abject poverty and starvation.
- Try to nullify the TV commercials by showing how *you* decide what to buy.
- Distract the children from dwelling on the subject. Read to them, watch TV with them, do things that are free. Picnic in the park, go to the public library, walk in the woods, stay away from stores, help in a hospital, visit old friends or grandparents (not requiring much gasoline, much less airfare). Such distractions must be enjoyed on a routine basis, not as a "band-aid" to patch up the family after a fight.
- Help the children find ways to amuse themselves without spending money by making homemade toys and decorations made of scraps, for instance.
- Teach children to manage their money. Teach about saving and budgets. Be a model of restraint. Establish policies and values concerning credit buying, high interest rates, and accountability.
- Teach children to share what they otherwise might want only for themselves, such as toys, books, candies, crayons.
- Help children acquire values apart from money. You can be as lovable in a shirt from K-Mart as you can be in a designer cotton. Who needs an alligator or polo pony logo?

The money issue needs to be separated from other matters. (See Section X, #44.) No family is without money considerations. All children benefit when they learn that family ties are more important than the size of the family income.

Multiple Caretakers Raise the Kids

The traditional family is now atypical. Mother has helpers. Child care extends beyond the parents. More than 50 percent of mothers work outside the home. Some estimates are as high as 70 percent. The typical school-aged child has a mother who is outside the home a number of hours a day.

Time spent away from a child can be of great benefit to parents and children. It can also create stress (1) if the parent feels guilty, (2) if the caretakers are not caring, or (3) if there are marked inconsistencies among the caretakers. Inconsistencies cause children to feel unimportant, unloved, and insecure.

Symptoms of Stress

Symptoms of stress usually show up as:

- Prolonged, exaggerated expressions of despair at time of separation.
- Listlessness, failure to show warmth and responsiveness to anyone, even animals.
- Agitation, a sense of continuous discomfort in any setting.
- Physical rejection of any adult; the child doesn't want to he held or kissed.
- Demonstrations of lack of trust of adults, outbursts such as, "You don't care where I am," or, "You never come when you say you will."
- "Sometimes I don't know who my mom is and sometimes I really don't care," is a sign that the child may feel unimportant to all of his or her caretakers.

If such comments or problems occur frequently or consistently, it is essential to discover why the child is so unhappy. You may have to take time to observe closely the interactions between the caretaker and the child as well as to evaluate how much attention you give.

Before reviewing ways to minimize or prevent stress, consider these benefits of a multiple-caretaker way of life.

The Benefits:

- The multiple-caretaker approach can enrich a child's life. Children learn that they can be loved by lots of people! They adjust to various styles of handling and assorted home environments, which may reflect unequal incomes.
- In daycare centers, children are introduced to routines and materials which may abet their future school adjustment.
- For parents, work time, time alone to pursue personal goals, join friends, travel, or accompany a spouse are important.
- The traditional pattern involving "leaving the children with Grandmother" is rare. A business arrangement has benefits. Though caretakers really love children, they may feel free to discipline or

manage them with greater objectivity than a grandmother might. Also, there may be continuity of care. Some children go to the same sitter for years. This provides security. When grandmother, from far away, arrives to babysit or as a visitor or for emergency relief, the children may feel uneasy at first. A grandparent from afar may be more of a stranger than a familiar babysitter.

- Many older babysitters today are surrogate grandparents. They may be free of a lot of pressures that younger sitters face. They may offer tranquility and a mellowed-with-age outlook. They provide a grandparent's approach combined with a businesslike manner. Some, however, may be a bit short-tempered or impatient.

Strategies for Support

- Introduce your children with great care to the sitter before you leave them for the first time. Welcome their questions. "Why is Mrs. Jones so fat?" "Will I call her Mrs. Jones or Martha?" "Does she like to fix spaghetti?" "Will she make me take a nap?" "Will her kids always be there?" "What if I don't like them?" Answer these questions and remain optimistic.
- Inform the sitter about your child. Go beyond name, food dislikes, and when to take naps. Talk about ways your child responds to scoldings and affection. Tell about favorite TV shows, books, activities, and responsibilities. "Patty loves to help set the table while Patrick loves to run errands." This will help to create a sense of comfort and serve as a bridge from home which may help keep stress at a minimum.
- Be sure that your children understand that Mrs. Jones knows what is okay and what is not okay at home. Write down important items such as what you do when Patty hits Patrick, and when Patrick refuses to eat. You cannot remodel the way Mrs. Jones takes care of children, especially if she has her own children and a number of others, but the differences in your styles of caretaking are understood. Children do modify their behavior according to what is expected of them and adjust to different ways of adult handling. There are many successful, useful ways to manage kids and still keep a handle on stress.
- Don't compete with a sitter, day-care center teacher, or other caretaker. Children relate on so many different levels and find different loving qualities. There is no need for you to feel insecure because your child loves his sitter or teacher.
- Don't overinterrogate on a daily basis. It may come through to your child that you are too critical, looking for something with

which to find fault. This is unfair to the sitter and your child.

- Don't overreact to a child's complaints. Many children find fault with almost everything. This can be a symptom of stress. If complaints are real and consistent and you perceive that the child is really unhappy, you should investigate. But bear in mind that children are great manipulators, and complaints are common and predictable.
- Don't continually threaten to "find a better sitter"—one closer to home, less expensive, younger, older, or with fewer kids in the home. Children are entitled to a meaningful attachment to sitters and this may be undermined if they hear that the relationship may be cut off shortly.

Other stress management strategies for the children:

- Infant care. At first, separation may be a major problem, especially if it involves a daily shift from breast feeding at home to bottles at the sitters. Allow enough time. Tell the child that you will be back even though the child is too young to talk.
- Be on time. A child is not clock-conscious but can become very insecure if he or she experiences your absence as unduly long. With toddlers, try to say, "When the sun goes down, I will be back," or, "When you get up from your nap I'll be back." Some children take many weeks to adjust to the pattern of being left and then picked up.
- Let children take familiar clothes and objects with them, or leave some at the sitters. Do not chide if an older youngster wants to bring along a blanket or stuffed animal or doll.

For yourself

- Take time to evaluate the persons or institutions that help bring up your children. Evaluations give you a sense of comfort.
- Get comfortable with the fact that Mrs. Jones handles Patty differently from the way you do. She may be more firm or more permissive. This will not damage your relationship with Patty, or Patty's self-esteem.
- Accept that your child may be closer to a Mrs. Jones than to you. As Patty bursts in the door, she may spontaneously tell Mrs. Jones all about what happened in school today. She may be excited or cry. Mrs. Jones may have the time to listen to every detail. Your time with Patty is a conglomerate of a dozen things to do—the drive home, the mail, phone calls, dinner, dogs and cats, house cleaning, *all the other kids*, homework, bathing, planning, spouse time. Patty has told her stories about school. She has had answers,

questions, sympathy, or encouragement. Is it reasonable to expect her to take time to repeat it with you?
- Let go of some of the responsibilities with the children that you think a mom or dad should have. For example, Patty may enjoy doing her homework with Mrs. Jones.
- Consider letting caretakers go in your place—or with you—to school conferences and school performances, for instance.

Multiple caretakers are part of the new look in the contemporary family. The relationships can enhance your well-being and at the same time meet the needs of your children.

The Knowledge Explosion Undermines Parents' Self-Confidence

The knowledge explosion about child development has influenced family life. The distinction between raising children by the book and raising children by instinct and personal experience is no longer clear. This is confusing for some parents and creates stress. Dr. Spock is a great guide. He provides the Bible of baby care. At the same time, bookshelves abound with other useful guidebooks beginning with pregnancies, home deliveries and midwifery, through all the details of how to provide a maximum, protective environment for your child. Volumes deal with special problems and special situations. While parents are grateful for expert advice, just the availability of so many how-to books imposes feelings of inadequacy. Furthermore, philosophies do vary from permissive to authoritarian, expressive to strict and repressive. It is not always easy to choose one style of parenting and stay with it, nor is it wise to change your style of parenting every time you read something new on the subject.

The knowledge explosion today encompasses professional help for personal problems. Although intended to be a boost to parents, for many it undermines their confidence and becomes a source of stress. No longer are problems within the family sacrosanct and private. Many still regard seeking help from outsiders as a sign of weakness. "If my parents could put up with that, how come I seek help?" If parents observe that the family as a unit or one person in the home is markedly unhappy they feel insecure. Reports from school that Johnny is mischievous are embarrassing. They are not put aside as just a kid acting like a kid. His parents infer that they are being judged as inadequate. They tend to blame Johnny and this further complicates matters. Parents may ask themselves "What's normal behavior anyway? Do we really need to go for help?"

Many parents don't want to admit that they need outside guidance, even from school personnel. Definitions of such terms as emotionally disturbed, learning disabled, or incorrigible are useful. Professional help from psychiatrists, social workers, psychologists, or therapists is essential in some instances. Unfortunately, there are not enough qualified helpers to handle the number of persons needing or wanting their services. Also, help may be too expensive, too far away, or too infrequent to be of benefit. Headline stories of failures reinforce the notion that when a child or family goes for counseling or therapy, it is usually too little and too late. John Hinkley, Jr., who attempted to assassinate President Ronald Reagan, may be a case in point. Scientific definitions of illness or character problems are often too sketchy to offset this erroneous impression. And the process of therapy may be misunderstood or underrated. (See Section XVI, #70.)

When children become involved in peer groups such as Adoptees Anonymous or Alateen, parents may not get involved. This needlessly reinforces parental feelings that they have failed.

Some parents say, "Kids had better learn to be tough. Life isn't always easy and there isn't always someone available to lend a hand." This provides an excuse not to use professional help. A negative attitude toward therapy, professional counseling, or peer support cheats some children of the assistance that may improve a coping style and damaged self-esteem. Parents should welcome assistance that may yield lifelong benefits and strength.

Here are some reminders that may reduce parental stress and therefore benefit everyone.

- Most complexities in society which produce stress are not of your making—economic problems, social tensions, violence, and discrimination, for instance. You and your children are entitled to professional help in order to get a clear perspective about this.
- Competition in schools, on playgrounds, in Little Leagues, at piano recitals, dance contests, and beauty contests affects everyone. Even when you negotiate carefully those activities in which your child participates, stress may result. You have to orchestrate approval and support to offset feelings of incompetence, inadequacy, or arrogance. If your efforts prove ineffective, the support of a counselor, coach, or teacher should be considered.
- If a member of the family is so unhappy that everyone else suffers, professional help can turn things around. One cruel member causes stress for all. It is important to ascertain why the person is obnoxious and find out what to do.
- If a change in the family constellation is recommended which requires one person to leave for a time, this does not mean failure on your part. Intense unhappiness, a symptom of severe stress, has *many* sources. Professionals can suggest and implement a myriad of suggestions to improve situations.

- If you have made a decision, such as to get a divorce, consider consultations with professionals for all the family as stress prevention or reduction. All family members will have deep feelings. (See Section XI.)
- Take the same attitude about professional help for adjustments and stress management as you would about using the skills of a physician to set a broken leg.

Many contemporary family problems have become too complex or severe for amateur solutions. Happily, children have been introduced to counselors, nurses, and special services in schools and clinics, and may encourage their parents to confer with helpers.

All of us want kids to be happy. Accept the fact that kids are not sheltered anymore. David Elkind describes them as "hurried."* TV has preempted the parents' role as the fountain of information. Even though basic changes have caused parents to feel displaced, the expertise of professionals can help to repair the damage. You are encouraged to see professionals as supporters, not as people ready to criticize. Many professionals are parents, too, and they understand about kids and stress.

15. THE LIFESTYLE OF A FAMILY AS A NON-TRAUMATIC SOURCE OF STRESS

Have you heard a friend say, "Our family is just a bunch of individuals living under the same roof?" Or have you listened when someone exclaimed, "We are a close, loving family?" Another person may comment, "We know Dad's the captain and the kids tow the mark." Each is describing the lifestyle of a family—not who makes up the group but the characteristic way the people interact. The lifestyle includes the way the members treat each other. Some are expressive, others reserved, some distant, others intimate. Family holiday traditions and patterns are important in one household while another family is casual, even helter-skelter. A lifestyle encompasses a style of parenting and the varying activities of all family members. "All" may extend to in-laws, cousins, and close friends.

The family lifestyle may be a source of non-traumatic stress. Little Jake is embarrassed to invite his friends to his house because it is a mess. The dishes are not washed and dirty clothes are deposited in piles on the floor. Abby hates to have the kids come over because her grandmother is grouchy. Everyone in the family is tense and irritable.

The family is a social system. Each person is affected by the others. There is always some connectedness. Because it is a system, it means that

---

*See David Elkind, *The Hurried Child*, 1981.

every part is important, just as the heart, lungs, stomach, and brain are all essential parts of the body. Children learn from parents and siblings as they interact in the family system. The system creates stress when the needs of a member are unsatisfied or when arguments, fights, harshness, and hurt feelings result in disharmony and rejection.

At various times every person within a family will experience stress. Both adults and children contribute. Some ride out the storms more easily than others. "We can handle it—all except Becky. She's so hot tempered," or "Paul needs everything planned—the rest of us are spontaneous," may typify a family. Relationships and alliances shift. "This year Ken and Harry seem to be ganging up on Jay. Last year it was Jay and Ken against Harry." Shifts delineate underlying loyalties and love even though certain relationships are stressful at times. The family lifestyle is important because it is describable and familiar.

Some Examples of Lifestyles

The Musical Family

The Martin family life centers around music. The father, Len, plays the clarinet and the oboe, and sings in the church choir. The mom, Nan, plays the piano and accompanies the others. Both girls, Penny and Pam, have become competent violinists, while young Danny enjoys the cello. Sunday evenings are concerts at home. Everyone practices hard and, up to now, looks forward to Sundays.

This family's lifestyle is characterized by common interests, similar routines for the kids, and intense competition. Father and mother still insist on practice and the pattern even though Penny is fifteen and wants to spend more time on studies and with her newly-acquired boyfriend. She says she's done her "music things," and wishes she'd taken up a wind instrument so she could play with the school band. Already, Dan, at age ten, dreams of being a drum major and complains that Dad is too bossy when they all play together.

Potential sources of stress are popping up. Pam feels that she isn't as good as Penny and wants more recognition. More and more frequently she has a Sunday evening "headache" that keeps her from participating or cuts short the concert.

Although the family's lifestyle reflects the parents' enthusiasm, the sources of stress differ for each one. They derive from: (1) the father's authoritarianism, (2) the ages of the children, (3) "too much of a good thing," (4) the competition, (5) one child's becoming rebellious, (6) other interests that have had to be put aside.

Symptoms of stress among the kids include headaches, irritability, and refusal to cooperate. No one is unduly unpleasant, although the sisters criticize each other more and more.

Suggestions may seem obvious to the outsider, but both Mr. and Mrs. Martin want to hang on tenaciously to the family lifestyle. They are quick to say that they have the right to establish patterns and insist that the children stick with them. "It's the least they can do for us. A few hours a week is not much to ask. When they get older, they'll be grateful." It would be appropriate for the parents to try to negotiate. Perhaps the musical evening should be reduced to every other week, or Pam should be allowed to quit for a time. Or the parents could remain determined that the Sunday events shall continue and plea for the children to be "good sports"—pleasant, enthusiastic, and appreciative. There is no guarantee that the children will cooperate. Nonetheless, there is the need for family negotiations in order to reduce stress.

The Martin family's lifestyle provides benefits for all.

- They pride themselves on their knowledge of music and their ability to play well.
- The children feel that their family is very special and tell their friends and acquaintances about their musical way of life.
- The parents have helped the children establish patterns of self-discipline and practice.
- Their proficiency as musicians has prepared the children to participate in fun, rewarding activities such as the band, orchestra, concert bands, or private musical groups.
- They have all learned to love music.

The Angry Family

Everybody in the Swan family is angry. Making sarcastic, biting remarks is their lifestyle. Underneath there is loyalty but all conversations have a sting to them. Outsiders feel uncomfortable. Jeff and Debbie admit that they are embarrassed to bring their friends home. Mother and father are very close. Jeff, the oldest, has had privileges and consideration way beyond what Debbie and Carl have had. The younger two feel as if they are unimportant except to build up Jeff. Jeff monopolizes the conversation. Jeff gets everything he wants. Debbie and Carl have asked, "Why did you bother to have us anyway?" If the family is going out for supper, Jeff gets to choose where they go. Every menu at home is planned around his allergies. Debbie and Carl lean on each other, but most of their conversations are critical and sarcastic, too. One day, Debbie told her friend, "I guess Jeff's happy. And Mom and Dad have a great thing going. But being at home is a drag."

Swan family members are all good workers. Both parents like their jobs and all three kids do well in school, but there is considerable stress in the home because: (1)Parental closeness represents the ideal couple but creates a marked remoteness from the kids; the younger two, in particular, feel unimportant; (2) Jeff, the oldest, appears to be in an alliance with the parents much of the time; (3) The lifestyle is not open to compliments or loving remarks because of the sarcasm and criticism; (4) The younger children can't discuss their problems with their parents. When Debbie, now thirteen, wants to tell her mother about "girl things," she knows that her mother will tell her dad and she'd be embarrassed. There is no privacy with either parent; (5) The younger two, who are constantly compared to Jeff, don't like their brother at all.

Various symptoms of stress show up in the Swan family. Jeff plays up his allergies. Because he is dominating, callous, and obnoxious, he has few friends. His biting remarks are considered cute by his parents but alienate him from others. Debbie has headaches. She is very nervous, tense, and whiny. Carl, now eleven, is withdrawn and unhappy. No one seems to notice him. He excels in school and hides out in his room to study and be alone. He occasionally has trouble with his bowels and has to take mineral oil. He is secretive. He feels it's the only way he can escape the biting remarks. Once in a while he explodes and throws his books around or slams doors.

How can each child be helped and what benefits does this family's life-style provide? Strategies that might help:

- Debbie and Carl might make a conscientious effort to become close to the mother or father of a friend to compensate for the barriers that exist between them and their own parents.
- The children can tell the parents how much the sarcastic remarks really hurt. Expressing their feelings helps, though the remarks continue.
- The children can tell their parents that they are embarrassed to bring their friends home because, "No one ever says anything nice except to Jeff. And no matter what he does, it's so great!"

The benefits are:

- The children are learning that a husband-wife relationship can be fulfilling and happy, even though the children may feel secondary.
- The younger children learn to look to each other for support.
- The importance of doing well in school has been established, perhaps as compensation for little acclaim or praise at home.
- The younger children wisely reach out to non-family people for support.

The Traditional Family

In the Ambrose household, the old pattern is established and maintained that, "Children should be seen and not heard," even in these days of more progressive thinking. Everyone accepts that Mr. Ambrose is the star of the show. His opinions are not to be questioned. Although his prejudices make others uncomfortable, no one dares to challenge him. Mr. Ambrose has worked hard to give the family this home, modest though it is, and he expects his wife and five children to be grateful. The family lifestyle is justified by cliches, such as, "That's how it was when I was growing up and that's how it's going to be here."

The children are trained to be quiet when Daddy is home, to let him dominate the scene, make all the decisions, and be the disciplinarian. Stress comes from the mother's passivity. All five children feel that she's overworked and underappreciated. Stress comes from the feeling that their family is very different from the Macks next door. The Mack kids are allowed to speak up and express their opinions. The Ambrose children, ranging in age from four to seventeen, complain that it is like a prison at home. Stress comes from watching Mrs. Ambrose clench her fists in order to hold back from contradicting her husband when he is too severe. The children are not going to rebel at the system or defend the mother or themselves. They wouldn't dare. All the children love to play together, have friends, enjoy reading and are interested in school.

Some symptoms of stress are evident. Sandy, aged seventeen, talks on the phone to her girlfriends. She became upset when required to write a description of her family for an English class. She urges her mother to speak up for herself but to no avail. Sandy's an anxious girl. She seems to have a lot more fears than most girls her age. She won't date, refuses to socialize with boys at school and is critical of girls who wear tight clothes. She avoids her father as much as possible.

The other Ambrose children show stress by being too dependent. They seem unwilling to make decisions about what to wear and whether their hair is too long. They demand endless help with their homework. They give the details of all the mischief and misdoings at school in order to portray themselves as very straight, almost angelic. They all lack spontaneity. Even the four-year-old has difficulty adjusting to the flow of a nursery school. The lack of a powerful male figure at school bothers him, and he is not willing to touch unfamiliar toys or games. All the children are afraid to express their opinions or ask questions.

Even though the family lifestyle is not going to change, the parents could: (1) Encourage the individuality of each child, even under such a strict family regime. (2) Talk about fears. Help the children understand that feeling protected at home may cause them to exaggerate how bad things are elsewhere. (3) Encourage them to visit in the homes of their friends and to notice that all families have strengths and weaknesses. (4) Point with pride to Dad's accomplishments. (5) Explain that the family is not running any kind of competition with the other families. They like the strict family lifestyle. (6) Reiterate that parents do not want to harm their kids. They do what they know how to do and what they believe is right. (7) Point out that when the kids have their own families they will create family lifestyles, too. (8) Find a way for the children to express their emotions—write poems, make up stories, become absorbed in emotional parent-child series on TV, for instance. When children can express emotions, without causing arguments and fights, stress comes down. (9) Help the children confront the fact that they feel as if mother abandons them when Daddy comes home. This is one predictable aspect of this particular family lifestyle which the children really hate. But there are benefits:

- The lifestyle is predictable.
- Mother and father present a united front.
- All the kids are in the same boat.
- The pattern helps them to understand other families that have similar stressors.
- The children have learned to withstand such peer influences as truancy and drugs. The price of isolation is expensive, but it is beneficial to know limits. Parental disapproval may be scary or repressive but it offers needed guidelines.

Other family patterns

The Fishing Family

This family enjoys trips, loves the outdoors and the whole fishing experience—tying flies, studying water conditions and operating boats.

Sources of Stress	*Benefits*
Too competitive.	Fosters togetherness.
Boring for some.	Unpretentious.
Takes away time from other interests.	Expands interests.
Expensive.	Encourages children to earn money for equipment, thus establishing goal-setting patterns.

The Athletic Family

This family takes sports seriously, goes on team trips, is interested in health, exercise, and fun and makes friends with those of similar persuasion.

Sources of Stress	*Benefits*
Competition may be too intense.	Child-parent participation.
	Children self-disciplined.

Burn-out possible.
Family overly critical of
coaching, refereeing, etc.
Children compelled to live up
to parental expectations.
Other interests crowded out of
their lives.

High standards of
sportsmanship.
Learning life-long skills, such
as tennis, skiing, bowling.
Basis for friendships.

The Funny Family

The funny family enjoys jokes, tricks, laughter, high-spirited get
togethers, and family traditions.

Sources of Stress
Competition.
Cover-up for real feelings.
Intolerance for people who
are somber.
Inappropriate humor—
wrong subject, wrong
place.
Victims—some jokes are
brutal, hurtful.
May be the only level on
which family members
relate.

Benefits
Fun quality of life, a great
reprieve from other stresses.
As performers, feel confident,
poised.
Creativity encouraged.
Learn to applaud each other.
Proud when friends want to come
to their house.
Improve vocabulary.
Extend humor to reading, writing.

The Studious Family

This family enjoys books, classical music, fine art, museums,
lectures, exhibits, a home studio, intellectual conversation, stimulating
friends, school activities such as debate, foreign exchange groups, and
service organizations.

Sources of Stress
Intolerance of less intellectual
families.
Too much criticism of teachers.
Too much seriousness.
Scorn for non-intellectual
activities such as rodeos,
some athletic events, for
instance.
Vocabulary tends to alienate
neighbors, classmates.
Feelings covered up.
Isolation.

Benefits
Lifelong interests, pursuits.
Enriching activities.
Exposure to culture.
Parents giving children
worthwhile values.
Stimulating discussions at
home.

Family Lifestyle: A Recap

The lifestyle, in effect, demonstrates how your personality and philosophies mesh into patterns and habits.

You may want to assess your pattern as a possible source of stress for your children.

Symptoms of Stress

Your answers here provide an inventory of the symptoms of stress that your children may display. Do your children:

- Appear overbearing or too passive?
- Appear detached from you, intent on being too independent?
- Constantly compete with someone else in the family?
- Complain that someone is always critical of their decisions?
- Frequently comment that you are unfair?
- Seem insecure, uncertain because you are too permissive?
- Remark that other kids don't want to come over because, "We are too snobbish?"
- Complain excessively about having to make excuses for the family, parents or brothers and sisters? Do you hear them explain to their friends, "We can't do that because...

My mom would worry."
We have no money."
My dad might lose his job."
We never do anything different."
We'd never be allowed to do that."
Our household is too disorganized."

My brother is on drugs."
We're supposed to be home all the time."
It would take us too long to get ready."
My parents don't understand kids."

- Tend to stay away from home?
- Hang on to illnesses?
- Seem apathetic.

If You Want to Change the Family Lifestyle

(1) Make a list of the "we messages" that describe your family lifestyle.

"We believe the children should earn whatever money they need."
"We use grounding to punish the kids. Nothing else seems to work."
"We watch TV all the time."
"We can talk about anything."
"We are not an affectionate family."
"We never miss church on Sundays."

"We urge the children to bring their friends to the house."

(2) Observe your children. Note how they react when you remark about any of the "we messages." Ask them for their answers to these questions:

Does our family:
- Welcome changes?
  "We like it when Mom introduces new treats for us to eat." "We're going to have family meetings to negotiate jobs. That's new for us. Our parents give us orders about everything and that's going to change."
- Resist changes?
  "Why can't we do things the way we have always done 'em? Eating dinner at the table is stupid. We like to eat in front of the TV."
  "No, I don't want to share my room with Lillian. I like having my own room. Let the others double up."
- Encourage expression of feelings?
  "I like it when Mom and Dad tell us how they feel. We're learning to talk about emotions. Seems like every family should be like ours."
- Encourage talking about needs?
  "We're learning to be sensitive about each others' needs. Now I can understand when Dad says he needs quiet or Jane says she's got to have extra time to fix her hair."
- Handle painful situations such as a death by supporting each other, or toughing it out alone?
  "I notice that Dad pulled away when his father died but Mom seems to like to talk over her feelings with everyone! Dad really got upset when we asked if we could help!"
- Confront each other when we are indirect rather than outspoken?
  "The little guy still tries to whine or beg his way into whatever he wants, but the rest of us have learned to be open. We use the question, 'What's the issue?' a lot because then we don't have to guess about things. We like that."
- Encourage each other to feel comfortable with our different personalities and interests?
  "Mom always tells us, 'Each one of you is different—be proud!' She never makes comparisons. She keeps telling us, 'We don't have any carbon copies around here!'"
- Resist traditions, belittle sentiments?
  "We make a fuss at Christmas but we don't notice birthdays. I'd like to change that around and so I'm going to buy some balloons and decorate the house for Dad's birthday. Maybe I can talk Mom into making a cake!"

"We celebrate everything at our house—even the anniversary of when we got the dog!"

- Seem split or disloyal?

"I hate it when the family seems split. Even when Mom and Dad come at us as the 'grownups,' I feel bad."

"There are so many kids at our house that the big ones hardly know the little ones. They're like strangers."

(3) Talk to the children about these lists and observations. Ask for their ideas on what changes to make and how to make them. Don't defend every "we" statement—especially those that you would justify by saying, "But we have always done it that way," or "I was raised that way and I'm not about to change," or "You will have to convince me to change."

(4) Together select one area for improvement to work on. "Let's cut down the sarcastic remarks!" or "For every sarcastic remark, you will say something nice."

(5) Plan a once-a-week, half-hour time to find out what's happening and how everyone feels about the changes. Praise the kids and save some for yourself, too.

(6) Realistically, because each person will react to the family system in his or her own way, some private agreements will be made and must be respected as such. In private, Mother may urge Father to cut down his praise of Lou's baseball ability because it discourages Jim from playing.

Repeat these six steps as frequently as possible. They reflect your awareness that parts of a complex family lifestyle can change when you make the effort. It is not something that just happens. When the family sets goals and makes an effort to change patterns, everybody benefits and stress is reduced.

In conclusion, you are urged to express your pride in the family, its heritage and traditions. Keep telling yourself that you want your family life to be happy. You know that there may be personality conflicts, that you will hurt when your children fight and are openly hostile to each other. You know each individual will find things to complain about and things to love. Encourage family members to communicate, to share their feelings. It is one good way to prevent or alleviate stress. Make sure that everyone gets the message that in order for a family to run smoothly, each member must assume responsibility.

Every family is unique. There is no such thing as an abnormal family. Single parents, gay or lesbian parents, old/young couples, step-parents, and multi-generation families have one common hope—that there will be love and respect for all. Don't overanalyze all the interactions. Smile when you see the children doing nice things. Praise them and give yourself a pat on the back.

The Individual
in the Family

"Blood is thicker than water"—is that good or bad? Family ties and family relationships are immensely complex and entangled with feelings and expectations, while there is an underlying sense of belonging. "I've always been proud to be a Wilson," Robert tells his friends. "I can't imagine living in another family!"

It is not surprising that many people experience more stress at home than they do with their friends, lovers, classmates or fellow workers. Perhaps it is the intimacy or overexposure that creates tensions and misunderstandings.

Sources of Stress at Home

There will be quarrels. It is as if parts of the webbing snap when kids tease, belittle or compete unnecessarily. Predictably, when one member of the family is in pain, others may hurt, too. If one young child is crying, others may cry as well. Older siblings worry about each other and defend each other against outsiders.

Family standards are stressors. How often have you heard someone say, "I can't do that. What would my family say?" Nobody wants to lose the love of the family or any of its members. Yet it may be difficult to consider family standards and at the same time foster your personal interests and values. Maintaining your own individuality becomes a stressor. Each person may find that his or her interests or personality is not readily understood and accepted by Mom, Dad, Sis, or Brother. How does a person balance "me" with what he's expected to be or do as a member of a family? The struggle to stay connected and at the same time be independent reaches a peak during the teen years. With so many diversified lifestyles, it is no surprise that children and young adults experience stress as they work to placate parents and family on the one hand and make their own choices on the other.

Communication or lack of it can cause stress. Some brothers and sisters can be best friends, others may be like strangers. Sometimes they may split off into factions or even gang up against one person. Sometimes the strongest bond they have is a commitment to care for the parents or maintain family property.

There is no perfect family. Stress at home is not unusual or bizarre. The place each person fills will have unique stressors. Each individual will have to adjust as best he or she can as personal problems or circumstances are etched within the family constellation.

16. THE FIRST CHILD AND POSSIBLY THE ONLY CHILD

It is thrilling to have your first baby; each day is more fulfilling than you ever imagined. At the same time, you appreciate that this first child is the "practice child." You may feel uncertain about what to do and how to do it, but children weather the storms and you enjoy their wonderful learning. Your number-one child gets a lot of attention, fanfare, acclaim and *power*. The child feels very important. The only child becomes masterful at controlling the household. All the adults want Junior to be happy, to not cry, to be free to make all kinds of discoveries. Junior may even be given freedom to interrupt adults, refuse foods, and dominate the play when children come to visit. His parents frequently act like a fan club and Junior loves the applause. He feels very secure. Most first children and only children do. Many parents smile when they read that an expensive government research project established that there are no negative effects of being an only child. They would have been happy to tell you that they knew it all the time!

The old cliché, "The only are lonely," may be true. The child may not have round-the-clock companionship, but may appreciate and enjoy privacy and time alone.

Is being an only child a source of stress? The answer has to come from your family and your only child. Some children thrive on being in the spotlight, having two parents hovering over them! Others feel smothered and monitored and are subject to being either corrected or commended for every move that they make.

Symptoms of stress the pre-school-aged only child may display:

- Disturbed sleep patterns denoting anxiety.
- Extensive temper tantrums to get what he or she wants.
- Nonstop demands for attention.
- Inability to be distracted.
- A self-defeating willfulness that causes a lot of child-parent battles.
- Inability or unwillingness to amuse himself or herself.

- Destructiveness.
- Selfishness with toys, books.
- Appearance of self-consciousness and lack of spontaneity as if preparing for a presentation. "Look, my tooth's loose!" or "See the picture I made."

When the parents of an only child ask me for advice, I frequently suggest, "Pretend you have five kids and then figure out how much of a fuss you would be making about this incident." If one kid had the flu, one was in a school play, and another had to go to a piano lesson, you might say to Jerry, "You'll have to handle that on your own!" This pattern of adding four kids is surprisingly helpful. In effect, it redistributes your energies, money, and time and gives you a chance to back off from some of the intricacies in the life of your child. You let the child have more freedom and you permit yourself to ease up from stress.

If your school-aged only child is under stress, these symptoms may show up:

- Extreme secrecy.
- Rudeness and disrespect. "Stay out of my life!"
- Efforts to belittle and criticize the parents.
- Indications the child is embarrassed to have his or her parents around in front of his friends, teachers, and classmates.
- Nonstop demands for material things or service.
- Bids for attention on his or her terms, a tendency to interrupt, and to challenge adult authority.
- Very dependent, seeking help or advice when perfectly capable of doing the task independently.
- Unusually inept in relating to other kids. May want the limelight, insist on being the boss, be intolerant of other kids' weaknesses or demands.
- Unusually passive with other children as if grateful for the company.
- Evidence of many psychosomatic problems which come from parental overanxiety. Parents may have the attitude "He's our *only* one. We have to take special care of him." The child may react by asthma attacks, hives, allergies, for instance.
- Child may be very choosy, fussy about what he or she will eat or wear—in short, a "spoiled brat."
- May be angry at parents because he or she is an only child and feels deprived. An only child tends to romanticize about the happiness and fun that siblings have. It may be difficult to picture that jealousy, fights, hostility, rivalry, and competition are all parts of sibling relationships and that such children may hurt a lot.

- May be intensely involved with an imaginary brother or sister. This is predictable up to four or five years of age.
- May be stormy and stubborn about being forced to play with others, share toys, take turns, etc. May appear disinterested or turned off by babies. May show that they really do not like other kids.

This assortment of symptoms may not describe your only child at all! The *benefits* of being an only child are synonymous with the characteristics of a first child:

- Highly motivated toward a goal.
- Intellectually curious.
- Set high standards for themselves.
- Tend to mature earlier; may be very verbal.
- Enjoy the philosophical position that their parents are aware of world problems and the overpopulation crisis, and are contributing to the controls that are essential.

Only children are very likely to do better in math, English, abstract reasoning, reading comprehension, and even IQ tests. They are usually less sociable and more prone to spend more time in intellectually artistic or solitary activities than children with siblings. They are not very often conceited or lonely.

Only children are usually encouraged by the parents to show interest in both male and female activities. In her only child, the mother is happy to see sensitivity and female characteristics. At the same time, the father welcomes male qualities such as dexterity and orderliness. (See Section X, #45.) The androgynous attitudes seem to provide a special degree of comfort to both parents and prevent, for example, a single boy from being forced into all-boy activities which he may not like at all.

Although the single child may miss out on the normal give and take of a sibling relationship, he or she thrives on having the single-minded love, warmth, care, and attention of both parents. Often only children will announce gladly that they do not want a brother or sister.

17. THE ONLY CHILD ISN'T AN ONLY CHILD ANYMORE: THE SECOND CHILD ARRIVES

"I've got a new sister so now there are two of us. But I'm still bigger and older," little Roger announced. Roger, as number one, appears to love the baby. Other young first children display ambivalence. They are not hesitant to ask you to take the baby back or give it to a neighbor. It's hard to learn to share Mom and Dad. The adjustment has to do with age, preparation, self-assurance, and relationship with the parents, as well as the way that he or she is involved with the baby's care and the quality of time alone with the parents. Older first children may appear more sophisticated, even ultra-mature and maternal or paternal.

The first child may not experience stress. The adjustment to the new baby may be genuinely exciting and smooth. If, however, you notice any of these behaviors, the first child may be under stress.

With or without words, the child exhibits stress.

Symptoms of Stress

The child:

- Resorts to baby behaviors.
- Is very passive.
- Overplays the role of mother's helper.
- Exaggerates displays of talents, such as playing the piano or reading.
- Acts out anger against parents.
- Becomes excessively demanding and unreasonable.
- Acts aggressively towards the baby.

Strategies for Support

The best strategy to follow is to make certain that the first child does have certain privileges. He or she:

- Can stay up later.
- Has alone time with you.
- Is not exploited to help take care of the little one.
- Has an opportunity to express jealousy and love.

18.   FAVORITISM AS A SOURCE OF STRESS

Favoritism may erupt at any time. Sometimes it is only a matter of the children's ages and how "cute they are." Sometimes it is a matter of different personalities and how they interact. One child is bossy, one is complacent, one is habitually ill-tempered, another has a cheerful, happy disposition. You may be quick to note, "Susie is just like my sister was, and we never got along," or, "John is the spittin' image of my dad's brother and he was everybody's favorite." Such statements have an immeasurable impact on a child. In effect, they are labels which reflect attitudes and determine expectations.

Children learn to believe that Mom prefers one type of kid to another. The same for Dad. "He's Dad's pet because he gets good grades and Dad's a brain," can be an accurate picture. Mom has made it clear that Gayle's whining drives her up the wall. "She's a whiner and I can't stand it," Mom frequently exclaims. Gayle can't let go of the label, even though the whining is a symptom that she needs more attention.

Children label themselves and many times they reinforce the idea that "John is her favorite. I'm the troublemaker," or "I'm the helper." Such descriptions expose family patterns. Labels can be delightful or disastrous. Whether self-imposed or picked up from others, they influence relationships and the stress level in the family system. A child who gives himself a negative label, such as "I'm sloppy," or "I'm dumb," has a built-in excuse for being the unfavorite kid. This hurts. It prompts anger, jealousy, fighting and other behaviors which denote low self-esteem. When children accuse you of playing favorites, hear the accusation as a symptom of stress.

Parents can help.

- Confront labels. If they accurately describe a problem, work for a solution. "I'm sloppy" may mean Chris needs more shelves in his room, fewer toys to straighten up, or your attention when getting dressed.
- Establish complimentary labels for each child. "You are so thoughtful and dependable."
- Help children to get rid of labels which no longer apply. "You used to be silly, but you're not any more."
- Extinguish competition wherever possible so that no one feels inferior or unwanted. "Let's take turns on the trampoline and not go with a system where you have to do two flips to get on."
- Give the child who sees himself or herself at the "bottom of the pile" special attention. This may relate to birth order. Youngest children may need frequent reassurance that they are important, too, especially if the older child is an outstanding person.
- Note how symptoms of stress at home may disturb relationships outside the family. Work with your child to overcome bad habits which may stem from labels. "You seem to like being sloppy but even your friend complains that you won't clean up when you play at his house." "You seem to be proud that you are the most sarcastic member of the family. We are learning to ignore you, but you hurt people's feelings. Your friends won't go for that."
- Listen to the defeatist labels the little ones may express, such as, "I'll never be as good as Patty. She is so pretty and smart, and I'm little and not smart." This may reflect that the first child has been dominating and demeaning. You have to address this issue. Act promptly to safeguard the self-esteem of all the children.
- Little kids usually admire big sister and big brother, yet they are jealous of their power in the family. Big sisters and brothers may echo similar complaints. You have not failed as a parent when

kids protest, "But you always let Jennie have the front seat," or "You always help her and you never help me." These protests are warnings for you to heed. Are labels or favoritism contaminating your family?

Stress in the family is to be expected. Even animals adjust to a pecking order. Happily, as human beings, we can rearrange relationships so that no chick feels unwelcome in the yard. Children want to feel that they are all loved equally. Even favorites can hate being favorites because a sibling is being hurt. They want to be free of the problem, to see you as fair and appreciative of everyone.

19. THE BABY OF THE FAMILY

Recently at a wedding reception, I watched an elderly couple greet a lovely girl, "Oh, you're Lisa, *the baby!*" She protested, "I'm not a baby. I am a twenty-year-old woman."

Lisa used to enjoy her position in the family. She could turn on her little-girl smile and her parents would give her almost anything she wanted. They would explain, "But she's so little and she's our last." At other times, she bore the brunt of parental annoyance. Her older brother and sister would set her up to do something forbidden and when she got caught, they were nowhere to be found. Lisa's protests were to no avail. "It'll have to be a lesson, Lisa, on when to say no." Nevertheless, being the baby was fun. Besides, there was nothing she could do about it!

If the youngest is pushed to grow up in a hurry, there may be many problems. The child gets the feeling that he or she is a burden and that the parents are tired of dealing with little people. They appear to want an instant grown-up. The boy or girl facing unrealistic expectations from the parents imposes unrealistic expectations on himself or herself. This creates stress.

On the other hand, some discover that their efforts to grow up and be more independent are thwarted and discouraged. The message from the folks is, "We love having a baby in the house and can't bear to face the day you leave." This makes some children very angry while others play the game, enjoying every minute of it. A lot depends on the number of children in the family and the friendship patterns that have developed among the siblings.

Symptoms of Stress

These are symptoms of stress to watch for as the youngest child grows:

- Babyish mannerisms, whining, tattle-tale games, and manipulative, coquettish behavior.

- An attitude of helplessness.
- Unexplained outbursts of anger denoting insecurity or reaction to too-high expectations.
- Possible resentments expressed to older siblings because of their detachment from parents. In effect, the baby feels as if he or she has been left holding the bag.
- Problem relationships with peers; too demanding with friends.
- Unsatiated need to get older siblings in trouble.
- Pouty, passive behaviors as a bid for attention.
- Incredible need to be on stage, the main attraction.
- Compulsive need to live up to brothers and sisters.

Strategies for Support

- Sit down and discuss the child's feelings about being the baby of the family—what feels great and what may be a problem.
- Intervene if older children persist in teasing and taking unfair advantage of the littlest one. Children understand about fairness.
- Make sure your leniency and permissiveness with the baby doesn't arouse jealousy in other children.
- Set limits if the baby persists in tattling, bothering the others, interfering with their toys, messing up their rooms and demanding to be noticed all the time.
- As the baby matures, let go of the word *baby. Our youngest* is more respectful.
- Be tactful. Even though you really may be thrilled to have this "last child," make certain that your enthusiasm does not leave the other children feeling unimportant.

Benefits

The older brothers and sisters of the baby constitute a built-in support squad! And they are wonderful teachers in almost every way imaginable. Even though there may be stress on the youngest, the benefits of being part of a group are numerous.

Circumstances may benefit the youngest child. Sometimes the economic situation of the family has stabilized by the time the baby comes along or becomes a teenager. The gift of a car or stereo or college tuition is possible for this child while the older kids had to work for theirs. Parents don't need to be defensive and neither does the youngest child.

20. THE MATURE YOUNGEST CHILD

As the youngest child matures, it is not unusual for him or her to feel a special sense of responsibility for the parents. He or she has been in the home most recently so is more aware of the problems and pressures that the parents face. It is natural to want to reach out to them and, depending on the age of the parents, the youngest child may offer to stay in the home to help. If one of the parents is deceased, the youngest child may feel very strongly that it is his or her place to take care of the surviving parent. The resulting conflict between being independent and being caretaker may cause considerable stress. The child may decide to follow the independent lifestyle of the older siblings and then feel so guilty at abandoning the parents that he or she decides to return to the home. The youngest may be the one to negotiate with siblings about joint responsibility for the parents.

21. THE MIDDLE CHILD

Child-development experts give the middle child a lot of press. There are numerous articles in the women's magazines about how to make certain the middle child has a proper and special place in the family.

Who is the middle child and do they have distinguishing characteristics? In the family of three, the one born in the middle may be the second girl, but the third child is a boy. Is this little girl a middle child? The girl may prefer to see herself as the little sister to one sibling but as a big sister to her brother and not feel as if she has been squeezed in between.

Being the middle child is more attitude than placement.

Symptoms of Stress

For those who really seem to function as the center of a cookie, possible symptoms of stress may show:

- An exaggerated sense of insecurity, or shyness, a tendency to be a tattle-tale in order to get the others in trouble.
- An unwillingness to express an opinion, as if what he or she has to say "isn't important anyway."
- A tendency to find excuses to be away from the family.
- An all-pervasive anger, perhaps masqueraded behind illnesses such as asthma, allergies, skin problems, or nutritional disorders.
- Many signs of jealousy. Belittling remarks, such as, "How come she gets to do that and I don't?" or, "It seems as if you have to be a baby in this house for someone to come and kiss you goodnight."

Almost without exception, the symptoms of stress may be seen as a plea for love. This child needs to feel appreciated for special talents and for his or her uniqueness. The symptoms may reveal that the middle child feels that the first child and the baby are favorites.

Strategies for support

- Avoid making comparisons. "At your age, Janie was helping with the dishes and Julie is still too young."
- Structure schedules so that you have time alone with each child. The little one can go to bed a half hour early. The older child can go to his room to read or listen to music. Now you can spend undivided time with the middle child. This may not be possible every day, but consider once or twice a week as minimal.
- Ask yourself, "How well do I know my middle child?" Describe him or her as best you can. *Then fill in the blanks!* What does the child like or dislike about school, who are his or her friends, what badges is he or she working for in Scouts or Camp Fire Girls? Will he or she make the soccer team? How well does your spouse know this child? Does he or she happen to be a favorite of either of you? Do you note symptoms of stress and rationalize that this is just a phase that the older one went through, too? (See Section IV on ages and stages.)
- Compare the amount of attention that you bestowed on your first child at this age and ask yourself if the middle child is receiving a fair share. If not, begin today.
- Have you left a lot of the caretaking to the older child, who in turn may be impatient, angry or disdainful? If so, start a plan which will change this situation.
- Make certain that the preferences and opinions of a soft-spoken middle child are not overlooked.
- Program the middle child into different activities from the others.
- Make the same effort to get to the middle child's piano recitals or ball games as you did for the first child.
- Take time to talk to the middle child about feelings. A middle child may ally him or herself with the youngest for protection from the first child and receive as a bonus a more generous amount of the loving that the youngest one gets.

The personality descriptions of first children emphasize their aggressiveness and need for power and approval. The descriptions of the other kids are less definitive. But all children in the family need approval and have the right to take turns being bossy. Middle children are frequently described as easygoing, less intense, sweeter, and more considerate. These complimentary adjectives may describe your child. Don't let the nice description deter you from observing whether the middle child is under stress.

22. THE WRONG-SEX KID

But I Was Supposed to Be a Boy (Or a Girl)

This is an endless source of stress to many children. They have heard the comment numerous times and it never loses its sting. I have heard little ones ask, "Then why didn't you give me back and get a new one?" Parents are quick to respond that they would never do that, but the stress has not been relieved. Older kids will just joke about it, even though their personalities may be affected by the problem.

Symptoms of Stress

If the "wrong-sex" kid is a girl

(1) She may act like a boy—demand trucks, cars, guns or male-type clothes to try to make up to the parents what she visualizes that they are missing. She may act out her feelings of being unwelcome and unwanted by belligerence, defiance, or pre-delinquent behaviors such as lying and stealing.

(2) She may overplay her femininity in order to win over her parents. She may acquire seductive mannerisms as early as two or two-and-a-half years old. She may strive to be like mother—a good cook and dressmaker, for instance. She may become very competitive with her mother for the father's attentions. She may display an exaggeration of sex stereotyping or a total rejection of your reassurances that she is loved and appreciated. As a young adolescent, she may become sexually promiscuous.

If he is a boy

(1) He may exaggerate his masculine interests in order to impress Mom and Dad that he is acceptable, because he is super-boy. He may show off, do risky things such as climb dangerously high in a tree. He may become self-conscious about everything—he may make weird faces, and seem strained and tense all the time. As adolescents, he may take to drugs to ease the stress resulting from the self-consciousness and feelings of rejection.

(2) He may become overly ambitious to prove that he is a worthy member of the family. He may put himself under too much pressure to succeed at school or in athletics, or may become emotionally disturbed. He may avoid peer friendships.

(3) He may just give up and become very passive, convinced that he is in a no-win situation. Consider Martin, now ten years old. While his parents haven't mentioned their disappointment in several years, he thinks of it every day. His passivity comes across as depression, low self-esteem, and lack of ambition. At this point, he needs professional help.

Other family dynamics can add to the stress these "wrong-sex" children feel.

- The maturity and adjustment of the mother and father.
- A possible division. Mother wanted a girl, Dad "had to have a boy." This polarity itself may indicate problems in the home.
- The child was to replace a child who had been killed or died.
- The family name was to be carried on by a boy in spite of the new non-name-change ways of today.
- The parents had themselves been "wrong-sex" babies and unwittingly set up the same stress for their own children.
- There was a real desire for a mix and match family! There were two boys already and they wanted a girl.
- An older child or children had "ordered" a brother or a sister. Such a fantasy may harm the sibling relationship for years to come.
- In some religious groups, such as Orthodox Jews, there are special services and celebrations to herald the arrival of a male. A young girl may feel she has let her family down by being a girl and depriving them of the tradition so important to the heritage. In the ongoing family lifestyle, the role of the girls is very stressful for some while others appear to be more comfortable and less rebellious. (See Section VIII, #41.)

Strategies for Support

What can a parent do now? What do children need?

- If planning a pregnancy, consider amneocentesis (a procedure not without risks) so that you may know the sex of your child before the birth. Work through any disappointments ahead of time with someone you trust, such as a doctor, or minister, in order to let go of any attitudes which may permanently damage your child's self-esteem.
- If you were a "wrong-sex" child, reaffirm for yourself that everyone disappoints Mom and Dad on some level at some time, and let go of this emotional garbage. Everyone has both feminine and masculine qualities and can achieve a well-balanced personality.
- If your child is an infant or toddler, stop verbalizing your disappointment. Babies cannot comprehend and toddlers are in love with life and can withstand your remarks. Give children non-sexist toys, such as blocks, and both sex toys such as dolls and trucks.
- When school-aged, the child needs repeated reassurance that he or she is loved as a person, not as a person of masculine or feminine gender. If the wrong-sex concept is deeply implanted it is difficult to erase the damage. *If you still harbor disappointment, get help*

for yourself; look at your own hang-ups about being masculine or feminine.

- Try to avoid such expressions as "Well, that's not bad for a girl!" or "Boys are supposed to be able to fix their own bikes." (See Section X, #45.) The wrong-sex child will overreact. Be aware of his or her sensitivity, whether it is verbalized or not.
- Consider the name of your child and whether a nickname would be a good idea. Did you want a boy whom you planned to name George and have a girl with the substitute name Georgia? Perhaps, if the child is young enough, it is time to try a nickname like "Gee-Gee." Nicknames can offer a reprieve.
- Talk to your teenager and explain the history of your attitude. This may alleviate misunderstandings and your guilt. Teenagers need such a discussion with repeated expressions of love and welcome. If your child asks, "How come you're talking about this *now?*" explain that you are aware of the problems you have created and that you want to straighten things out. Furthermore, it may help prevent their imposing a "wrong-sex" burden on their own children.

23. THE REPLACEMENT CHILD

The child born following the death of a sibling may be in a stress-unlimited situation. Many things will influence the life of this new child—the deceased's sex, age, personality, and the cause of death. Will the parents try to mold the new baby after the dead child or expect and accept differences?

Such stress is predictable. However, most parents are happy indeed to have the new baby; they do not become overprotective or unrealistic in their expectations. If problems begin to arise, consider these suggestions:

(1) While the infant is still very young, talk to someone you know about your feelings. If, for example, the deceased child was a victim of Sudden Infant Death Syndrome, take time to use support of members of the organization. This may require a number of visits.

(2) Try to stop all comparisons.

(3) Keep sentimental memorabilia to a minimum.

(4) Help all extended family members to accept the new baby as a very welcome addition to the family. Discourage a recital of memories and grief.

(5) Discipline yourself to avoid comments such as "She is sweet, but little Mary was sweet, too," or "She is a darling baby, almost two now, but Mary would have been six and just starting first grade." Such remarks

keep the new child under intermittent stress that can damage self-esteem.

(6) Express depression away from the child.

(7) Enjoy the baby!!

Symptoms of stress will appear in infancy if the child-parent relationship is suffering because of the circumstances. The symptoms will be similar to those displayed as a result of impaired bonding. Older children may be depressed and insecure. Everyone may benefit from professional help.

24. THE FERTILITY-WORK BABY

The prospect of this new baby is immeasurably exciting. This baby was certainly planned and worked for. Doctors had given Helen and Steve every reason to believe that the child would be fine—and he is. What possibly could be a source of stress? Money—the thousands of dollars spent for medical and laboratory studies and procedures. Anxiety—the special plans to be carried out for the "special baby" or an overprotective attitude to make certain nothing happens.

Remember all babies are special! The basic ingredient for the parent-child relationship is love, generously expressed in the care that mothers and fathers intuitively show. Try to avoid being overprotective because you worry that the loss of this baby might necessitate a repeat of all the difficult medical procedures.

Children don't understand the intricacies that surrounded their conception and birth, and if they become aware they are entitled to careful explanations. It isn't necessary to burden children with inappropriate details which may be misunderstood. No matter the circumstances, they are welcome in the family. Let the stressful circumstances be history.

25. THE CHILD OF THE "LATE-IN-LIFE" COUPLE

The child whose parents are in their late forties when he or she is born faces some interesting situations which may become sources of stress. The deferred child is becoming increasingly common. Couples marry later; remarriages occur in the forties; and some career-minded women prefer to wait to have children until they have achieved certain goals. It can be a matter of choice or a matter of chance!

When the child is old enough to realize his or her unique situation, the question that will come up is "Was I a mistake?" If there are older children, with perhaps a gap of eight to twelve years, the child will at some time ponder about being an unwanted child. Parents usually draw the picture with such comments as "You were a happy surprise!" or "We thought we were through with diapers, babysitters, and the PTA and then you came along!" These intended-to-be humorous remarks need to be backed up with a lot of reassurances and sincere indications that the couple is, indeed, delighted to have this child. I have heard couples say, "We worked on the first three kids—this is the one to enjoy!"

Symptoms of Stress

- Does the child seem to be forcing himself or herself to be independent in order to avoid being a burden to the parents?
- Does the child seem to avoid the parents in an effort to stay out of the way?
- Has the child developed habits of apologizing for all kinds of things that do not warrant apologies? This can be interpreted as a basic apology for interfering with their plans and mature lifestyle.
- Is the child reluctant to bring home friends for fear of messing up the house or bothering his older mom?
- Does the child take advantage of his special position by being obnoxious, attention-seeking, and demanding?
- Does the child appear embarrassed when his parents attend a school function or Scout meeting? How does he react when one of his classmates says, "I thought they were your grandparents?"
- Does the child seem passive with his parents? Does he or she take the position that his parents are unduly set in their ways and there's nothing he can do to change it?
- Does the child seem obsessed with his parents' age and worry about their becoming infirm or dying?

Strategies for Support

- Get the issue out of the way, settled once and for all. Make it clear that the child is a welcome member of the family who enriches the lives of all of them.
- Avoid the expression, "You keep me young."
- Don't push yourself to get involved in activities which you do not enjoy for the sake of the child. Suppose that you are in your sixties and your child is in junior high school. You are extremely busy with your work and activities, and the child pushes you to become a skier, a jogger, a weaver or whatever. Your other interests, other children and commitments determine how many new pursuits you can undertake.
- Don't overplay all of the child's accomplishments to your friends. Many of them, as you may also be, are into a grandparent role and may be burned out on the doings of eighth-grade kids.

- IF YOU ARE A GRANDPARENT, it is important to show as much enthusiasm for your child's school, friends, and interests as you show for your grandchildren's activities. Your child may feel displaced by or jealous of his or her nieces and nephews.

Look at all the advantages your late-in-life child may have

- The family may be more secure financially. Older brothers and sisters are out of the nest, so there is more time and money for the new child.
- An add-on kid is sometimes overindulged by all the family. Relationships with nieces and nephews can be very loving and close and provide the companionship which may not be possible with older siblings and older parents.
- The child may have a set-up similar to that of an only child and love every minute of it! (See Section VI, #16.)
- The maturity of the parents may mean considerably less friction about such issues as clothes, which were troublesome when raising other siblings.
- The parents may feel rejuvenated and excited about being a part of younger parent groups. The attitudes of younger parents, as well as those of their own older children, may make parenting this child easy, delightful, and fulfilling.
- Current issues which face the child of today are brought home for your consideration. The child may challenge you about nuclear energy, space, computers, genetic engineering, careers, or religious cults. You may have to confront prejudices or old attitudes which you have had and be motivated to update them!

26. THE CHILD OF THE ELDERLY FATHER-YOUNG MOTHER

The name of the game may be confusion. The crux of the situation may be whether Mom and Dad agree on how the child shall be raised. Is one parent more modern or progressive than the other? Is the "old man" full of old-fashioned ideas? Or does he sit back, simply adore this young person and become totally permissive?

Children can sense if one parent is more manageable than the other. They play manipulator with great proficiency. There are sources of stress for this child when he or she is old enough to be aware of the picture.

- The child may feel that he or she is never out of the spotlight and feel that as a symbol of the love between this couple, he or she should take on the responsibility to keep things loving and smooth.
- The child may feel very remote from the older parent.

- The child may feel insecure if the lifestyles of his parents are markedly different—if the father is the sedentary TV addict; and the mother is athletic or involved in business or volunteer activities.
- The child may feel defensive about his or her parents. This may not be evident until the teen years.
- If the parental relationship becomes strained, the child may feel that they are staying together for his or her sake. If they separate, he may assume unwarranted blame.
- There may be an unusually close alliance between the young mother and the child, almost a two-against-one pattern. The two may be bound together around the issue of the father's age and health.

Parents are almost always thrilled when they have a new baby and the older, established father (often in a second or third marriage) is no exception. The role that he chooses to play is an important key to the child's adjustment. Does he become an active caretaker or a benevolent by-stander? Do business commitments keep him absent a great deal of the time? The issue is not age but the pattern of family life. The child may occasionally be defensive about dad's age but this need not be construed as a symptom of stress. On the other hand, it may be a great family joke.

27.   THE CHILD CONCEIVED BEFORE PARENTS WERE MARRIED

For a baby or toddler, the meaning or possible implications for the child add up to zero. If a three-year-old hears, "If it weren't for you, we wouldn't be in this mess," the words have little meaning. Jennie thinks mother is mad because she spilled jelly on the floor. Usually a child begins to absorb the message after the age of six or seven and usually only when an unhappy, stressful home situation has evolved.

The child, when old enough to understand, may ask disturbing questions.

- Would Daddy have married you if it weren't for me?
- Would you have been happy if you didn't have to be a mom?
- Is Daddy mad because he has to take care of us?
- Would you have gone to school or taken a different job if I had not been on the way?
- Did you and Daddy want to get married when you were so young?
- You and Daddy loved each other then—do you *now?*

Children asking any of these questions may discover that their parents ask the same ones. In answering, the parents can clarify issues, sometimes with very positive answers and sometimes not.

The question, "Was I wanted?" creates stress. Children can convince themselves one way or the other. If the answer is positive, the question of time of conception does not create stress. If negative, the child may suffer serious adjustment and ego problems.

Symptoms of Stress

- The child appears agitated.
- The child demands constant reassurance on many levels.
- The child seems to be in constant search for ways to please adults.
- The adolescent may become very critical and express disapproval that mother was pregnant before she got married.
- The child may pop up with questions such as, "Why didn't you put me up for adoption?" or, "Why didn't you have an abortion?" These questions may solicit reassurances or may be a bid for information, asked out of curiosity.

The child needs reassurance. He also needs to know that neither his mother or father dwell on the circumstances surrounding his or her conception.

If, as a parent, you wonder how the child found out, remember that all children want to know about how things were with you before they were born, about the pregnancy, delivery, and their babyhood. Their baby books can be fascinating. They want to know about your babyhood and childhood, too. If a child asks questions, don't misconstrue it as an inquisition. If you are oversensitive, you may think the child is trying to embarrass you. This is not so.

Do not tell about unnecessary arguments or fights or the demands or attitudes of your parents which may have influenced your decision to get married. This may create some misunderstanding between your child and the grandparents.

Don't ever say to a child, "You were a mistake." The child already knows it. Express the positive. "We were happy to have you. You are special to us." If appropriate, you may talk to teenagers about sexuality, impulsivity, or the influence of drugs or alcohol.

28. THE CHILD OF TEENAGE PARENTS

Almost one fourth of all persons who marry are teenagers—high school sweethearts, the girl or boy next door, the person who works on the adjacent machines—romantic, exciting, and optimistic. When a baby arrives, this can be "My every dream come true!"* The fun, unsophisti-

---

*The baby of the unwed teenage mother who is brought into the family may not have to face these potential sources of stress. The baby is usually cared for by mother or grandparents as well as by doting aunts and uncles. (See Section X, #45.)

cated ways of teenage parents may be the envy of older folks. Teenagers don't seem to worry as much or make big issues of things. Fresh from school and homework, they find it easy and natural to ask for help or advice. They are not defensive or embarrassed about it. Close bonds with the child usually form. Nevertheless, there are some issues that need to be looked at realistically. They can affect the emotional well-being of the baby and influence how he or she learns to cope.

Sources of Stress

(1) The number one problem may be money. How will this family make it? Babies are expensive. Beyond housing, there must be provision for medical care, food, clothes, and babysitters. If the father is still in school, someone has to pick up the tab. School and work? Work only? One job or two? Both parents? Help from grandparents—yes or no, possible or impossible? Teenage parents are not prepared to confront the money issue. Money matters can cause serious friction and family stress which then affects the baby.

(2) The second problem may be the immaturity of the parents. The child of teenage parents learns to live with a mother and father who display emotional swings and moods characteristic of the pre-twenty age group. These swings can become a source of stress.

(3) Many teenagers marry for reasons that can undermine the stability of the marriage. Some will readily admit, "It was to get away from home." Others were pregnant, hated school, or were following the example set by an older sibling or the kids in the neighborhood. Many times it was an impulsive, "Let's do it" event. With the arrival of the baby, both parents have some serious growing up to do. They suddenly realize that they have to finish school or prepare for a better job or career while they maintain a home. If the precipitating problem was an unhappy home situation or poor relationships with their own parents, this can cause considerable stress for all.

With all these issues, it is not unusual for teenage parents, while they love the baby, to find themselves resentful of the effort and responsibility which the baby requires. Many teenage marriages fail. The subsequent problems may be traumatic for some—at best, the parents will be depressed, insecure and upset for some time. Most infants weather such problems quite well, but older children may become anxious and insecure. (See Section VI, #27, and Section XI, #47-53.)

Strategies for Support

Young parents must consider these issues.

(1) If money is a problem, think through your attitude about borrowing. There is a time and a place to borrow, and though you may

want to be independent, it may reduce a lot of worry and friction if you decide to borrow. Many grandparents would make every effort to help out, if asked. They would rather see you happy than overwhelmed by money worries. The rule: Be businesslike. Treat the arrangement in such a way that you protect your self-respect and your parents respect the plans that you negotiate with them. Loans are far easier to deal with, for some persons, than gifts or handouts. If you are concerned that borrowing money will open the door to too much parental interference, save the situation by writing down the details. Include the pay-back arrangement and small interest costs to keep the desirable businesslike structure.

(2) If your relationship with your parents causes you a lot of grief, anger, or worry, go for help. Talk to your minister, school or college counselor, or someone you respect. Until your relationship with your parents stabilizes, the relationship with your own child may be harmed. For example, without realizing it, you may be wanting—almost demanding—that your child be close to you because you are still disappointed that your mother was never able to let you be close to her. This can create a stressful way of life for your child.

(3) When a disagreement or problem pops up with your spouse, try to remember the phrase, "Hey, we are young. We are both growing up and we won't agree about everything! Adults don't—why should we?" Be fair with each other about time away from home with friends, just as you would if you were still involved in activities at school and just dating. Plan to equalize baby-care time.

The Grandparent's Role

If you are the parent of teenage parents please consider these suggestions.

(1) Make certain that you do not have the attitude that, "You made your bed, now lie in it," when or if your children reach out for help. The grandbaby is going to add so much to your life. It is really important to let go of any hard feelings you may have if your child eloped or proceeded into a marriage of which you didn't approve. Any rift between the young couple and yourself will create stress for all and the vulnerable baby may be the unwitting victim.

(2) Bear in mind that these kids are still kids, with a big load to carry.

(3) Applaud the many good decisions that they make. Even though they are married and have a family, they need the same consideration and tolerance that you would show if they were still living at home.

Statistics show that immature teenage parents, when upset, may be more prone to lose control than older persons. This loss of control may

result in harsh handling of the baby, cruel punishments, or even battering. It has been suggested that teenage parents may attempt to try to
ease their stress by excessive use of drugs and alcohol. As a grandparent
you may decide to be assertive and confront certain issues with the young
couple.

At first, they may demand that you let them work things out on
their own, but your recommendations, tactfully repeated, may prove
important to all. The child of teenage parents benefits from the energy
and enthusiasm that young people have. The parents may refrain from
unrealistic expectations that older parents frequently impose on their
kids.

29. TWINS

The days have passed when parents heralded a set of twins with the
announcement, "We were totally surprised." Almost all parents-in-wait-
ing have weeks, or perhaps months, to prepare for the multiple birth.
This planning time gives the couple the opportunity to think about all the
problems and complications that twins may bring and provides a chance to
discuss costs, how much help will be needed, and what provisions will be
necessary. They will have time to visualize how to give equal attention to
each child, how to try to keep comparisons down to a minimum, and how
to find time to enjoy the babies.

Twins are fascinating and fun to watch. So many questions are asked
about them. Is one brighter than the other? Do they want to be dressed
alike? Which one is dominant? Do they mind being separated? Have they
developed their own language? Do you have a favorite? The most
commonly asked question is, "How did you survive when they were babies
with so much work to do?" Thoughtful parents reflect their philosophy of
raising twins with the statement, "I want each child to have individuality
and not feel that he or she only counts when one of a pair." Through
normal give and take, each personality will become distinguishable. One
twin is friendly and one twin is shy. Mary is self-confident, Marty is not.

As infants, some twins are easy to manage and some more demanding. Within three or four months, however, they learn to watch each other
and react to each other in so many ways that the stress of newborn weeks
on the parents drops dramatically. This changes the quality of family life
from somewhat frantic to joyous.

Within the first year, stress may result if

- Fatigue prevents parents from cuddling and handling their twins.
- The small size of the babies creates unusual worry and concern to
  the point that parents may become overprotective.*

---

*Many twins are very small at birth, some due to preterm delivery. Although there
are studies about problems relating to preterm deliveries and mother-child bonding, they
are not included in this book.

- The personalities of the babies (or just one of them) is demanding and difficult.
- Mother's possible slow recovery causes problems.
- Parents are not able to get extra help, even from the neighbors, older children, grandparents, or paid help.
- Expenses are overwhelming.
- Either child exhibits developmental problems.
- The children overreact to being in the spotlight.

There are three different kinds of twins—identical, fraternal same sex, and fraternal opposite sex—with similar and different sources of stress among them. Identical twins can be confusing to all caretakers. The switches and tricks that the kids may play as they grow up are fun to hear about, but they can also be a puzzle to parents, teachers, neighbors, or friends. Some competition may play a big role with some fraternal as well as identical twins. Others may accept the dominant/passive positions and not be noticeably competitive. Boy-girl twins seem to demonstrate the more traditional sibling rivalry.

In general, there are many advantages to being a twin!

- Companionship
- Loyalty
- Independence from parents
- Sharing
- Cooperation
- Understanding of differences

These disadvantages may result in stress

- Too much competition
- Lack of individuality
- Feelings of being a burden
- Favoritism
- Parents too stressed to meet the needs of twins
- Too much dependency on each other
- Feelings of being pushed out or of less importance than the other, especially if one develops more slowly
- Feelings of being forced to do what the other wants to do
- Resentment from other brothers or sisters

Symptoms of stress may be difficult to distinguish from the personality of a twin. Consider Tommy and Tim as examples. Tommy, a withdrawn child, has adapted to Tim, who is overbearing and very outgoing. He does not struggle to be in the limelight and though he may feel jealous, he accepts his position in the family and appears to be stress-free. Tom's passivity becomes a source of stress when social relationships outside the family are hurtful and unsatisfactory. Tom has great difficulty making friends; he feels unwanted and unimportant. Tim lets him be a tag-along. Other kids don't play with him or cater to him the way his parents do. It is a difficult situation for him.

Symptoms of Stress

Unmet needs—unrelenting need for attention and approval; may stem from one twin getting more or neither twin getting enough attention because of parents' personalities or fatigue.

Combativeness—social situations become competitive, out of proportion; twin must be the first in line, sit next to the teacher, argue and quarrel to prove he or she is always right.

Too dependent—child refuses to make a decision on his or her own, consistently defers to the opinion or preferences of others.

Too independent—child refuses to be associated with twin, won't dress alike, play same sports, read same books, for instance.

Overprotective of twin—child feels the need to be the twin's protector at all times and may interfere with peer interactions on behalf of twin.

Strategies for Support

Strategies for support must address one or more of three areas.

• Does the twin feel insecure as a person, not sure who he or she is? Is the child without a satisfactory coping style?

• Does the twin feel alienated from the parents?

• Does the twin consider being a twin a burden? Is he or she struggling to become free of it?

Positive strategies require the parent to evaluate the symptom, talk to each child, and make certain each feels respected. Make certain that your interactions with each child are unique. For example, one of your twins may court closeness while the other is uncomfortable when you ask personal questions. If one is struggling for identity, you may have to insist they enter different activities or be placed in different classes. Teenage twins may be adamant about separate activities and friends.

In general, twins enjoy each other. The benefits of stress from their relationship are apparent when they proclaim that they feel sorry for kids who have to go it alone.

There are more than two million pairs of twins in the United States. And twins tend to beget twins. A woman, herself a fraternal twin, has one chance in fifty-eight of bearing twins. A number of persons alive today who have lost a twin brother or sister at birth or in infancy, are described as obsessed with being a twin and unknowingly suffer from unresolved grief. Nancy Segal, a twins researcher, says that they experience survivor's guilt. If this should be your situation, take time to find help for yourself. The unresolved problem may not affect how you parent your twins, but you are entitled to clarity and happiness.

30. THE GIFTED CHILD

The gifted child is invariably under stress. Personal expectations include the need to excel and to be perfect. An accumulation of years of attempting to live up to others' expectations also creates stress. Feelings of frustration and inadequacy frequently result.

Predictably, the symptoms of stress may be similar to those of any anxious child, including nervous habits, inappropriate responses to persons and situations, or retreating into a book or TV. Retreat prevents involvement with others and the acknowledgment and expression of emotions. Stifling emotions is not healthy, and it is important to ascertain what other expectations the child may be hiding which create stress.

There are ways to help the gifted child cope with stress.

- Explain sources of stress completely and carefully.
- Anticipate questions and suggestions.
- Encourage the child to express emotions. Ascertain why it is important to the child to control his or her emotions when others "fall apart." Help the child to let go of such a pattern.
- Don't push adult control on the child even though verbalizations may be very sophisticated.
- Allow the child privacy.
- Encourage creativity—an established way for a child to deal with death, in particular.
- Appreciate the child's needs to reach out to others. Some gifted persons have an unusual awareness of the needs of others. (Others are disinterested and self-involved.)
- Anticipate that some gifted children will react to certain stressors by staying with a task such as practicing a musical instrument for hours and hours. This can be regarded as a healthy way to cope as long as it doesn't go on indefinitely and there are other outlets for emotions.
- Involve the child in as many decisions as possible. The gifted have remarkable insights and judgments to offer.
- Let the child brainstorm for solutions (for example, what would be the best use of time before a move, or of money for investments left by deceased parent). Listen to the answers and accept workable suggestions.

School is the major source of stress for gifted children. Be aware of the school program provided for your gifted child. Be assertive. Make certain the child isn't bored with redundant busywork. The regular classroom has some advantages. Children participate in some competitive activities which satisfies school mandates, parents' realizations of the child's potential, and which reaffirm for the child the superior quality of learning of which he or she is capable. The democratic basis of the regular classroom is invaluable if the needs of the gifted are being met.

In a school class of gifted, to the exclusion of others, a great deal of stress may result for some. *They may be brilliant and in some ways very mature, but they are still children.* They need to understand that there are individual differences among the members of the select group. This avoids the unnecessary pressure of trying to emulate the giftedness of others. For example, some children have far better fine muscle control than others, enabling them to excel with instruments and tools. The advantages of the class are inherent when the learning is geared to originality, problem solving, scientific methods, and the processes of analyzing, synthesizing, and evaluating. Furthermore, many of the special programs for the gifted and talented do not require grading. The kids can be free to use and expand their minds without the stress that comes from unnecessary competition, though many love to compete in games. They are usually very selective about what and who they like and dislike.

A disadvantage of gifted-with-gifted groupings on a full-time, exclusive basis is that the groups become stratified on unique levels, and the stratifications inhibit or unwittingly diminish the self-esteem of some. This is particularly evident in the social skills. Some gifted leaders may become overbearing, while their gifted classmates assess the situation and may choose to be tolerant and passive, to their own detriment. If the more reticent ones were in a class with non-gifted learners, their own leadership capabilities would stand a better chance to be nurtured and developed. One frequently sees the gifted at home as very bossy. If the child has learned well but has poor work habits, is consistently sloppy, tardy, and disorganized, these undesirable habits must be confronted. The remediation of such deficiencies is preparation for the career world ahead, where genius is judged and respected but responsibility and accountability are equally important.

The Gifted Child in Family Turmoil

The gifted have unusual insights into most problems even before they are brought out into the open. A child may try to take steps to improve the situation or prevent a crisis. If the adult resists or discounts such efforts, this may result in alienation and ill feelings between parent and child. The child feels as if he or she has failed if parents separate, or fighting or drinking continues.

The gifted experience the same emotions as the other family members when a crisis occurs. They may, however, appear more intensely upset and overreact. They may display inappropriate or unnecessary hostility to peers, disdain for authority, or resort to alcohol or drug abuse.

It is important to provide many diverse experiences for your gifted child. The youngster may resist and appear single-minded, but when mature he or she will be grateful for the wide exposure to life situations. Gifted children benefit from some stress because they learn to rely on their thinking skills and unusual insights. If stressors become overwhelming children can fail to see any inherent benefits and become seriously depressed. As a parent, do not hesitate to ask piercing questions in order to assess what help is needed.

SECTION VII

Stress from
Personal Problems

31. THE ILL CHILD: LIVING WITH A CHRONIC ILLNESS OR HANDICAPPING CONDITION

The ill or handicapped child is forced to cope with complex, difficult stressors. Their world is both deprived and rewarding, threatening and satisfying, painful and comfortable, frustrating and gratifying. That's a lot for anyone to understand and live with—especially a child.

It is important to remember that:

- The adjustment of the child will be very much influenced by age, mental and emotional development, ability to conceptualize, and the nature of the illness. The time of onset is extremely important. Has the child had years of normal development or has he or she been ill since birth? What other problems does the family face, such as poverty, lack of medical or therapeutic support, or troubled relationships?
- The child with a handicapping condition is more like than unlike non-handicapped persons. The child has the universal needs to feel acceptance, competence and *love*.
- With the exception of extreme retardation, the child with a handicap may function normally in many areas or have outstanding talents. Handicapped children are usually highly motivated to be independent and to find ways to be creative and productive.
- Handicapped kids love to teach someone else what they have learned. This builds self-confidence.
- Parents are to be applauded for their continuous efforts to avoid unnecessary segregation of handicapped kids. Excellent TV programs promote understanding.

Public Law 94-142, The Education for All Handicapped Children
Act, may be seen as a significant addition to civil rights legislation.
The goals are to provide opportunities within the public schools to
move handicapped children from a segregated status in special
education classes to regular classrooms whenever feasible, thus
allowing them to benefit from the give and take of interactions
with non-handicapped peers. More than 7 million school-age
children are emotionally, mentally, or physically handicapped. Not
all of them will qualify for placement in a regular classroom either
full-time or part-time. In any case, the purposes of the law must
be made clear to all. Its effective implementation is essential
whatever the cost, which in 1982 was about $3.1 billion.
- Qualifications for placement in a regular classroom are tied to
limitations resulting from the handicapping conditions. The success of the placement of your child will depend on the preparation
and attitude of everyone concerned.

With or Without Words: The Child Exhibits Stress

The child with a handicapping condition or chronic illness may be a
very happy, well-adjusted person or unhappy, volatile, and difficult to
manage. This is, in part, determined by the condition itself. All of the
children will experience frustration and stress. Occasional symptoms will
show up. For example, the child with limited ability to speak has to act out
by crying, being extremely obstinate, hiding, hitting, running away, or
clinging. The youngster who is immobile may occasionally scream, be
unusually irritable, throw things, or regress in other ways.

As a parent, you may hear yourself say, "Oh! That's just Susie" and
be reluctant to think of her behavior as a symptom of stress. Symptoms
vary; changes may denote increased stress.

- Does your child seem unusually agitated?
- Is your child exhibiting more babyish, less mature behavior than
usual?
- Is your child doing something unusual such as wetting the bed or
sucking his or her thumb?
- Are there unusual pleas for attention, holding, comforting,
closeness?
- Is your child unusually anxious to talk to you, to tell of fears, bad
dreams, or new problems?
- Does your child appear unusually listless, defeated, unhappy?
- Has your child stopped trying to be independent or to overcome
some problem he or she has been working on?
- Does your child cry or daydream excessively?

- Does your child talk about death or express a wish to die, or express nonstop self-pity or guilt at being a burden to the family?
- Is your child exhibiting self-destructive behaviors?

The Child Goes to School

Other reactions to stress, subtle or significant, may indicate how a handicapped child adjusts to the regular classroom. These reflect the child's personality, past experiences and the way parents and teachers handle the situation.

- Indications of being overwhelmed.
- Fatigue.
- Insecurity, crying.
- Signs of jealousy or misunderstanding of classmates.
- Show-off antics—aggression or marked passivity.
- Exaggerated displays of handicapping condition.
- Vivid denial of weaknesses; bravado or unrealistic stories about achievements.

Parents and teachers need to be encouraging and patient. It is hoped that within a short time these symptoms may dissipate. New teachers, new classmates, the challenge of new activities, and the feeling of being one of the group can help the youngster let go of self-consciousness and the initial stress behaviors. While your child may be one of 7 million handicapped youngsters who need public concern, *this* child needs your special understanding!

The Middle-School-Aged Child With a Handicapping Condition

Middle-school-aged children harbor a need for closeness to adults and attract it with their enthusiasm and sparkle. They may freely seek counsel, comfort, and advice. These patterns may be exaggerated by the handicapped child. Above all, children want friends and acceptance at home, in the neighborhood, and at school. Some may continue to behave in babyish ways and their more sophisticated peers may be scornful. Mom and Dad should help them understand that all kids of this age are trying hard to grow up, and that is why they are intolerant of babyish behaviors.

If the handicapped child has always been carefully protected, he or she may overreact to the characteristic thoughtlessness of peers. There is a tentative quality to many peer interactions which the handicapped child may misperceive as callous, uncaring, or hostile. Adults should interpret these misperceptions. Many middle-school-aged children today appear to emulate their older brothers and sisters in almost everything they do. This results in uncertainty and confusion. In effect, they are catapulted from childhood to adolescence with too little time to try out their own ways of doing things. The handicapped child faces an even more complicated task when surrounded by peers who may be smoking pot or reading *Penthouse*. This creates feelings of alienation. The child may become more self-conscious, self-critical, and depressed. Help the child to learn tolerance and to understand that everyone matures at his or her own rate.

The Adolescent With a Handicapping Condition

No date on the calendar is marked, "Adolescence starts today." The onset of puberty, the need to be with a gang or a clique, the struggle to become independent and to set career goals and develop a sense of self-mastery are part of the adolescent realm. This may not describe the progress of the adolescent with a handicapping condition at all. To some, he or she may appear "too young to be so old" and in other situations "too old to be so young." The handicapped teenager may have great wisdom and a philosophy of life from which parents, friends, and siblings derive much strength and courage. In other respects (again depending on the nature of the disability), the judgment and demands that the teenager displays indicate that he is still immature.

The years of preparation for adulthood have been full of adversity. They have learned to cope. One sees compensatory behaviors, acceptance of limitations, courage, a spiritual acceptance of the handicap, development of some talents, parental support, and important bonds with friends, family, and professional helpers. One also may note low self-esteem, loneliness, repeated expressions of inadequacy and failure, anger over being a burden or worry to parents, discouragement, and confusion.

The handicapped teenager may have a great sense of humor, school spirit that won't quit, and enthusiasm for new activities such as learning to play the guitar, that will be an inspiration to everyone around. Some of the teenagers give the impression that they are out to conquer the world—and they do.

Others become increasingly depressed. As they begin to look ahead, they are angry about or they fear their dependency. Money matters can become very important. Resentment about their condition or illness builds up to larger-than-ever proportions. Questions about dating, sex, and marriage come up to cause heightened feelings of being cheated, inadequate and bitter.

As the parent of a handicapped child, try to distinguish between the normal ups and downs of teenagers and any special attitudes or problems of your youngster. Your child needs to know there are times when all the kids feel this way. Be certain that your child has a chance to talk with other teenagers. While this may sometimes be difficult to arrange, it is very important. Kids may benefit more from talking to others with similar problems than they do from therapy and program activities.

In the case of the chronically ill teenager who must be hospitalized periodically, it is comforting to see the camaraderie that the kids in the ward build. As much as possible, they tease, scold, laugh, and joke with the staff. They show great sensitivity for those who are suffering and display an admirable bravery themselves. Visitors may show more depression than the kids. Nurses and attendants often complain, in a good-natured way, that they get tired just keeping up with the high spirits of the kids. They also report that kids today get hooked on TV serials—an interest that sometimes interferes with the characteristic group quality of the wards in the past.

No ill or handicapped person, teenager or not, can be expected to act like all the others all of the time. However, be aware that this may reflect age and not how problems are handled.

What Handicapped or Chronically Ill Children Need

- As much certainty as possible. Uncertainty has a profound impact on the patient. Many illnesses or conditions are difficult to diagnose. Wrong diagnoses may have been made. Multiple surgeries may have had to be endured. The whole family may have gone through years of uncertainty. *The children need explanations they can understand.*
- To be *surrounded by people with a positive attitude.* Loss of hope is the worst disability of all.
- Help and support to face changes. Diseases with remissions, handicaps which respond to new therapies, braces or machines result in shifts in a child's hopes, dreams, outlook, and goals. Most children remain very optimistic if those around them have the same attitude. If they feel very discouraged, accept their feelings and assess the situation. Depressions can deter some recovery.
- Lessons in how to handle stress. Learning to give up something you love to do, like skiing, and substituting swimming in a warm pool may be very tough. Help the children feel enthusiastic about the new people they meet at the pool or in a yoga group or in the physical therapy room at the hospital. Just staying active keeps the stress level down. Coping by retreating to a TV set may be necessary for some but may be overrelied upon by too many others.
- Experience in coming to terms with visible evidence of disability, such as hearing aids, crutches, a walker or wheel chair. Most children adjust quite well. They need to be surrounded by accepting family and classmates or to have a buddy or two nearby. Oftentimes, the fear of being conspicuous or of isolation is more difficult to adjust to than the equipment itself.

- Help in coping with an invisible disease, such as childhood diabetes, early-stage multiple sclerosis, or controlled epilepsy. These children are privately ill. No one has to know that they have a chronic illness unless they tell or have some kind of episode or breakdown at school. There may be days when they are not energetic. They may be pleasant one day and surprisingly short-tempered the next. They need a sense of emotional well-being that will permit them to talk about the disease without embarrassment. They must be open and direct. Acceptance is the key. Self-esteem leads to acceptance and an attitude which promotes friendships. In the world of children, friends come first.
- The child whose illness causes a loss of control suffers an added source of stress. The youngster who experiences breathing difficulties or seizures, who stumbles or drops things, the blind who may fall against a misplaced chair, need to know that even the non-handicapped have clumsy moments and drop things. Remind the child that all people goof now and then.
- Children who must take medicine at school usually do not attract any attention at all. Some schools require the children to come to the nurse's office for their pills. It becomes routine. The child will smile or greet the secretary in the office on the way to the nurse's room without any unnecessary fanfare. The child needs to be aware when medication is changed so that he or she will not be frightened if there are any side effects. Parents would be wise to notify the teacher and school nurse of such a possibility.
- A chance to help others become comfortable with their handicaps or illnesses. Teachers, friends, parents of friends, teammates, or neighbors may be very uncomfortable not knowing how to help or even to talk to the child about it. The child gains much by talking about real feelings, especially anger and fear. These experiences help the child make the point that while a handicap may be a real nuisance, it can be put on the back burner of the mind. Little Kathie has childhood diabetes. As a fifth grader, she could remember times when she was dizzy, sweaty, couldn't sleep, and had to be rushed to the hospital. She says she's glad they found out what was the matter. Now her parents aren't so mad at her for being cross. She says she would rather have a shot every day than wonder what was the matter. She smiles when she says, "You know, I only think about it in the morning, and when I can't eat candy, and when I have to go to the doctor. I wish my mom and dad wouldn't talk about it so much!"
- Freedom to ask for rest periods or to be given shorter assignments or to change deadlines. After a day at school or a therapy session

at the hospital, the child may rebel against having to do the dishes or feed the dog because he or she is too tired and doesn't realize it.

- Encouragement, encouragement, encouragement—the kids need as much as they can get. Help each child discover strengths and talents that they never dreamed they possess.

Strategies for Support

As you read about the needs of handicapped children, I am sure you were saying to yourself "I could help her do that!" or "I could talk to him about that" and you probably have in mind at least three or four things that you want to try right away. Or perhaps you are pleased and satisfied that your child's needs are all being met. Great! I invite you to read over this list of strategies—one of them might be a good addition to your present repertoire.

- Remember that the handicapped or ill child is learning a different lifestyle from those who do not have such problems. This requires you to be tolerant of expressions of sadness and fear that you never imagined your child would have. *Be open and let the child express any feelings to you.*
- Prepare yourself to support the child in whatever school setting he or she fits. Think through all the benefits of mainstreaming, of special classes and training programs. Mainstreaming the handicapped with non-handicapped can be a most successful school arrangement. Your positive attitude is essential.
- Keep in mind the importance of friends; promote ways to keep the youngster in a social setting.
- Try to capitalize on strengths at all times.
- Listen to what the child wants to learn or to improve upon. Would mastering a word processor or computer be helpful?
- Help your child set realistic goals in many areas—home chores, schoolwork, and outside interests.
- Encourage independent decision making whenever feasible.
- Make frequent efforts to help the child develop new interests and creativity. Provide toys, supplies, and books.
- Handle the subject of sex, grooming, and relationships with the frankness appropriate to understanding. If your teenager has had a limited background in social situations, an understanding of relationships will be missing or misconstrued. Take time to read books together, go to the movies, watch TV, and talk about the relationships that you observed.
- If your child shows special talent (for example, a blind student who plays the piano, or a deaf person who composes) make certain he or she is planning to use the talent for monetary and *emotional* gain.

- Don't overreact to outbursts. Teenagers may be acting out for the first time. The handicapped adolescent may be reacting to years of forced overdependency or overprotection.
- Keep in mind the wider scope of interests and job opportunities which are developing. This means new methods of evaluating work and forecasting for the future. Be open minded about non-competitive school placements or training situations, and living facilities which promote independence.

The teenager with a handicapping condition is confronted with the normal crises of adolescence. Combined with the ongoing difficulties of the past, these may upset some of the established ways he or she has learned to cope. This may be very upsetting to the child and his parents. Remain optimistic. All young people need support to handle the regressions, demands, and problems that lie ahead.

Ernest Siegel offered, in *The Exceptional Child Grows Up* (page 212), a summary statement that fits the context of this discussion: "There is an obvious connection between degree of disability and level of potential. The factor of adjustment, however, cutting across all levels and types of exceptionality, has relatively little to do with severity of impairment. In the long run, a person's well-being is influenced less by the disability than by his adjustment to it."

Every adult in the life of a child is a teacher. Teaching involves the effects of our behavior on the feelings and learning of others. This requires insight into self. Once we understand ourselves, we can begin to understand others. *Understanding the needs of your handicapped child must take priority over understanding the disability itself.*

Welcome the reminder that our concern is for the integrity of the whole person, for his or her finiteness as a human being and the comforts that can be established and maintained in the complex world of human relationships.

32. STRESS FROM A TRAUMATIC ACCIDENT

A traumatic accident requires emergency medical attention. It will cause sudden stress. Fear, pain, and all the necessary medical procedures combine into a package of unknowns. After the crisis, there will still be unknowns. "Will my arm be okay? Will I ever be able to use it again?" or in the more serious situations, "How long will I have to stay in the hospital? Will my mom and dad be able to visit? What about school? How many operations will I have to have? Will I ever be okay?"

Medical professionals care. They don't want to make matters worse or more traumatic than necessary, but they have procedures they must follow. In a crisis, physical problems take priority over psychological or emotional considerations. Doctors and nurses try to comfort the child and provide as much support as they can. Yes, accidents are traumatic events and yes, the child will recover from the stress—some more readily than others. All will leave some scars, emotional and sometimes physical, and these will become less troublesome after a while.

Accidents Requiring Hospitalization

Kenny, aged five, was in a car wreck in which his mother was killed. He suffered two fractured legs and a broken pelvis. They were en route to visit grandparents almost 800 miles away from home. Kenny's father was in the service in Germany. It was almost twenty-four hours before the grandparents could get to the hospital. Doctors kept Kenny sedated, but by the time the grandparents arrived, he was alert and in a state of panic. In time, Kenny recovered and adjusted to the loss of his mom. His body healed but he is not the carefree boy of pre-accident days. Except for his underlying sadness, no other important symptoms persisted.

Symptoms of Stress

At the time of a traumatic accident, expect:

Evidence of panic, overwhelming fear.
Mutism.
Uncontrolled crying, screaming, especially at night.
Refusal to eat.
Almost total withdrawal from caretakers.
Physical symptoms of shock, such as blood pressure changes.
Extreme passivity, unresponsiveness.

As the child improves, other symptoms may show up:

Fears about being alone without someone nearby to help if needed.
Anxiety about disfiguration, handicaps.
Belated grief when appropriate.
"Hospitalitis"—child becomes cranky, hostile, restless or very critical, depending on length of stay.
Seeking guarantees that he or she will be welcome at home.
Anxiety about peer rejection, losing ground at school, poor grades, or having to repeat.
Exaggerated self-involvement.
Nightmares, disturbed sleep patterns, especially if sedatives or pain shots have been reduced or discontinued.
Guilt over attention taken away from the siblings at home.

Depending on the age and maturity of the child, some become obsessed with a fear of dying. Others become negative and depressed.

Children have a remarkable capacity to bounce back. They want to make new friends among the hospital personnel and other patients. As they improve, they may strain to show each new accomplishment and how they have learned to compensate for a cast or immobility. This is wonderful to watch.

Strategies for Support

Strategies for support have to be modified for each patient, but some can be grouped together.

Physical needs, medical matters

During the critical days, be there, be comforting, and don't press for responses, smiles, or laughter.

After the critical days

(1) Be prepared for the child to be demanding, have a very short attention span, cry easily.

(2) Share the facts in a supportive way. There is no use in making predictions that may not come true, but you can express hope, for example, that nerves in the arm will be restored. Talk about pain. There may be pain for a long time.

(3) Discuss with the physician and the child what signs of improvement to look for and a possible timetable. Even young school-aged children can understand accurate reports and prognoses.

(4) With older kids, discuss the necessity of adhering to a medication program without constant parental nagging.

(5) Make it clear that there will be appointments that will interfere with school activities and outside interests. Talk about home routines and plans, taking into account that the child may get unusually tired.

(6) If further surgery is necessary, prepare the child far enough in advance so that all questions can be answered but not so far in advance as to cause prolonged worry and stress. In some instances, let the child choose the date—for example, spring vacation for plastic surgery or skin grafts.

Non-medical matters:

(1) If the child is disfigured or now has a speech or hearing impediment, take as much time as necessary to deal with feelings. He or she fears peer rejection the most. Explain that at first people may react to bandages and scars, but this doesn't last.

(2) Explore feelings about any aspect of being in the hospital. Each child will adjust in his or her own way. Don't make comparisons with the

kid in the next bed. "Why can't you smile like he does?" This won't cheer up someone who is sad or terrified. Be as positive as you can, minimizing criticisms of food service or the availability of the staff.

(3) When appropriate, describe the recovery of others who have had similar accidents, such as burns, broken bones, or loss of limbs. Call on hospital personnel and specialists to spend time with you and your child. The child needs to know from experts how bones heal, or how skin grafts work. The angry child may not accept such information from a parent, thinking that you are only saying optimistic things in order to cheer him or her up.

(4) If the child becomes grouchy about shots and tests, remain businesslike. Nobody likes shots, but inappropriate sympathy won't help. The child may need a great number of shots in the months to come.

(5) Consult the doctor and see if your child needs help to work through the trauma of the accident. It may take months, even years, for some children to talk about being hit by a car, or being thrown off a bike. On the other hand, some children stay on the topic and go into great detail about it again and again. Talking about the accident is an effective way to diminish stress. Prepare family members to be listeners.

(6) In preparing the child to go home, discuss what may be expected. Siblings may be resentful of all the time that parents have spent with the accident victim and they may need and want more attention now. Others will be delighted to have the sibling home, anxious to be helpful, ready to bring water, flowers, and medicines, to play games or watch TV together. In general, as long as the child feels well, you can expect excitement at going home.

When the child returns to school, arrange for a shortened day at first. This may mean that you have to play chauffeur or ask an older brother or sister to pick up the child. Some school districts have adjusted bus schedules and this might help. Negotiate with your child as to which subjects he or she would like to concentrate on. And consider getting a tutor. Grades are not all that important. Resuming a normal social life is the child's top priority.

If your child runs into problems with teasing, a teacher can deal with student insensitivity. If it is necessary for the child to give up a favorite sport, go to school and confer with the teacher to find alternative, challenging activities.

Finally, if you feel guilty because of the accident or the treatment your child has received, get help for yourself.

33.   ONE INVISIBLE DISEASE: LEARNING DISABILITIES

(For others such as childhood diabetes and heart disease, see Section VII, #31.)

Chris's mother noted in his baby book that as a toddler he would overreact to any change in routine. When the family stayed in a cabin in the mountains, Chris was frightened—too many unfamiliar sights and sounds. As his vocabulary got bigger, he was puzzled when a word had more than one meaning. He couldn't conceive that Mom plays bridge, Daddy drives over the bridge and Grandpa has a bridge in his mouth!

His problems became more apparent when he started preschool. Teacher said he was hyperactive and bright, restless and inquisitive. He didn't like to be touched and his temper tantrums indicated that he was immature and had poor impulse control

By the end of first grade, his teacher recommended that Chris be tested for learning problems. He already gave signs that he felt unsure of himself, was "no good" at anything, and wanted to stay home. His invisible disease was no longer invisible. The adults in his world recognized some of the symptoms. He was one of the lucky ones. Chris got help.

Over 90 percent of all boys who are sent to reform schools, detention centers, or jails have significant learning disabilities. The affected youngsters act out their stress against society and are consequently often punished by the society they offend. Such children come from all walks of life and all kinds of schools. Over 10 million kids have learning disabilities, many of them never diagnosed or given any help. One out of every ten boys (a ten to one ratio more than girls) suffers from some learning problem due to a neurological source. They handle their stress the only way they know how—with anger and impulsive or inappropriate behavior. Some take drugs as an escape. Many get very depressed.

Identifying the Problems: the Source of Stress

Symptoms of learning disabilities are difficult to distinguish from symptoms of stress. If a boy is not reading, is it because his eyes are not functioning properly or because he is so frightened that he cannot attend to the words? Learning disabilities are usually discovered *after* the child has failed to progress properly or displays consistent problems. When he or she is seen struggling, it is called "trying hard" or "putting forth a lot of effort" and not identified as a symptom of stress. *Stress for these kids stems from continuous or intermittent failures and the resulting loss of self-confidence.*

Chris's mother had to learn that there is a wide range of different impairments or dysfunctions, both within a child and between one child and another. Some aspects of development are normal and some are not. These inconsistencies contribute to the child's fragmented sense of personal worth and create a high anxiety level. They confuse adults. Work with these children is complex and taxing. Parent and teacher are confronted with three goals: (1) the remediation of the learning or communication problems, (2) the repair of self-esteem, overcoming defeatist attitudes and discouragement, and (3) the training necessary to develop a successful coping style.

Symptoms of Stress

The symptoms of stress replicate symptoms of communicative, social, and personal learning disabilities. It is almost like the chicken and egg dilemma—which came first?

- Impaired, hesitant speech.
- Inability to concentrate.
- Illegible handwriting, heavy strokes, white-knuckle hold on the pencil.
- Disorganization; the child loses things, and is very sloppy.
- Exaggerated anxiety.
- Immature reactions to changes, shifts, surprises.
- Mood swings.
- Poor peer relationships for some.
- Poor judgment, inappropriate behaviors of all sorts.
- Depression.
- Task avoidance, refusal to go to school.
- Anger, hostility, or extreme docility.
- Inability to take teasing, jokes.
- Use of drugs and/or alcohol as an escape.

More detailed indications of learning disabilities include the following items.* These contribute to a sense of frustration and stress.

Verbal Disabilities

Cannot understand what is said.
Has small vocabulary, recognizing one meaning only for each word.
Repeats many questions.
May refuse to speak, or speech may be halting, slow, or slurred.
Tends to be forgetful of what he or she is saying.
May use large words but not comprehend them.
May be two or more grades below grade placement in oral reading
    ability.

---

*List from Spice Chart of Learning Disabilities (1975) R. P. Arent, C. A. Berryman, Denver, Colorado

Motor Disabilities

Walking may be clumsy with frequent tripping.
Handwriting may be labored, illegible.
Buttons, shoelaces, zippers may give difficulty.
Onset of fatigue is rapid.
Child may become disoriented in large, open space.
May have difficulty participating in games that involve running, jumping, skipping, hopping.

Visual Disabilities

Cannot put pictures or letters in proper order.
Cannot copy letters or numbers accurately.
Cannot write a list of words, numbers, or letters in a column.
Reverses or rotates all or part of written letters or numbers.
Cannot maintain eye contact.
Has difficulty copying from chalkboard or book.
Cannot remember words from sight vocabulary after many presentations.
May complain of tired eyes.

Auditory Disabilities

Cannot locate sounds.
Cannot follow oral direction.
Cannot remember a series of three directions.
May cover ears when room is noisy.
Cannot attend to a story when it is read aloud.
May attend to part of a spoken assignment.
Tends to forget what he has heard.
Cannot use context clues to correct wrong discrimination.

Strategies for Support

All strategies must be geared to

- Improving self-confidence and self-esteem.
- Providing a predictable environment to minimize disturbances.
- Strengthening of the child's abilities.

For young toddlers

Strategies build from an understanding that the child with minimal brain injury will be extremely irritable and have unexplained outbursts. The outbursts are described as a breakdown in all the controls the child has acquired. They are frequently confused with the tantrums of the spoiled or willful child. They are signs of the child's internal disorganization.

These are useful management ideas

- Require orderliness and regularity to fix habits; *routines are essential.*
- Limit assortment of foods to the familiar. For example, hamburgers, peanut butter sandwiches, and cereal may be the only foods the child will eat. Limit sugar intake.
- Provide quiet, to avoid stimulation from TV, radio, or loud stereo. A child may respond well to soft music.
- Keep tensions to a minimum; perhaps allow the child to eat alone or before the others, and to play in his own room at times.
- Put away fragile items such as easily-tipped lamps because the child may be clumsy and awkward.
- Choose clothing that closes easily.
- Repeat explanations of limits and consequences as often as necessary.
- Follow through with medication as prescribed.

For school-aged children

This is the time when problems in learning, reasoning, abstract thinking, and problem solving will become apparent. In my experience as a therapist, I have noted that more than 80 percent of adult male patients had adjustment and emotional problems because they had learning disabilities which were never diagnosed and/or properly remediated. Almost without exception, the problems involved their eyes. Yes, they had been tested to see if they needed glasses, and many did not. Yet they continued to be unble to *visualize* how relationships work or the outcome of such decisions as a job change. This inability, combined with a history of school problems, self-doubt, and confused relationships resulted in painful debilitating stress.

If you find that your school-aged child displays a number of the symptoms of stress plus specific learning problems (for example, he or she cannot spell), it would be advisable to have him or her checked for visual-motor *function* difficulties. This examination is usually performed by an optometrist who specializes in the field. Children, teenagers, and adults respond well to exercises which will improve perceptual difficulties. Such an examination is an essential diagnostic measure.

Strategies for Support for The Young Child With Learning Disabilities

- Be predictable.
- Offer a consistent approach to *all* situations. TV viewing must be regulated.

- Give one-step instructions; too many words are confusing.
- Offer protection from being teased or ways to manage cruelties.
- Arrange for special considerations at school, perhaps special placement. Learning problems become progressively worse unless effectively remediated.
- Limit special events such as birthday parties, or the circus, because there are too many stimuli.
- *Give encouragement.*
- *Show warmth, expressions of love;* remember some children may not want to be touched.

In some classic works, human stress has been defined in chemical terms with descriptions of imbalances and deficiencies based on reactions to pressures and events. These reactions can be diagnosed through blood and urine studies among other biochemical indices. Some symptoms can be alleviated through the use of vitamins and diet adjustment.

During the 1960s, the use of drugs, such as Ritalin, had become accepted practice among pediatricians in the handling of hyperactive children. Dr. Linus Pauling, Dr. Allan Cott, and others discovered that the addition of megavitamins helped children to behave and learn. This became known as orthomolecular treatment. Although controversial, much research supports the use of well-regulated and monitored intake of megavitamins and minerals. Without consideration of the chemical well-being of the brain cells and related nutritional or metabolic findings, the child with learning disabilities may continue to experience body stress that adds immeasurably to the stress resulting from other physical, functional, or emotional sources.

Parents and school professionals may feel defeated when a child fails to progress after many weeks or years of skillful teaching. In many instances, the brain has not been chemically receptive to changes.

Strategies for Support for Adolescents with Learning Disabilities

These strategies are intended to overcome fear of school and to maintain good feelings about family and friends.

- The school program must not isolate the student. If the child is placed in a special program, vocational training center or the like, contact with non-disabled learners must be provided.
- School programming must be geared to future survival in the community, offering preparation in the social and work skills areas.
- Money management merits the special attention of parents and teachers. The learning-disabled student may be ripped off, cheated, or conned out of money by others who take advantage of his vulnerability.

- Parents must help the adolescent maintain realistic goals. The teenager may be very aware of the successes of others and make comparisons. He or she may become very depressed. Parental understanding of the child's moods, inconsistencies, demands, and changes is essential. This may be difficult because parents also are often worried and depressed.
- If your teenager gets unusually depressed, urge him to participate in a group of other persons with similar problems. There are a number of such groups around, in schools, and some community mental health centers, for example. It is necessary to explain the facts about learning problems. Remind him or her of those things that he can do well, such as drive a car, or use a calculator.
- A predictable home environment with clear rules and equally clear enforcements decreases stress.
- To offset a major problem—loneliness or lack of friends—provide some family patterns that include cousins or the children of friends. Within a relatively protected setting, a youngster can practice social skills and may feel most successful.
- If a brain-damaged child has siblings who are callous or unkind, the parent must be assertive and not let uncaring habits persist.

The Learning Disabled Child in a Family in Turmoil

This is a very difficult struggle. Give repeated explanations of the problems, couched in words and simple concepts that he or she can grasp. One can predict many questions from the child for a long time to come. You are asking the child to see the nuances and comprehend consequences and feelings that he or she may not be able to visualize at all (such as, the concept of ambivalence).

These difficulties are especially true when trying to help a child understand abuse. More and more studies show that it is often the disabled child who is singled out for child abuse by a battering parent. The healthiest child needs an enormous amount of help to understand complex family problems. Realistically, the disabled child will need even more. If, for example, it becomes necessary to remove the child from the home, this must be handled with immeasurable skill and caring and requires repeated explanations. The stress is overwhelming even to a child who is not an impaired learner.

34.   LIVING WITH A LIFE-THREATENING ILLNESS

The daughter of a friend of mine died as a teenager. She had nephrosis. She had been hospitalized frequently. She couldn't stand straight, and used to call herself "the crooked one." Before she died, she wanted time with her sister who lived far away. She died at her sister's.

The mother let the sister select a burial site. It was underneath a crooked tree.

Children with a fatal illness experience stress that cannot be experienced by anyone else. They know that they do not feel well, that something is very wrong. They rebel against being different from well people—family, friends, kids on TV. Depending on age and development, first they want answers that are hopeful; later they want the truth about their future and about death. In many ways, answers provide them with a way of life, with a format for dealing with profound stress. Each child develops a way to cope whether it involves sharing feelings and fears or maintaining a kind of quiet privacy. Children adjust to their own emotional swings at separation from family and friends when they have to spend time in the hospital. They often become very intuitive and philosophical.

There are some fine booklets distributed by the Leukemia Society of America, and the Cystic Fibrosis Foundation, for example, that give great insight into the experiences of the children, their siblings, and their parents. The initial impact of the diagnosis of the disease will create more stress for the parents than for the ill child. It may be months, perhaps years, before the child is told the truth. The child must be given sufficient information to insure his cooperation with medical treatment and his emotional well-being. You, in the meantime, must answer the questions of relatives and other children without frightening the child who is ill. The teenager, in contrast to a five-year-old, may demand answers or draw his own conclusions about the nature of the illness and the prognosis. All ill children need much support, regardless of age.

Sources of Stress

Sources of stress, when presented as a list, seem mundane. Nevertheless, they provide a picture of the tests ahead for all members of the family. Again, the age and the personality of the ill child will be pivotal to his or her coping style.

For the Child	For the Parents	For Siblings
Wants to feel better.	Medical decisions.	How to deal with fear, anger, curiosity.
Wants parents, doctors to make him well.	Feelings. How to approach others.	
		How to know when to ask for something for themselves.
Fears treatments, separations, missing school and losing friends.	Spouse agreements or disagreements. Financial matters. Hospital stay, visits. Concern for others.	How to deal with jealousy of attention ill sibling gets.

For the Child	*For the Parents*	*For Siblings*
After remissions or in late stages of the disease:	How to communicate with the sick child: what to/not to tell.	How to give support to ill sibling, parents.
Wants to be certain parent is near.	How to program a child during remissions or when "feeling better."	Questions about their own well-being.
Wants doctor near.		
Wants help to talk about illness, death.	How to balance expectations/normal child vs. ill child.	
Wants time, a chance to say good-bye.	Discipline, excuses, sympathy as problems.	
Wants to decide how things will be distributed.	Making plans for funeral, burial of a child. Anticipating life without the child.	
Wants to be reassured that death doesn't hurt.	Seeking answers, cures, spiritual guidance.	

Descriptions of children with a fatal illness may include such words as pensive, angry, searching, realistic, hostile, passive, intuitive, unresponsive. When such children feel well, they are frequently described as conscientious, eager, delightful, reserved, anxious to please and friendly. At certain times in the illness, symptoms of stress range from deep depression to temper tantrums and refusal to talk. Realistically, all of those behaviors are manifestations of the childrens' awareness that they are ill, that they are different, that they may die. Their priorities may shift rapidly. For a while a child may be intent on spending a great deal of time with parents, siblings, and friends. Within a short time he may want to spend hours reading as much as he can, learning about aviation, or studying trees or history.

Strategies for Support

How can parents help to alleviate such stress? If you are a parent with an ill child, I am certain that you give immeasurable support to your youngster. So that others may benefit from the lessons that you and other parents have taught us, this summary is presented.

(1) Remain at the hospital with the infant, toddler, or pre-school-aged child. The child is apt to be more devastated by the separation and fear of abandonment than by the illness.

(2) Be prepared for angry outbursts and don't overreact. The child may scream "I hate you!" because he or she feels that somehow you have let this happen to him or her.

(3) Express hope, understanding, and realistic reassurances. You can't make a promise that the child will never have to go to the hospital again or go through painful tests and procedures. But you can reassure the child that you care, that others care, that the doctors and nurses will do the best that they can and that they care, too.

(4) At home, keep the family as near normal as possible. Continue holiday celebrations, routines, events for the siblings, and traditions. This helps the ill child feel less guilty about interfering with family life.

(5) If the child is going to school, urge the child to be honest with teachers and friends. This prevents misunderstandings when the child gets crabby, can't keep up, or complains of not feeling well. If the child is embarrassed to handle this, offer to go to school with him or her and handle the problem together. Some young children may discuss heart disease, liver problems, cancer, or other diseases with peers in a matter of fact way. Others are reluctant to do so. The child may feel betrayed if you tell without his or her permission.

(6) Older students will accept hospitalization more readily when you make arrangements with teachers for lessons and tests. There is no way to predict the outcome of a disease for a patient, for your child. Some teenagers with Hodgkins disease or leukemia may become young adults—into their twenties—and will make every effort to be independent and self-sufficient. They are, therefore, entitled to the same skills training, learning, and career counseling as others.

(7) Listen to the child's protests if he or she feels that you are being overprotective. Back off or explain your decision. There will be times when you can make decisions together—about bedtimes, exercise programs, clinic schedules, or responsibilities at home. When they are not feeling well, most children accept dependency without too much of a struggle. They welcome freedom and responsibility when they feel better.

(8) If the child is being teased by peers—such as being called "hairless" as a side effect of chemotherapy—be assertive. Parents' and teachers' assertiveness must be focused on being fair and kind.

(9) Reflect on your spiritual or religious beliefs regarding life and death. Share these with your child. Seek help for yourself from any sources that you respect. This support gives you more energy to cope with the many pressures that you face. It goes without saying that your ill child will benefit from your attitude and strength. (Parents sometimes report that one of the most difficult adjustments to be made after the death of a child is where to direct, and how to use, this ready reserve of energy.)

(10) When you become aware that death is imminent, your presence is the greatest reassurance and comfort the child can have. Dying at home allows the child to be in the place he or she has loved, surrounded by people, especially parents, whom he or she loves. This is not always possible or wise. In the hospital, the dying child, though very weak, perhaps semi-conscious, needs to know that you are there. If possible, having his or her much-trusted doctor there also eases the way. You may want to ask the doctor to stay nearby if it can be arranged.

Stress on the child with a life-threatening illness cannot be compared with any other stress. We all want to know what we can do. Underneath, we all feel so helpless. The children may show us the way to compassion and humility. For this, we can all be grateful.

The *benefits* for the well persons in the family include:

- Opportunities to be supportive, express love, be helpful.
- An introduction to the realities of death and dying, even though this is sad and unpleasant. An opportunity, perhaps, to learn about the concepts that Kubler-Ross describes and to participate as the patient goes through the stages. This encompasses an understanding of the emotions a dying person may express, anger, denial, depression and resignation. (See Section XII, #56.)
- The fact that emotional ties for all members of the family may be strengthened. The appropriate and sensitive expression of feelings is a pattern that helps through the days of distress and as preparation for all relationships.
- A chance to determine values—what counts most in this life. It reaffirms the importance of compassion, unselfishness, sensitivity, and non-materialistic goals.

In your interactions with a dying child, listen to his or her agenda— let the child ask about the flowers in the garden or the puppy. You are there to comfort not to ask questions which may require strength to answer. Show your love. Accept his smiles.

Chronic Stress at Home

35. LIVING WITH AN ALCOHOLIC PARENT

One out of every nine adult Americans is an alcoholic. Twelve to fifteen million children live with a parent who has a serious drinking problem. Accurate statistics for drug addicts are not available, but their problems are similar. The stress the children live with is profound and confusing. Parental addiction results in damaged relationships, repressed feelings, fragmented bonding, and anxiety. Inevitably, the children face the future asking, "Will this happen to me?"

Alcohol is a legal drug. In 1956 the American Medical Association recognized alcoholism as a disease. Almost every reputable organization dealing with the problem, ranging from the U.S. Department of Justice to the World Health Organization, is in agreement. All affirm that this disease, like other addictive diseases, is treatable.

Alcoholics and others with addictions are ordinary people, men and women, young and old. The only thing that makes them different is a chemical dependency that they cannot control. It is easy to blame the pressures of modern life for the increased use of drugs. Ultimately, it is a personal disease that requires a personal decision to seek treatment in order to overcome the dependency.

Characteristics of the Alcoholic Family

Deception and unreliability are perhaps the two most easily recognized characteristics of the alcoholic family. These create stress for children. Some parents may hide their drinking while others may pass out on the living room couch. Children are deprived of honesty and consis-

115

tency. Unanswered questions and unexplained behavior add to the problems. Irresponsible behavior frightens children. It's scary to feel, "I don't know where Mom or Dad is," or, "I can't understand why Dad is so hateful today when he was so loving yesterday."

On a deeper level there are three issues that these children must face: parental detachment, role changes, and repressed feelings. A parent who is absorbed in his or her own gratifications cannot be expected to develop or maintain a normal bonding situation with the children. (See Section III on bonding.) Sometimes the child will feel cared for and other times the child will feel neglected. A feeling of being detached or maybe being abandoned can result. When role reversals are necessary and the child takes care of the parent, the child misses a close and loving parental relationship. At the same time, the child learns to stop asking questions. It is not difficult to recognize that when asked too many questions, the parent gets angry and ends up consuming more drinks. Children, seeing cause and effect, back off. They don't want to make their parents mad, and more important—they do not tell their parents how they feel. If they admit to being scared or embarrassed, it may simply start another scene and Mom or Dad will hit the bottle again.

Stress results from having to be secretive. Children are naturally social persons who freely share almost all their thoughts. They learn quickly that talking about a parent's drinking is a family taboo. It is a lesson which can affect all of the child's relationships. The message kids get is to stay businesslike with teachers and have fun with friends, but not to talk about family to outsiders or discuss feelings with the other members of the family. Even brothers and sisters remain remote from each other.

Being a child of an addicted parent may force a child to take on different roles. Betty, a daughter, became a rescuer. If Mom was drunk, Betty would fix dinner, do the laundry, or look after the other kids. Matt, a son, took on the role of hero. He tried to make things better for the family and worked diligently to improve the situation. Because a parent who drinks needs to drink more and more, the hero is always losing ground and feels consistently inadequate. This feeling of inadequacy is well hidden by the obvious, visible success of the family achiever. The role of the hero is to provide self-worth for the family. He pays a very high price in terms of nonstop stress.

Some children become scapegoats. These children choose to pull away from the mess and stress in the family. They attract attention by doing things that are self-defeating. They may run away, get pregnant, use drugs, or provoke significant problems at school. In providing distraction away from the alcoholic parent, the child protects those he or she loves. Stress in the family is thus compounded instead of relieved.

Symptoms of Stress which children display

Some are easy to observe. Others are more subtle.
- No positive self-image. "I don't like me."
- Inconsistent feelings about parents. "Sometimes I love my mom and sometimes I hate her."
- Uncertainties about who they are. "Am I a kid or a grownup?"
- Adult-child confusion. "Sometimes I have to take care of them!"
- Lack of respect for parents.. "I can't respect my parents. They tell lies."
- Feelings of helplessness, incompetence, pity, fear, anger, despair, and embarrassment that may not be openly expressed. "I can't do anything when my dad screams at us or when my mom blacks out." "I've learned I'd better not tell anyone how I feel."
- Need to be a self-reliant perfectionist. "No one takes care of me so I have to take care of myself and be the *best* I can be *all* the time."
- Depression, signs similar to anyone who suffers loss.
- Withdrawal, reluctance to ask for help. "I am the one who is supposed to be a helper. I shouldn't have to ask for help."
- Lack of self-esteem. "I feel guilty when I stand up for myself. I don't deserve all this attention."
- Uncommunicativeness. "I learned the best thing to do is to say nothing. I'm not going to be the one to tell. Maybe if I don't talk about it, it won't hurt so much."

The parent *must* have two important goals. The first is to solve his or her own drinking problem. *This means to stop! A commitment to a therapy or support program is imperative!* Group therapy in an inpatient or outpatient facility can be intensive and can hasten recovery. Alcoholics Anonymous is one of the most effective programs, though it lacks the intensity of the inpatient setting. Related programs like Alateen and Al-Anon are designed to help children and mates of the alcoholic.

The second goal is to repair significant relationships as far as possible. Help the children with feelings and adjustment problems. Be open and communicative. Help each child learn that he or she can cope with life without the use of alcohol. This is important. Today, too many boys and girls of eight, nine, and ten years of age are already addicted to booze or other drugs. These children—and all others—need help to recognize the symptoms of an addiction and to do something about them.

The Characteristics of an Alcoholic

- You drink more and more because you really enjoy it. Actually, there is something wrong, but you can't pinpoint it; you are powerless against it but you think you have it under control.

- You need "one or two" drinks nearly every day.
- You get drunk almost every weekend.
- You keep "going on the wagon."
- You think about booze a lot.
- You arrive at parties and social affairs already "well oiled."
- You begin to lose friends quickly even if you make them easily.
- You have blackouts—that is, the next day you can't remember what happened while you were drinking.
- You drink to get rid of a hangover.
- Once you take a drink, you find it hard to refuse another. In fact, you hardly think about it.
- You make excuses about your drinking.
- Your family makes excuses about your drinking.
- You get into trouble because of your drinking.
- Once you start drinking, you can't stop. You go on long binges that you can't help.

Strategies for Support

Note: If parents are still having addiction problems, another adult may have to be the support person.

(1) Help children understand that they are not responsible for the fact that their parents cannot show love. Addictions distort emotions.

(2) Help children understand that parents who drink have impaired memories. They don't show up for conferences at school or for birthday parties; that is part of the addiction. Parents do not intentionally hurt their kids. The parents are victims of their disease.

(3) Let children know that they can confide in responsible adults, such as other family members or school counselors. (It is estimated that 90 percent of physical abuse is alcohol related.)

(4) Respect the child's wish not to take sides, to maintain a certain loyalty to both the alcoholic and non-alcoholic parent.

(5) Help the child learn to play. Many children from an alcoholic family have had to be caretakers as young as five years of age and this meant playtime was gone. They have an overdeveloped sense of responsibility and approach life in a serious, sad way.

(6) Expect that the expression of feelings may be very, very difficult. Be patient. This may be a problem for many years to come. Experts in the field of alcohol treatment state that crises from childhood experiences may be acted out in the late twenties by angry fights or sexual promiscuity, for instance. Acting out may precede verbal expressions of feelings.

(7) Encourage the kids to get involved with other kids from similar backgrounds. High school students might want to join SADD—Students Against Driving Drunk. This group was founded because kids suffered so much grief when their friends and siblings were killed in car accidents. Ten thousand people between ages sixteen and twenty-four die in alcohol-related motor vehicle crashes each year. No other single cause kills more people in this age group.

(8) Remind kids about the effects that alcohol has on an unborn child. Even though it may sound preachy, tell them about fetal alcohol syndrome in which newborn babies of drinking mothers are born drunk and need detoxification. Tell them about impaired development and mental retardation.

(9) If your family has broken up because of drinking or other addictions, make sure that the youngsters understand what happened. This is consistent with one theme of this book: that children are entitled to know the facts in order to build and maintain a successful way to cope. *The alcoholic family has a higher rate of divorce, incest, death, money problems, violence, and neglect than any other.*

The child of an alcoholic lives in an environment inundated with stress for everyone. Although the problem is shared by the entire family, that doesn't make it any easier. The aim of treatment for the problem drinker is to make him or her stronger, happier, and more self-aware without the need for alcohol. Repair of the parent-child relationship is an essential part of the program.

The benefit of living with an alcoholic parent may be that a child will become aware of how alcohol has damaged the lives of so many people and he or she may develop a way to live a drug-free life.

36. LIVING WITH AN ILL OR HANDICAPPED PARENT

A parent's handicap may be a very private matter. Some kids are embarrassed by it. Very young children might believe that "all moms can't hear" and "most daddies are in wheelchairs." Learning to take care of a parent, to help on a daily and often very personal basis, is a way of life for millions of youngsters. Situations vary dramatically. So much depends on the other helpers available, the degree of the handicap, the attitude and expectations for all. There is no typical pattern.

Sources of Stress

As a source of stress, these children do have some things in common.

- Their home life is different from that of families where no one has a handicap or chronic illness. Although children adjust to life with a handicapped parent and learn what is expected of them without fanfare, there may be an undertone of resentment. "It's not fair that *my mom* has arthritis so that she can't walk. Sometimes I think it's not fair that I have to take care of her so much."

- Fear is ever present. Will the parent get worse, have to leave the house, and go to a nursing home or die? Will they run out of money? Some children wonder, "Will I be taken away?"
- Children feel overwhelmed that there is so much to do to take care of the parent—and perhaps the other kids and the house. When things don't get done, they feel guilty and embarrassed. They may not manage to keep up with school assignments and this contributes to stress.
- Older brothers and sisters can become unusually protective of younger siblings to make up for what a parent can't do. In turn, they may put aside their own responsibilities about school or outside interests such as music, Scouts, or athletics. Marital problems are common. These affect everyone. The children become confused about dependency and helplessness. They want to see the parent get better and become more independent. If Rose, a fourteen-year-old girl, helps to bathe her partially-mobile mother every day, she knows that she is important to her mom. When Rose herself wants help with homework, she is reluctant to ask.
- The expression of feelings becomes a problem. The ill parent may put on a brave front all the time so as "not to worry the others." This way of coping with disability and pain is a powerful message. The ill parent who complains, whines, and looks for nonstop sympathy also creates a situation where expression of feelings is difficult. Sharon, age eleven, is in this situation. She really feels sorry for Mom, but expressing sympathy is hard. She feels some anger and disappointment sometimes because Mom doesn't "try to cheer up." Sharon seldom expresses herself. She may break down and shout, "Oh, for once Mom, why don't you smile?" Then she feels guilty. The stress she feels comes from the dual life she leads—junior nurse and developing school girl.

With or Without Words: The Child Exhibits Stress

- The child appears too serious, depressed, or worried all the time.
- The child is afraid to leave the house for fear the parent will not be properly cared for. It is difficult to concentrate at school.
- The child has disturbed sleep patterns, fearful that the parent's middle-of-the night plea for help might not be heard.

- The child gets embroiled in disturbing fantasies, imagines the worst, and can't seem to control such feelings. Children as young as age five may become obsessed with death and dying.
- The child is angry a lot, flies off the handle, or is moody. The need to be controlled around the ill person causes stress. There are times when the child is jealous of attention that the handicapped or ill parent receives.
- The child withdraws, feels as if he or she cannot ask for anything (attention, help, or money) because this might deprive the handicapped parent. I remember a child who appeared neglected. He refused any new clothes, and protested against Christmas presents because, "Mom needs a new wheel chair."

A child who displays any of these symptoms needs someone to talk to. Most children who show extreme stress are not given enough details such as who will be there with Mom or Dad, who will fix lunch, help with bathroom matters, bathe, or change clothes. Once they are made aware of daily routines, their stress levels will come down. Sometimes a vacation or a trip or visit away from home will help.

Sometimes the child's stress level will increase when they overreact to a parent's statement such as, "I love to have you here with me." Conflict ensues when the child interprets this as, "Don't leave me!" The child needs to be told about the predictable emotional ups and downs of a handicapped or chronically ill person.

Strategies for Supporting the Children

(1) They need thanks, compliments, and much appreciation. Taking care of a handicapped parent becomes routine, humdrum, like brushing your teeth, but the children need to be thanked.

(2) They need to understand that everyone depends on others to some extent and that circumstances change. Remind them that they were babies once and their parents took care of them! Now it has to be turned around.

(3) Children need to be helped to see the "wellness" the parent displays—efforts to be independent, cheerful, helpful with school work, and ways the parent attempts to compensate for one deficiency by being proficient in something else. The kids need to be reminded that Mom is a person first—a person with a handicap or illness—deserving of their respect.

(4) Beyond the wellness, children want to admire a parent. In some instances, this may require looking back on what a parent had accomplished in the past. This is important.

(5) Children need to be given a realistic picture of what is ahead, in terms that they can understand. No one can predict the course a disease will take. But children want people to "get well and live happily ever after." When this will not be the case, help them to accept reality. One doesn't have to be morbid. The thrust is, *"Let's make the best of every day we have!"*

In a handicapping situation such as that of a post-accident quadriplegic or progressive multiple sclerosis where change is slight, children will seldom ask questions about what's ahead. They need honest answers to whatever questions they may pose.

(6) Kids need to be allowed to be kids! Family patterns, if at all possible, must leave lots of time for kids to enjoy their own friends and activities.

(7) If a parent becomes terminally ill and death is near, the child may need special support. (See Kubler-Ross' Section XII, #56.) for the steps to follow to help a child deal with the anticipated loss of a loved one.) Hospice personnel give excellent information and advice.

(8) If possible, provide a chance for them to talk with other kids who help to take care of a mom or dad. Peer exchanges can be great.

(9) Give the kids an opportunity to tell their peers of the patterns in the home. Make it a learning experience for others. Most children do not have a poor-me attitude. And this mature, accept-life-as-it-is attitude is a fine example for other children and adults.

Benefits

I'm certain that you have already pictured a number of benefits that these kids have—and they are very real benefits.

(1) They learn that life can be a struggle. The struggle will mean that you have to learn to be strong, unselfish, and adaptable.

(2) They learn that living in a home where there is a problem doesn't have to be a problem! Patterns are worked out. People do adjust. "That's just how it is at *my* house!"

(3) They can become committed to doing something meaningful in the field of the parent's illness. Daniel's father had multiple sclerosis, and as a young boy, Danny decided to become a doctor to "find out about my Dad's illness." It may lead to a career choice or participation in an organization as a volunteer.

(4) They learn that you cannot run away from some problems.

(5) Many adapt a spiritual attitude about life and use this in order to make an adjustment to parental or family stress.

(6) Some become philosophical and adaptable. "Oh, Dad's back in the hospital getting some tests" is announced with a degree of nonchalance and comfort. Other children may become hysterical at the very thought of hospitalization.

Remember that most children adapt readily or seem only moderately or appropriately caught up in the ups and downs of the parent's disability. However, some children become unduly upset and may over-react, especially if the handicap results from some traumatic event such as an accident or a fire.

Children of a chronically ill parent seldom exhibit bitterness. Almost always, they contribute a sense of liveliness or serenity to the home. Their love of life can be maintained and the wellness of the ill or handicapped parent is thereby enhanced.

37. LIVING WITH AN ILL OR HANDICAPPED GRANDPARENT

You may find that your child is having problems being tolerant of a live-in grandparent who is ill. The child is not as concerned and loving as you would like.

Pertinent questions to consider are:

- How long has Grandma lived here?
- Did you bring her into your home to take care of her because she is infirm?
- Were the children prepared for it?
- How has it changed your life? Do you have only leftover time for the kids?
- Do the children resent Grandma? Or are they glad to have her with you?
- How much do the children know about Grandma's problems, her illnesses or senility?
- Are they constantly worried that Grandma is going to die?
- Did the children expect that Grandma would be more lovable and companionable than she is?
- What family patterns have had to be changed in order to accommodate Grandma?

Your answers to these questions provide hints as to how well your kids are adjusting to living with Grandma. It is worthwhile asking if they would behave this way if Grandma weren't ill.

Symptoms of Stress

Most children do not become disturbed when a well grandparent moves in. (See Section VIII, #40.) They may protest a bit or find minor complaints to fuss about, but you can expect them to be accepting, or, perhaps remote and disinterested. A few children will become closely involved in the care of an ill grandparent. In time, some of these children may show symptoms of stress. *Do not expect serious symptoms of stress.* These symptoms are frequently transient.

- Unusual demands for attention such as hurting the dog, leaving messes, or using obscenities.
- Considerable sibling bickering.
- Unusual withdrawal, isolation, or extended TV time, as if escaping from contact with the family.
- Expressions of anger. "Why did you have to bring Grandma here? Why couldn't Uncle Charlie have taken her?"
- Fears appropriate to anxiety about death or loss, such as disturbed sleep, or bedwetting.
- Numerous expressions of guilt. "I should do more for Grandma but she never says 'Thank you' and she's boring," is the way a child may describe the reactions of a post-stroke grandparent. Or, "It seems like she's been sick forever, and I guess I've learned to ignore it."

Strategies for Support

The strategies for support do not differ dramatically from those for the child living with an ill or handicapped parent. In most instances, it is only a matter of needing reassurance that the child is important to you. When they feel secure they will adjust readily as circumstances change. Kids are primarily concerned with their friends, school, their relationships with brothers, sisters and you. Relationships with grandparents are commonly less intense. They may love the grandparent very much but do not have the same sense of responsibility that they have for a parent.

There are *benefits*, not unlike the ones that come to children when living with a handicapped parent. In short, children will:

- Learn tolerance.
- Exhibit patience, hear endless stories about childhood experiences, for instance.
- Adjust to sharing their parents with the grandparents.
- Adjust as the grandparent becomes increasingly ill or dependent.
- Be glad that they could contribute to the care and at times, offer levity.

38. LIVING WITH A HANDICAPPED OR CHRONICALLY ILL SIBLING*

Many mixed emotions characterize this situation.**

Factors that determine how much stress the well children feel include:

- The nature of the disability. The degree of handicap. Is the child mobile, bedridden, totally dependent, improving, terminal?
- The time of onset. At birth or later?
- Whether the well child is older or younger.
- The attitude of the parents. Are they devastated, accepting, oversympathetic?
- The necessary financial adjustment and sacrifices the family must make.
- The quality of the relationship between the siblings. Were they close, competitive, very dependent?
- The family lifestyle that has developed to adjust to everyone's needs. Are people encouraged to be independent? Does the illness govern housing, vacations, meals, parents' work?
- The adjustment of the handicapped child. Is he or she demanding or pleasant?

Symptoms of Stress

Symptoms of stress reflect the adjustment that the well kids make. No symptoms mean that needs are being met. Negative feelings and attitudes will be expressed when the child is unhappy. They also may occasionally feign illness to get attention; or may do poorly in school.

In general siblings show sympathy and may say, "I wish I could fix Jim up!" In some instances, unpleasant or unaccepting remarks may be heard. "I get tired of always having to hear about Mary's problems. Just once, I wish someone would ask me how I feel." "When I look back over the last ten years, it seems as if *every* decision was based on what will happen to Eric." "I can remember how my sister manipulated Mom and Dad. She'd forget her pills or pull an attack just when they were supposed to come and see me play basketball!" "I couldn't believe how we all put up

---

*If the ill child has severe emotional problems—unmanagable temper, destructive behaviors, violent attacks on animals, people and things—these patterns may not apply. The resentments and fears of the other members of the family create significant stress. Decisions that need to be made can be very disturbing for all.

**If the handicap is mental retardation, the child may or may not experience considerable stress. (See Section VIII, #39.)

with Alice's nastiness. She would make biting remarks or be sarcastic, and we were supposed to excuse it because, after all, 'she has diabetes.'"

Strategies for Support

- When the well kids express negative feelings, don't be harsh. Expect some envy of the attention the ill child gets.
- Remind them that all kids, sick or well, can be moody. All kids can say things that they regret.
- Encourage them to be as tolerant of their handicapped sister or brother as they are of their friends.

The well child who is overly solicitous of the handicapped or ill sibling may be sending one of these messages:

- "I really love Ellen!"
- "If I pay a lot of attention to Ellen, maybe Mom and Dad will appreciate me."
- "It gets boring, but this is what I'm supposed to do."

The normal pattern of adjustment is to seem more involved on some days than others or to appear as if the parents can handle things and that there is no point in getting upset. In some instances, kids will take advantage of the sick or handicapped sibling. They may snatch his things and run away with them or not share a toy or game. Sometimes, it is best, to ignore such incidents. Teasing is part of the sibling game and a bit of it is to be expected in any household. If the teasing seems excessive step in on behalf of the ill child.

Benefits to the well children

The benefits of having an ill or handicapped sibling are numerous.

- The well children learn as much from illness as from health.
- They learn compassion.
- They learn to team up with parents on behalf of their brother or sister.
- They become aware of the importance of humor, unselfishness, and loyalty.
- They learn to support the parents when the parents get discouraged. They can encourage the parents to go to parent's groups or join other support organizations.

In some instances, they may be asked to compensate for the unfulfilled dreams the parents had for the other child. When a member of the family is chronically ill, it brings out the maturity in everyone. The family's lifestyle adjusts to the handicapped or ill child without fanfare.

Brothers and sisters almost always become very protective of each other and of the family as a unit. It would be great if all families had the same cohesiveness.

39. LIVING WITH A MENTALLY RETARDED SIBLING

Thousands of families have retarded children. Everyone must make certain adjustments.

Most retarded children are happy and sociable. They enjoy certain foods, music, and some become hooked on TV, crafts, or activities. Some are antisocial, fearing unfamiliar situations and meeting new people. Most become close to the members of the family even though communication is restricted and much goes on that they are unable to understand.

Living with a mentally retarded sibling is a source of stress for many children. The degree of the problem depends on the degree of the impairment, size of the family, birth order, and parental management. Parental management adds up to attitude, distribution of responsibilities, and how the needs of all are met. If the retarded child receives a disproportionate amount of adult time or family money (for example, for private education), others may feel displaced, ignored, or unimportant. These feelings may be expressed in various ways which replicate *symptoms of stress*. Outbursts of anger or expressions of disgust are rare. Most siblings understand and accept that their impaired brother or sister cannot learn what they learn, cannot handle machines or understand abstract ideas such as appreciation, consideration, or anticipation.

From the point of view of siblings, the impaired brother or sister often just gets in the way. "She won't get out of my room," or, "Why can't she keep her hands out of my goldfish bowl?" a young child may say. If a retarded child is unduly stubborn, as many are, the others may complain, "She won't move away from in front of the TV and I can't see!" Again, parental management is the key to the stress level in the home. Will the parent be assertive and move the child away from the TV, or will the normal children hear, "But she doesn't understand and she likes to look at the TV. You go find something else to do."

Some non-impaired siblings become caretakers and protectors. A parent has not failed if one of the children chooses to ignore a retarded sibling. If the oldest youngster is impaired, a younger non-impaired toddler may be confused by the behaviors he sees. It is natural for toddlers to imitate. Parents may need to provide encouragement to urge the toddler to progress ahead. Some school-aged children feel guilty when they perceive that they can do things the older sibling can't do. They may be uncertain as to whether or not to tell their parents about certain successes for fear of hurting someone's feelings.

It is hard to parent a mixed family. Yes, all families are mixed because each person is unique. The mixture that contains a retarded child is more complex. Many difficult decisions must be made which relate to the degree of impairment. Mild retardation means that the child is educable and as an adult can be minimally self-supportive. In contrast, the profoundly retarded may require placement or nursing care. In between these extremes, retarded youngsters can communicate in limited ways. They can respond to habit training, for example, though they have poor social skills and need ongoing supervision.

The stress on the parents results in separation and divorce in many families. The statistics range from close to 45 percent to as high as 65 percent. These problems compound the stress for everybody.

Benefits

Benefits of living with a mentally retarded sibling are numerous. The child has

- The opportunity to show love, compassion, understanding and unselfishness.
- The opportunity to be supportive to parents and other non-impaired brothers and sisters.
- A lifelong search for values and an appreciation of his or her own talents.
- The opportunity to make financial sacrifices without having a martyr's attitude.
- The chance to make a commitment to be involved in organizations which provide services to the mentally retarded.
- The ongoing appreciation that family loyalty comes first and that in a family we all make adjustments for each other. They may not always agree with the decision the parents have made on behalf of the retarded.

The siblings of a retarded person are usually more mature and knowledgable about handicapping conditions and assume an accepting attitude which is exemplary for their friends, neighbors, and classmates.

40. LIVING WITH A MULTI-GENERATIONAL FAMILY

"Grandma, where are you?" little Claudia Ryan asks as she bounds in the door after school. Grandma is in the kitchen putting out cookies and milk. After a hug and a kiss, Claudia goes outside to play with her friends. She is eleven years old. Grandma has always been in the home. This is the only way of life that Claudia has ever known. Multi-generational relationships are relatively smooth. Grandmother is a primary caretaker of the little ones.

The Ryan family is in marked contrast to the Owens down the street. The grandparents moved in when they sold their home. They were very upset because they had to leave their friends and their church. They feel lonely and embarrassed. They cannot understand how the grandchildren are permitted to be so outspoken and demanding. Any suggestions that they make are belittled and criticized. Relationships are ambivalent and the lack of communication creates misunderstandings and hard feelings. Stress is mounting as everyone tries to adjust to a multigenerational lifestyle. The kids are caught up in the conflict. They have always loved their grandparents and respected their ways. With their own parents, they enjoy open exchanges and a relatively permissive home environment. Now the tensions and criticisms seem to destroy the harmony and compatibility they have always known with both the parents and grandparents. Symptoms of stress are becoming apparent.

Multi-generational families are becoming more common today in the wake of economic pressures. It is a two-way street. Young families move in with the grandparents or vice-versa. Some will make the transition without any significant problems. Others will have great difficulty making the adjustments.

Sources of Stress

These are some of the sources of stress when grandparents move in.

Grandparents (Physically Well) Expectations	*Children's Parents*	*The Children*
Children should be respectful.	Communication is essential. Children may not always be respectful. Grandparents should not be too critical.	Do you have to act one way with grandparents and another way with parents?
Responsibilities Some grandparents want a lot of tasks to do, while some want to be passive, as unnoticed and as	Uncertain how much responsibility to permit grandparents to have. Resentful if grand-	May be delighted grandparents are taking over their jobs. New responsibilities because of

Responsibilities	*Children's Parents*	*The Children*
little trouble as possible. Some believe children should have a lot of responsibilities "as we did when we were their age."	parents act like guests in the home.	larger family and grandparents' needs.
Money Issues Some grandparents experience a great deal of stress because funds are very limited. Some give money to children which parents do not approve of; may criticize how their children or in-laws spend money. Some grandparents are angry when forced to be dependent.	Parents and kids cost money. How do you make agreements with your parents or in-laws about money?	Children may be confused if parents and grandparents have different money values or management. Can become resentful if have to sacrifice for the grandparents.
Discipline Feel uncertain what their rights are. May criticize own children too readily which confuses kids.	May feel they have to change discipline style because grandparents observing, judging.	May learn to play one generation against the other.

When grandparents move in, the children and their parents (the nuclear family) may resent the loss of privacy. If space is limited and children now have to share a bedroom, you should expect to hear complaints. These complaints can be used to trigger important discussions. "We didn't have any choice, kids, and these are the arrangements. You will have to learn the give and take of living with your grandparents. We have to adjust to having them here just as they have to adjust to being here." This must be expressed in a positive way. *The importance of family is a meaningful lesson for all.* Europeans and Asians comment that merging generations under one roof is an American problem. Overseas, the multi-generational family is a revered tradition.

Symptoms of Stress

For those boys and girls who resist the pattern, several symptoms of stress may be expected.

- Babyish behaviors. "Grandma will do it for me!"
- Staying away from home (especially teenagers). "I don't want to have to deal with all the quarreling."
- Unusual demands for privacy, time alone. "I can't handle being around people all the time!"
- Anger, feelings of being displaced. "I can't watch what I want to on TV. It's always what my grandmother wants!"

When the pattern is reversed and Mom, Dad, and kids move in with the grandparents, other problems may appear. It may take a while until children adjust to new schools, neighborhood, and friends. They may feel unwelcome, like strangers, or have problems adjusting to the new household's rules. The problems of Mom and Dad may also add stress. The old relationship patterns and problems between the father or mother and his or her parents may resurface. Communication is the key here. If there is unfinished business, it is important to clarify the issues whatever they are—permissiveness, money matters, disappointments, and the like. Remind the children that the adjustment for the grandparents may be the most difficult of all.

Strategies for Support

- Discuss the plan ahead of time. Point out the many positive benefits that the children can anticipate. Talk about respect and unselfishness.
- Consider asking the children to involve the grandparents in their lives outside of the home. Ask them to come to soccer games, dance recitals, or class plays. Also, grandparents may be very enthusiastic when asked to help with projects for school or Scouts.
- Commend the kids for the thoughtful things that they do.
- Respect the children's desires to have time alone with you. Arrange for picnics, short trips, shopping days, or just quiet time together in the bedroom before they go to bed.
- If there have been problems, praise the children as they become more tolerant.
- If the grandparents are ill, this may create stress. (See Section VIII, #37.) Anxiety about illness and death must be confronted.

- If the grandparents are working outside the home, encourage the children to ask questions and be accommodating when they come home.
- If grandparents are babysitting, remind your children to be as pleasant to them as they used to be to Mrs. Jones.

Benefits of Multi-Generational Households

There will be benefits beyond financial matters. Grandparents have a chance to be full-time grandparents, giving the special love and attention that grandparents do! Some kids get along much better with their grandparents than they do with their parents. There is much to be said for a skip between generations. Count on these possible benefits:

- Children may have someone at home when they get off the school bus rather than being latch-key kids.
- Grandparents may be far less harassed than Mom and Dad, and this offers stability and comfort.
- Traditions and stories that grandparents pass on can enrich the lives of everyone. In turn, this can build a sense of family self-esteem. How about taping those great "I remember when" narratives about other times and places?
- The patterns of family life may change from informal dinner in front of the TV to enjoyable sit-down meals that Grandma may prepare while Mom and Dad are at work.
- If grandparents move in with the single-parent family, there may be many benefits. The single parent has a backup, more free time, and often less stress. This benefits everyone.

Above all, children learn that they have to cope with shifts and changes. They are not being displaced by Grandma and Grandpa, but their lives are being enriched. While there are new problems to solve, everyone can benefit. Mom, Dad and the kids can find satisfaction knowing that they can provide comfort for the grandparents.

41. RELIGION—STRESS OR SOLACE?

The old expression, "to keep peace in a conversation, don't talk politics or religion," implies that these are tender topics. Politics can change rapidly. An act of war may suddenly bring together political opponents who join for a common cause. Religious beliefs are not so changeable. For some persons, they are a lifelong source of comfort and direction; for others, religious beliefs cause conflict.

Regardless of format or formalization, religion can bind together family members in a loving way. It can also establish attitudes, prejudices, and practices which result in stress. People from all around the world defend their religions, even to the extent of dying for them.

The commonly recognized clusters or levels of religious involvement are:

(1) Disclaimers of any formal religion. May emphasize nature, natural forces, spiritualism, ancestor worship, or focus on interpersonal relationships, man's inhumanity to man, or methods geared to personal search. Social issues may be paramount.

(2) Casual concern for the teachings of the prophets, the Bible, Higher Power, prayers, mysticism. Does not prioritize religious practices or traditions. Tolerant of other groups with emphasis on the family, interpersonal interactions, perhaps social issues.

(3) Committed to regular religious observances. Strong identification with a specific religion. Bible or scriptures, basic teachings or interpretations may be inspirational as well as repressive and frightening. Traditions are important. Some prejudice against other groups. Strong clerical leadership.

(4) Cults or fanatical devotion as a way of life. All decisions build from the commitment to serve a religious cause. A total lifestyle encircles around the religion; every action taken is done so in the name of the religion. Situations may be strict and prohibitive with many constraints that require members to differentiate themselves from non-believers in clothing, non-religious celebrations, and financial planning, for instance. Expression of emotions may be restricted. All-pervasive attitude of judgment may exist.

Each cluster may create stress for some individuals. Each reflects powerful parental attitudes and training. If parents declare, "We do not believe in God. We're not giving our children any religious training," this is a powerful position. It is as if not to believe is to believe. The children feel stress by being different from other kids or ostracized by more devout persons in the community. At the other end of the spectrum, children raised in communes or fundamentalist families are subjected to equally powerful positions.

In some situations, children learn to repress all feelings. They may or may not feel close to their parents. Teachings of the faith frequently obstruct normal social relationships with children of other backgrounds. This produces discomfort and stress.

Stress from Ideologies

From a philosophical point of view, children experience stress when a religion instills guilt without a promise of redemption. I have patients in my office who have not found a way to meet their needs without an all-pervasive awareness of the Devil. Their stress, originating from religious training, has interfered with their fulfillment and happiness. Some religions have a strong sexist point of view which creates stress. The famous Navajo sandpaintings which denote spiritual messages are the domain solely of the men. Boys and men are afforded power and privilege throughout the Middle East as prescribed in religious texts. I remember a young Orthodox Jewish girl who came for therapy. She had never resolved her feelings of having disappointed her parents because they wanted a male. When her brother arrived, she felt even more unwelcome. When the brother, as a teenager, was killed, it was more than she could handle.

Adolescents commonly question their own faith as they question parental convictions. At the same time, they may enjoy church groups and activities and accept family religious customs without protests. You probably remember going through a similar search. Stress may result if the searching culminates in alienation, disrespectful confrontations, or threats from either family or friends. Stress comes from the many piercing questions they ask on subjects such as death, astrology, abortion, and celibacy for instance.

Many children today challenge parental authority and attitudes about religion. Peer pressure may lead impressionable teens to religious fanatacism, thus causing a rift in the family and subsequent misunderstandings and stress. Even in religious communities, teenagers may struggle with the teachings of the sect, groping for answers and for ways to adapt to outside pressures.

Stress from Family Practices

Parents want their children to understand about commitments, moral and ethical matters, faith, spirituality, and related convictions. Infants and toddlers are introduced to Sunday school and church. Just how much young children absorb or comprehend is difficult to determine, although many recite verses, prayers, or sayings with accuracy. Family prayers, religious events, and frequent references to the Bible or other scriptures remind children that their parents regard religion as important. Within a family, stress from religion comes about when

(1) Parent-child conflicts arise over idealistic or practical differences. For example, children hear about what others believe or see disturbing programs on TV and find parents unwilling or unable to discuss these differences. "They must think they're right and we think we're right. How come?" the young Jewish child wonders about Christmas and Santa Claus, neither of which is a part of his faith.

(2) Parents are so involved in religious or church work that children feel unimportant. "How come Daddy has time to help paint the church, but he can never help me with my homework?"

(3) Rigid family practices conflict with children's desires or other commitments. For example, Louise wants to go camping with the Scouts but her parents will not let her miss Sunday school.

(4) There is a double standard about church or synagogue attendance. Children have to go, but both parents stay home; or children have to go, one parent stays home. Differences between parents may make the situation even more stressful.

(5) Children become more intensely religious, more devout than parents approve of. The upswing in conservative groups among young people is nationwide. Parents feel they have lost control, that the children will adopt the values of an outside group, even though based on ethical values or a search for enlightenment.

(6) Children rebel at going to Sunday school or taking part in religious practices, causing a serious rift between the generations. By giving in, the parents abdicate their power, give up their in-charge position. This is an appropriate situation to use negotiations as a means to solve the problems.

In order to minimize stress, consider these five purposes of religion: to provide guidance, comfort, direction, spiritual enrichment, and security. For many, these offer a framework within which a person finds definitions of ethics, faith, morals, and life.

As a parent, you want your children to have those dimensions in their lives. You offer what you can, with or without religious intensity. If your children take a different direction from yours, try to assess their decisions against the purposes of religion. They may not accept your religious beliefs or practices; therefore they seek others that they can accept. Your own life may be enriched in the process, to the subsequent benefit of the child-parent relationship. In the case of cults, where estrangement and depersonalization may take place, it is very, very difficult to be objective. Parents may suffer more stress than the children. The brain-washing or persuasive tactics of the leaders of such movements provide followers with insulation and protection that is reportedly stress-free.[*]

Strategies for Support

Strategies for support require flexibility—a willingness to let go of some important convictions and to accept new ones. Everyone benefits when misunderstandings are cleared up.

(1) Be honest about your own beliefs. Talk about your conflicts. Tell

---

*Suggested reading: *Snapping* by Flo Conway and Jim Siegelman, 1979.

about experiences you have had. Discuss self-awareness, fulfillment, humility, service and such concepts in terms that children can understand.

(2) Accept their confusion, even their anger, if it is expressed. In order for a child to search for answers or for an identity it may be important to search outside family structure. Don't misinterpret a child's search as a rejection of you.

(3) Make certain that you are not misusing religion. Have you frequently used the threat, "God will punish you if you are not good?" Children will misbehave. It is part of growing up. Children want the approval and love that they get when they are good. If you establish a pattern whereby punishment is left to God, you are giving up your own authority and an all-pervasive stress is established. You become a practicing threatener. It is unreasonable to assume that children understand that misbehavior is a sign of immaturity or frustration. Therefore, if punishment is moralistic, they feel condemned without realizing that being naughty is part of being a child, and such stress damages self-esteem.

(4) Confront the inconsistencies that there may be between you and your children. Do you insist that the children go to Sunday school, Mass, or the synagogue while you stay home or play golf? Kids often feel that you ask things of them that you don't do yourself and wonder why you don't go to church so that you can learn to be fair.

(5) Do you perceive that your child is putting up a false front—being "good" to please you and God? If your child lacks spontaneity reaffirm your love repeatedly. Show affection. Talk about your own strengths and weaknesses.

(6) If your child has a morbid fear of death or is obsessed with fear of the future, he or she may be reacting to threats of punishment in the hereafter. Johnny, an impulsive six-year-old boy hears that a friend disobeyed his mother, climbed a ladder, fell off, and was killed. Johnny, who thinks God punished his friend for "being bad," now refuses to participate in rough play, hesitates to let Mom out of his sight, and fears that he, too, will be killed if he is bad. Take time to find out what Johnny is thinking and be as reassuring as possible.

(7) Emphasize the positive. Issues about right and wrong, morality, wisdom, prophecy, legend, caring, giving, and adventure are all part of the heritage of a faith. Children are entitled to a pride in their heritage and to be involved in the process of the many changes which are occurring today.

(8) Teach tolerance. With older children, be realistic about the strife that the world has known historically and continues to experience over religious differences. Ireland, India, and parts of the Middle East are

examples. If your children have strong beliefs, they must be taught that it is okay for other kids to have different but equally strong beliefs. Otherwise, religious upbringing may result in unnecessary social conflicts and peer rejection. Teach them to assess what prejudices they may have.

(9) If you are involved in self-awareness programs or human potential movements that have become important to you, tell your children. Explain how these activities enrich or dovetail with your religious convictions or your understanding of the purpose of religion. They do not have to conflict. They may reaffirm your identification or commitment to your faith.

(10) If your financial commitment to the church appears to the children to be disproportionately high, this needs to be discussed. Although the children may protest, you are entitled to make such decisions without apology. You are demonstrating actions which support your commitments and this is an invaluable lesson.

(11) Be open to discussions of issues such as reincarnation, karma, Eastern philosophies, and the extremist religious groups. Open discussion may help your children acquire attitudes which may prevent impulsive involvement in activities, some of which may be injurious to mental health. Such discussion enhances parent-child communication. Express your opinions, but remember that open-mindedness allows children to ask questions on all subjects. This supports a trusting relationship and enhances respect.

Benefits

Religion enriches. When you tell your children about visions, Biblical stories, heroes, heroines, and famous festivities you fulfill some of their desire to know all about everything! Their questions about nature, death, and birth may be considered both scientific and spiritual, depending on your point of view.

In your conversations with your children you are inviting them to seek meaningful ways to understand the abundance of knowledge to which they are exposed. What a great gift to bestow!

In some ways, religious and spiritual matters cause all of us concern and discomfort. As we select philosophies and answers, we grow. Such are the benefits of stress in the religious domain.

Stress from
Outside the Home

School and television are considered outside stressors because they originate outside the family; they do not evolve from a style of parenting, personal problems, or relationships.

42. TELEVISION—TROUBLESOME, TRAUMATIC, AND TERRIFIC

Your influence as a parent may be preempted by a TV set. Programs have an enormous impact on viewers. They are vivid. Children watch anything and everything—good, bad, and indifferent. Parents often don't have the time to monitor and help children select worthwhile shows; they are simply grateful that the TV set distracts or absorbs the kids when dinner is being prepared or the phone must be answered. The TV has gotten out of hand. In the movie *Fantasia,* the Sorcerer's Apprentice was amazed when the water got out of control. In many respects, TV content today is equally out of control.

The average child of five may watch TV for three to five hours a day. By the end of high school, a child will have seen 350,000 commercials. More important, children will have seen 20,000 murders and countless rapes and other acts of violence. There is no way to measure the stress that can result.

Certainly, some children are more vulnerable and sensitive than others to the realistic TV dramas they watch. Is it reasonable to ask a child to be impervious to the meaning that violence spells mastery? Can a child witness so many fights without thinking that somehow this is acceptable behavior? There are many reports that children explain their violent behaviors with the statement "I learned it on TV."

Above all, TV shows ignore the feelings of victims or survivors. There is not time for these feelings. Viewers are left to guess how the victim felt or how the survivors were able to cope, they may not give it any thought at all. Displays of compassion and support are ignored or cut short.

Symptoms of Stress

If you observe a child displaying nervous habits, becoming unduly irritable or fearful and you are unaware of other current stressors, take the time to ask:

(1) What have you been watching on TV?

(2) How did you feel when you saw _____?

(3) What do you think might have helped the people (or animals)?

(4) How did you feel when you realized that the person didn't get help or hurt a lot or would never see his father, mother, friend, or dog again?

(5) Have you had bad dreams since you saw that show?

(6) Do you realize that some shows (newscasts, documentaries) tell real stories but others are make believe?

Be patient. It may take a while or repeated questioning before a child may be able to respond. But reassurances from you are important. Your counsel, your interest in their reactions to scary TV, can nullify some of the stress. Express your feelings. Tell what you experienced when you saw a violent incident on the show.

Don't scold, "Why do you watch such stuff?" It is impossible to preview all shows, even selected ones, and the regular shows and newscasts will present unexpected, traumatic, and deeply frightening pictures.

Strategies for Support

The most useful position for you to take is one that reaffirms that:

- Even though you see such awful things on TV, it does not mean that it will happen to you or to us.
- Even though you see kids and parents argue, fight, and hurt each other, these are not how-to lessons for our family.
- All people have some problems; TV stories seem to point out unhappy problems because they are interesting.
- When you see things that upset or worry you, *please* come and tell me about them. If you don't, then your worries may grow and grow. You can become very upset and not even know why.

At what age should a child be approached? Any age. Little ones, nonverbal preschoolers may need to hear your reassurances even though they are unable to give you any answers. For example, if you have both watched a house burn down on TV, tell about your fears and fascination. School-aged children should know ways to escape or special precautions you take at your house. Be certain that they know how to dial 911. If the frightening show has to do with kidnapping, violence, car accidents, or getting lost, express *your* feelings and be reassuring. "You are here with me now," and "We take good care of the cars. The brakes are fine." Stories about kidnappings, for example, should be followed by your comments and instructions. "Not all strangers are friendly. Never get in a car with a stranger." "You can say NO!" You can say 'I'll tell!'"

Stress from TV may be inevitable. Parents frequently discount it or ignore it. TV may impair memory, reduce problem-solving abilities, inhibit verbal expression and overload a child with contradictions if used too extensively or if the "wrong" programs are viewed by the child. Any one of these impairments may contribute to problems at school.

In many homes, the TV set contributes to a fractured family. Dad appears more concerned about the fate of the Green Bay Packers than he does about the outcome of his son's tryouts at the local high school. Many housewives are soap opera addicts. Children can be demoted in the hierarchy of parental attention.

Benefits of TV

Inasmuch as this book focuses on stress, the negative aspects of TV have been emphasized. It is only fair to applaud some of the excellent programs. With the wide range of content and talent, there is outstanding material for kids to watch. Educational programs vary in quality but many children are truly proud when they say, "I learned that on Sesame Street!" Please maintain control over program selection. Everyone will benefit from your caring assertiveness.

43. SCHOOLS AND SCHOOLING

Have you ever been to a party and heard a person say, "I hated school"? Someone else adds, "I liked my friends and some of my teachers, but when it came time for report cards, I was a wreck!"

Many things determine whether or not school is stressful for kids. Grading and competition can annihilate the slow learner or the child with emotional problems. Problems at home may interfere to such an extent that the child can't concentrate at school. In addition, busing has caused immeasurable stress.

Stress at school depends on: (1) grade level, (2) personality, and (3) the talent of the learner.

With or without words, the child shows stress at school.

Stress in Kindergarten

The kindergarten experience may set the stage for stress that mounts in the years ahead. Originally, kindergarten was intended to give children early childhood experiences in independence, how to get along with others, to learn about games, toys, school routines and perhaps numbers or letters. Nowadays kindergarten in most places has become a junior first grade. The result is considerable stress on children. Some youngsters are not ready to be in school and the immature are penalized. They are totally unprepared for comparisons such as star charts that tell them that they are not as good as others. The immature child has a short attention span, perhaps a smaller vocabulary or undeveloped language skills, and may be ill-prepared to separate from the home or another caretaking situation. Such early stresses can seriously affect the child's self-esteem and attitude about school.

Symptoms of Stress

Symptoms of stress in the kindergarten-aged child may be confused with signs of immaturity. In observing your child in school, look for babyish behaviors you may not see at home or an exaggeration of these behaviors—wetting pants, thumbsucking, crying, clinging, unwillingness to talk, withdrawal from adults, stuttering, disruptive or aggressive acts.

Strategies for support

Strategies for support require answers to these questions:

(1) Is the child immature? (Perhaps all he needs is the gift of more time!)

(2) Is the child given too much freedom at home, to a point where he cannot adjust to the way the teacher manages the group?

(3) Is the child bored at school?

(4) Is the child feeling well?

If you're answer to the second question is yes, your child requires more discipline or more responsibilities. It is not difficult to start such a regime. Begin by asking your child to perform a single task, such as putting his or her dirty socks in the laundry, and build from there. (For suggestions regarding discipline, See Section III, #8.)

Regarding question three, bear in mind that many children have benefited from Sesame Street, Head Start programs, preschool, parental stimulation, books, and trips, and are overprepared for some kindergartens. They may be bored and as a result become disruptive. Gifted children may have taught themselves how to read or to handle computers or calculators and may seek sophisticated answers to many questions.

Take time to talk to the teacher. Find out what she considers important for your child and what plans she has to fill his needs. Unless these needs are met, boredom may lead to unacceptable social behaviors which may interfere with friendships for years to come—not to mention how it will affect the child's attitude toward school.

Regarding question four, some children pick up all kinds of "bugs" when they first come to school. They are exposed to illnesses they have never had. Be on the lookout for chickenpox, for instance. Also, look for first signs of learning disabilities such as hearing problems or visual problems which may have never been apparent before. Eye strain, hyperactivity, or inability to follow instructions may indicate perceptual problems. They can be handled. It is important to get professional help at this early stage before your child begins to see himself as a poor student or failure. (See Section VII, #33.)

Kindergarten should and can be a happy experience. Almost all children are eager to go to school and to make friends. The benefits of these school days are immeasurable for those children who respond to a stimulating and caring situation.

For most children at this level, there is very little stress after the initial adjustment period.

Stress in the Elementary Grades (one through six)

There are endless sources of stress in school. They derive from grading and competition, classroom management (grouping practices), methods of discipline, child-teacher relationships, peer relationships, special problems, and teacher personalities. Look for additional sources of stress in grades four, five, and six. Girls, in particular, may be more concerned about getting a smile from the cutest boy in the class than they are in doing well on a test. Stress results when:

- Girls are more aggressive than the boys and everyone ends up feeling uncomfortable.
- Girls lose interest in academics, causing school work to suffer.
- Peer relationships become increasingly fragile because some students are ready for dating, and going steady while others are not.
- The more sophisticated kids belittle or embarrass the less mature children.
- Serious students, athletic kids, "straight" kids pull away from the less sophisticated kids, thus splitting the class into factions.

Special sources of stress may affect your child if

- A boy adopts the attitude that he is not athletic, too skinny, not muscular enough or, if a girl feels she is too heavy, humorless, or snobby.

- He or she is a minority person in the class—foreign student, member of a racial minority, handicapped, or even the "new kid in the school." (See Sections XIV, #63 and VII, #31)

Few, if any, children go through school without experiencing some stress. Whether in a private school, public school, boarding school, or parochial-school setting, there are predictable times when the coping style of a child is put to the test.

Realistically, stress isn't always the teacher's fault and it isn't always the child's fault. There can be a teacher-child mismatch or there can be unfair practices. Some groups of kids can be mighty cruel to others. In my experience, kids are surprisingly accurate reporters on what is going on and who is doing what to whom. *Listen* to what they tell you and remain as objective as you can. Take time to question your child about being pushed too fast, being bored, having a grouchy teacher, getting into too many fights on the playground, the presence of gangs and those sorts of things. *If your child, from kindergarten on, gets in the habit of telling you about almost everything that happens in school, you can readily spot a source of stress.* The child's report on his or her day should be given time equal to the five-o'clock news. Second-hand reports from sitters need your attention, too.

Symptoms of Stress

Academic

Cannot concentrate.
Has trouble remembering.
Refuses to study.
Is apathetic, disinterested.
Constantly complains that it
  is too easy or too hard.
Displays test anxiety, gets ill,
  has headaches, stomachaches.

Child-Teacher Relationship

Too dependent.
Repeatedly says the teacher
  doesn't like him.
Feels teacher enjoys
  embarrassing him.
Shows anger when compared to
  older siblings.
Says teacher is impersonal, callous.

Classroom, School Management

Embarrassed by grouping
  (always in the slow reading
  group, for example).
Never gets to be in a group with
  class leaders.
Resents hearing test scores
  announced in front of the whole
  class.
Never has a chance to be alone.

Peer Relationships

Has no close friends.
Never invited to parties or to play.
Oversensitive to peer remarks.
Unduly bossy with peers.
Criticizes others, quotes criticisms
  of himself.
Intolerant.
Feels too good for others, appears
  to be a snob.

Classroom, School Management	*Personal Behaviors*
Feels teacher doesn't trust the class.	Persistently unhappy or depressed.
Feels discipline, punishments consistently unfair.	Uses drugs, alcohol.
	Threatens to run away.
	Refuses to go to school.
Complains that the teacher never tells anything about herself; feels estranged and unimportant to her.	Destroys personal or school property.
Tired of being asked to help others.	
Feels teacher doesn't grade fairly.	

Strategies for Support

(1) Avoid being too critical of how teachers conduct a class or how a principal runs a school. In most instances, there is little you can do. Instead, help your child get a realistic picture of his or her own behavior, attitudes, expectations, and interactions.

(2) Make suggestions about how your child can change his or her behavior for the better. If Charlie feels that Mrs. French really hates him, he has undoubtedly begun to react to this. Find out what he does. Ask him. Talk to the teacher. Then suggest alternatives. Let's suppose he is now talking to his seat-mate as a way of getting back at Mrs. French. He already knows that she will get angry and scold him again. Help him find *something* about Mrs. French to like. Sometimes kids have to be more flexible and controlled than the teacher. Don't scold. Maybe Mrs. French really is a pill. Charlie has to learn to cope with the friendly and the unfriendly. He may have a great relationship with some or all of his other teachers.

(3) If a situation has become destructive and your child feels totally rejected by a teacher, I think it is appropriate for a parent to go to the school and try to make alternative arrangements. This isn't always possible, but at least your efforts on his behalf will impress Charlie. As your child's advocate, you must be the one to challenge teachers and administrators. If you do not take risks on behalf of your child, who will?

(4) If your child is locked into an unhappy situation for 180 school days, make every effort to find enjoyable activities at home and out of school. He needs to feel successful and happy somewhere.

(5) Look back on the year you spent in a class with a teacher whom you didn't like. What did you do? What do you wish your parents would have done on your behalf? Develop a plan based in part on your answer to that question. Some teachers appreciate your input. Some changes may occur. Your child will appreciate your concern.

Stress in the Middle School (or Junior High School)

When seventh and eighth graders are asked to talk about their stress, four major subjects come up: school, friends, parents, and family problems. Most pre-adolescents love school. Many blossom academically. School is a friendly place to be. They like the responsibility they have been given and the freedoms. They enjoy moving from class to class and having study halls. There are more sports and more activities.

Sources of Stress

- Concern about grades
- Parental expectations
- Impersonal teachers
- Poor study habits from the past
- Problems with peers

Symptoms of Stress

Symptoms of stress for the middle or junior high school child approximate those described for younger children. Many have never had grades before and this creates stress. Children seek reassurance that they will do better than they have in the past, or that they will be able to continue to do well. Those who need special help may reach out for special classes, or tutoring labs. Middle school-aged students sense an urgency to master skills before they head into high school.

With the opportunity to attend classes on different levels—such as basic math versus geometry—certain cliques may form. Separation from old friends may provide opportunities to develop new friendships. Until new friendships are made, there is stress. Students may become agitated and show a lot of anger. A few will get discouraged and need a lot of support and attention from teachers and counselors. In some areas, the introduction of drugs and alcohol may become a problem.

Strategies for Support

(1) Be available. Kids need to be reminded that their school life is important to you.

(2) Negotiate about grades. Discuss which subjects are easy and which are hard. Decide together which subjects will be most important and what would be an appropriate grade to work towards. The push for straight A's or to always do better creates stress. Perfect grades may be easy for some children but hard for yours. Grades are not worth nonstop sleeplessness, headaches, depressions, or irritability. A child may get good grades and still have poor self-esteem. "I can study and do okay, but I'm still not important to anyone." *Too often, a parent knows more about*

the child's grades than he or she knows about the child. The child is confused, thinking, "If I don't get great grades, I'm no good." Parents *must* guard against saying, "Debbie is a dear but she is certainly not a student." The child hears only the comments that come *after* the word "but."

(3) Don't pay for grades. This penalizes the child who may put more energy into piano lessons or athletics than academics. The possibility of unnecessary sibling competition goes without saying.

(4) Attend conferences. Arrange to have your child present. Conferences should cover achievements and clarify where encouragement is needed. With Mary present, the possibility of misunderstandings is minimized. Teachers should encourage Mary to help prepare the conference and assure the child that there will be no surprises. Unexpected comments such as, "Mary is one of the brightest kids in the class" may give Mary the impression that this is for Mother's benefit and has no merit. If Mary knows ahead of time that her teacher plans to make that statement, she will have more confidence in all statements that are made. School-parent-child bonds are important and the conference is the most effective tool at all grade levels. Some disgruntled children may attempt to manipulate the home against the school and vice-versa. Such maneuvers are fruitless when parent-teacher-child conferences confront the facts. No one benefits if the child is allowed to continue to bad-mouth the school at home in order to seek attention or make excuses for his or her own inappropriate behavior.

(5) Continue your habit of being open and honest about yourself and possible problems. When you appear unhappy or detached without explanation, this creates stress for the child. Concentration in school is effected. Studying at home also becomes difficult if there are tensions or fights that the child does not clearly understand. At this age, children need explanations about such things as drinking problems or chronic illnesses. They are mature enough to want to help.

(6) Confront behaviors that you do not like. If your child is experimenting with pot, don't ignore it. The limits that you set must be maintained.

(7) Above all, try to set a good example for your child. Your commitment to education and school success needs to be expressed frequently. This does not mean setting unrealistic goals; it means you are there to help and encourage your child to do the best he or she can.

Benefits of Stress at the Middle School Level

Preteen students have crushes on teachers (usually of the same sex) and will try in every way to please. This attachment may be much stronger than any teacher-child relationship that the child has known in the lower grades. The teacher involved has power—almost magical power—to inspire the child to do well and to build self-esteem. With a special teacher as encourager, friend, and mentor, the child can more readily deal with stress at school.

Middle school years mark the beginning of self-searching. One of the benefits of stress at this age is that it speeds up the process. Many kids become introspective. They want to reduce the stress that comes from the daily ups and downs of relationships. The child at thirteen or fourteen may ponder: "Will I ever have a boy (girl) friend? How tall will I be? Will I get into a college? Will I ever be happy? What really is a friend?" They try to cope in many new ways and benefit from developing self-awareness. In order to do this, they may typically talk over their problems with a friend for hours. (Ask any parent who has a telephone!) They also learn to cope by doing something athletic—riding a bike, jogging, watching TV, practicing the piano or the like. They may also decide to put a great deal of effort into school work.

Stress in High School

In America today, there is such an assortment of high schools, such a collection of teachers, such a variety of students that one cannot describe a typical school. Nevertheless, it is accepted that there are some very high-stress high school environments. This is a result of the way the high school is run, the teaching methods of some of the staff, and student attitudes. Frequently, student attitudes and expectations reflect the parents who may be critical and nonsupportive.

Student stress in high school may reflect teacher apathy. The amount of violence against teachers is growing every day.* Teacher concerns about their own safety have to affect the way they relate to their students, their jobs, and to the community in which they work. As a parent, it is essential for you to be aware of the stress the teachers are experiencing. I urge you to get involved, to help in every way you can to make schools in your area safe, healthy, and productive. Results may be subtle and difficult to perceive but as the school climate improves to benefit the staff, it will be much less stressful for your kids.

---

*Violence Against Teachers—National Education Association Research Report, Feb/March 1979.
- 70,000 teachers (1 in 88) were physically attacked at least once.
- 250,000 teachers (1 in 8) had personal property damaged.
- 500,000 teachers (1 in 4) had personal property stolen.
- More than 3,000 of the teachers who had been attacked required medical attention in a hospital emergency room; more than 9,000 required attention in a school clinic or in a doctor's office. About 10,000 had to miss one or more days of school to recuperate.

Students want their high school experience to be *personal, relevant,* and *interesting.* When their wants are not met, stress abounds. Personal means the kids are asking for the school to be aware of their needs, skills, rate of learning, and special talents, and to provide a personalized program. They do not want to be shuffled from one class to another feeling unwanted, out of place, inadequate, or bored.

Relevant means the student wants school to help him adjust to the circumstances of his life today and the working world of the future. Many students look to their teachers and the content of classes to help them understand the intricacies of relationships, family disturbances, and such societal issues as nuclear wars and the computerization of America.

Interesting means the student anticipates that classes will be conducted in such a way that he will want to attend. Kids want to admire their teachers. Teachers who are creative, personal, and knowledgeable motivate students to do well, thereby keeping stress to a minimum.

Assuming that teachers do their part, there are still groups of students who will know great stress in high school. Included are:

- Kids who consider themselves misfits.
- Immature students who needlessly rebel against authority and are unduly critical.
- The turned-off kids who consider school a waste of time.
- Kids who experience too much pressure from home.
- Kids with low self-esteem who express it with anger.
- The slow learner or problem learner whose needs are not being met.
- The gifted learner whose needs are not being met.

You may ask if there are any kids who do not fall into one of those groups. Of course there are. Schools are full of kids who may fuss a bit but are into learning, sports, activities, school spirit, and the normal ups and downs of tests, grades, and reports. They have achieved a balance between good stress and possible debilitating stress. Expressed another way, they have developed a successful coping style.

Symptoms of Stress

When symptoms of stress at school are apparent, they should not be ignored. These symptoms are evident when the child refuses to go to school, pretends to be ill, gets "high" in order to face school, will not study, can't sleep, is apathetic, surly, or depressed.

In order to provide support for a teenager, parents must be the great jugglers of the world. As described in Section IV, #13, there will be times when kids are open to parental suggestions and support and times when they are not. Parents have to juggle their support between the blocks or barricades.

Strategies for Support

DO NOT	DO
Ground kids for poor grades.	Remember that many classes today are boring. Accept the fact that kids will do better in some subjects than in others.
Use cliches that kids consider unimportant. "When I was in school, I had to ..."	
Make threats such as, "You won't get into college with those kinds of grades!" There are many alternative ways for kids to get into college, including the GED tests and many colleges which are stepping stones to more difficult programs.	Take time to help with homework and projects.
	Negotiate grades.
	Encourage extra-curricular activities.
	Maintain limits—time to be home, time for homework, sports and other extra-curricular activities.
Ignore symptoms, assuming that "all kids that age hate school."	Discuss facts—most employers require a high school diploma.
Ignore the attitudes of your child's friends about school. They have a strong influence.	If your child needs to go to a different school or work at a different pace, accept this.
Ignore the fact that if there are problems at home, the child's attitude about school will be effected.	Consider alternative schools. (Seek professional or teacher's help when appropriate.)

In many high schools, counselors will want to team up with you to help your child. Go for it. It may lead to a new approach that neither you nor the counselor would have arrived at independently. An alliance between counselor and parent tells the student that his success is important to both of you.

Benefits of Stress in High School

(1) Perhaps in no other setting, except at home, is there the opportunity for so much good stress for children. If friends are loving and teachers are supportive, a child believes that school is great. Many children are excited about what they learn and must put forth a lot of effort. While learning may be a struggle, they continue to feel good about themselves. For others, learning comes easily and they set high goals for themselves and work hard to achieve them.

(2) In addition to academic effort, note the benefits of learning tolerance. Children learn to tolerate individual differences among the students and the staff. In turn, this helps them to accept personal strengths and weaknesses.

(3) Self-discipline is a benefit. "I have to study! I've got to learn how to use that machine."

(4) Self-control is another benefit of stress which comes from being surrounded by many different people. "If I get mad, I'd better play it cool," or, "Those big kids will push me around if I am a pest."

(5) An appreciation of one's special talents may result from pressure to excel. "I didn't think I played any better than anyone else, but when I had to do a solo, I began to see that I was pretty good. It was so much work, but it was worth it. I'm really grateful now."

(6) Peer relationships provide happiness, challenge, and comfort even when problems must be solved.

The day I graduated from high school was one of the saddest days of my life. I had learned to cope with lots of stress. I loved my school. Above all, I learned about the care and feeding of friendships. Today, more than forty years later, my high school friends are among those I love the most.

Social Problems That Create Family Stress

The social problems included in this section are broader in scope than television and school (Section IX). Each stems from societal or global issues. They are: the economy, alternative lifestyles (including sex stereotyping), and the future as a source of stress.

44. MONEY—STRESS AND DISTRESS

Children who live in slums may be ashamed of the way they live. Their world abounds in stress. They face many dangers—the busy streets, filth, violence, illnesses, and cruelty from other kids. Food and housing are chronic worries. School hardships are commonplace, the kids are ill-prepared or feel alienated.

Marginal farm families suffer, too. Young children of the rural poor only know bare subsistence. They are traditionally described as withdrawn and frightened. They reflect the hopelessness that their parents express. As children fraught with fear, they exhibit a gamut of stress symptoms.

Depending on the definition of poverty that you may select, more than 18 million children do not have enough to eat, much less adequate medical or dental care, or a childhood that underwrites positive self-esteem. Most are not minority children. Some learn to cope surprisingly well. They find energy to confront dangers and scarcities and they come up with a positive drive. Others depend on a parent, siblings, peers, or society for security and may be withdrawn, passive, or callous. However, the all-pervasive stress that results from being poor cannot be readily erased. For some it becomes lifelong defeat.

More than 10 million eligible workers were unemployed in the

United States in the spring of 1983. Television shows highlight their depression and despair. Interviews tell of humiliation, frustration, and anger. Most of these persons have had jobs. Unlike chronically poor families, many have known a secure place to live, adequate food and medical care, and, above all, respect. Shifting from security to insecurity can be earthshaking. The injured self-esteem of the jobless parent, accompanied by anxiety and a reduced standard of living, invariably creates interpersonal tensions. The children may have had a good start with stable family relationships, smooth school adjustment, and well-developed coping styles. Now that there is a crisis, parents and children are put to a test. Money matters determine the family lifestyle. Survival becomes a key issue for which they are ill-prepared. Stress abounds.

Children of affluent families experience stress, too. Money determines their lifestyle, but their visions of the future are optimistic. Children of affluence do not suffer basic anxiety about survival nor do they suffer the oppressive ethical shame from being a slum person. Yet some have very serious problems with relationships, values, and self-esteem. Some are embarrassed to have so much money.

In school, the daily performance of affluent children is frequently judged by the question, "How will this affect the future? Will the child get into Harvard, Stanford, or Princeton?" The slightest evidence that the child may not be concerned about the future alarms some parents. Parental expectations are backed by teachers. While some discount school because they know they will inherit a lot of money, others may feel insecure, believing that success will be measured totally by the money they will earn.

In addition to stress from pressure to perform, affluent children confront other stressors.

- They are inexperienced in accountability for money. They feel inadequate or ill-prepared to make decisions. Having always used mother's charge cards doesn't help one learn to judge if a price is fair, how to budget an allowance, or how to avoid being cheated.
- Parental absenteeism due to business or social responsibilities leaves much of the child care to others. The children may feel abandoned or neglected.
- Parental attitudes imply that material goods are more important than human relationships, and acquiring more money has priority over meeting the emotional needs of the children.
- Parental expectations for the children are restricted to financial success, which confuses and belittles the children.
- Children may be allowed to become demanding and greedy.
- Overindulged children feel alienated, as if bribed to stay out of the way.

- Children equate personal worth with the number of cars in the family, expensive homes, exclusive schools, or trips they take.
- Parental or children's snobbishness damages peer relationships.

Symptoms of Stress

Regardless of the economic status of the family, children show symptoms of stress that are strikingly similar.

- Children's needs take a back seat to the energy and efforts that parents put forth to get money. Whether by necessity or choice, this is a common family pattern. Explanations such as, "We are doing all this for you" are no substitute for time together and shared experiences. Intellectually, children may understand but emotionally they feel cheated, angry, and confused. These feelings are displayed as symptoms of stress.
- Family disturbances arise from insecurities. Children tend to be irritable, sullen, unmotivated, and angry. If a family has to move frequently this, too, may result in displays of exaggerated dependency and depression. (See Section XIV.)
- Parents and kids may use drugs and/or alcohol as an escape from financial stress.
- Antisocial behaviors, such as stealing, may begin in order to provide for the family or to support drug habits. Little Jimmy takes a loaf of bread from the store because his baby brother is hungry. Big brother Jack steals a TV in order to get money to buy booze and drugs.
- Children may have an inability to plan for the future. Children of poverty or those in transition show their insecurity by depression, alienation, disgust, or anger. They refuse to think ahead. Some affluent children may take years to decide what, if anything, they want to do. They may become very demanding and self-indulgent or hide out from the real world as perennial college students. Others will utilize their financial circumstances to better themselves and to improve the world around them.
- Domestic violence stemming from severe money problems is common. (See Section XIII, #61.)
- A male child in an affluent family may display an attitude of "Why try? I'll never be as successful as my dad anyway."
- Children may have a defeatist attitude and become isolated and depressed.

Strategies for Support

It is difficult to remodel the lifestyle of a family, especially in the areas of money and materialistic values. When circumstances are difficult, the parent must focus on the parent-child relationship. Children can withstand all manner of deprivation, neglect, or frustrations *if* their parents show them that they are loved.

As a parent,

- Take time to be loving. Even though harassed by important money concerns and responsibilities, take the time to be affectionate and to be a listener.
- Explain your attitudes about money. Share your experiences. Talk to the children about your worries and frustrations. Tell them how you feel when you do well. If you consider it appropriate, talk numbers, dollars.
- Help prepare your child for his or her survival in the world of money. It is part of their education to involve children at times in decisions and discussions about money. Children may not be able to picture what can be bought for $25, but they can learn about food prices, clothing, car expenses, and housing matters. Read the ads with them. It is okay for children to know how you plan and budget.
- Teach children to budget. Set firm limits on how much they may have. Children will make mistakes in the way they handle money even as adults do. If Bert spends all his allowance on video games at the store and has nothing left for school lunch, let him prepare a peanut butter sandwich and take an apple to school. Do not bail him out. It is especially important that both parents agree about this. If one parent undermines the decision of the other, the children will not acquire a realistic understanding about money.
- If your child works, permit him or her to contribute to the family if he or she insists. It may only be a token amount, but from the child's point of view, this may be very important.
- Some children will attempt to save *every* penny that they have. Look at this carefully. Is Mary Anne holding on to money as a way of feeling secure? Has she had many losses in her life so that now she only trusts that which she can hold in her hand? This may indicate that she needs emotional reassurances or that she is a planner—has goals, wants to be able to buy a video game, a bike, or even a present for someone else. Saving is important to some children and not important to others. If your child spends all his money to please others or to buy friendships, help is needed to build his or her self-esteem so that such largesse won't be necessary.
- Involve the children in as many decisions about money as you deem appropriate. If the family has to move, you may want to let the child be present when you go househunting or apartment

searching. (See Section XIV, #62.) Stress resulting from necessary changes in the family's lifestyle can be less disturbing when the children are told the facts. The children feel respected and can cope with stressors more easily.

Issues involving money test the strength of a family. We think of death and divorce as major sources of stress. Money problems may be devastating because they directly effect the self-esteem of a father or mother. In turn, self-esteem problems may lead to serious family problems. The family may split. Parent-child estrangement may result due to issues over money. Although money crises may be lethal, in some families they result in stronger ties and sensitive compassion.

Social Issues

A discussion of money as a source of stress must touch on some social issues. It is not enough to pass off a few descriptive sentences about life in a slum and the difficulties children face. The key issues of prejudice, poverty, inequality, justice, brutality, and lack of opportunity are addressed by politicians on many levels. Yet today, in the large cities, deterioration is on a rampage. Fear and despair are universal. The wasted human potential is indefensible. When teachers try to befriend and encourage the young victims, they meet with disinterest or even by a readiness to attack. Slum persons do not trust teachers who represent an alien value system, which increases rather than diminishes their stress.

Children who do not live in poverty are often curious about it. They ask meaningful questions. They want to be able to make things better. Poverty may become a source of stress even to the children of the well-to-do. Your answers will reflect your values. Describe your feelings to your children. Discuss issues. Encourage your children to use opportunities to get facts, hear diversified opinions, and perhaps visualize what they might do in the future to improve the situation.

Your children may become leaders in the political world. Take time to evaluate their concerns about money and stress. They need to learn about jobs and social justice, about families, violence, and inhumane conditions. Without your encouragement to look at social issues, they may experience the subtle stress that complacency brings.

45. PARENTAL CHOICES—ALTERNATIVE LIFESTYLES

All kids learn that their parents aren't perfect. At some point, they may tell them that they think that a lot of their decisions are dumb or not cool. Usually, they deal with superficial matters, such as, "Why did you buy *that* dress?"

Parents of today are making all kinds of basic decisions which affect children on many significant levels. No matter what lifestyle parents choose, the child will be well-adjusted if there are good, sustained relationships with important people. Because a parent chooses to be non-traditional does not mean that the child will necessarily experience stress. If, however, the child-parent unit is harassed by society or the child is ostracized, stress may abound.

Among the more familiar alternative lifestyles are multi-racial families, single parents, adoptions, and communal living.

Multi-racial Families

Back in the 1950s, the public was gently introduced to the concept of placing minority children with non-minority families. It started with the placement of black children into white families. This trend now includes bringing Third World people into American families. Today, multi-racial or multi-ethnic families have become part of the American image. Children in multi-racial families may experience stress when they run up against biased attitudes of outsiders or even disapproving grandparents. The unity of the family establishes a protection intended to offset such rejection or disapproval. Increased acceptance of multi-racial families today should permit the youth to make their future decisions with an open mind. Cultural stereotyping doesn't need to be a stopping point anymore.

Single Parents

More and more persons are choosing to be single and to raise children. Women seek the fulfillment that comes from pregnancy and motherhood. Single persons are opening their homes to minority and hard-to-place youngsters. Children in single parent homes can be very well adjusted.

In the instances where a child does not know one or both of his or her natural parents, questions will come up. Don't equate questions with rudeness or a personal attack. Children want answers to unknowns. Kids want clarity about their heritage. Clarity contributes to a sense of completeness and well-being. Your honesty enhances your relationship. The unknowns are stressors. The stress comes from very basic questions. "Who am I? Who are my parents? Why don't I know them? What if I get some disease which I've inherited."

The concept of illegitimacy is a source of stress for many. There are reportedly 115,000 illegitimate adults who have formed a group to safeguard their rights and to give each other support. The issue of identification and parental lineage comes up often in passport applications, some college and job applications, and insurance company matters, for instance. It is as if the problem will never go away. Some harbor resentment that affects all relationships. Even though the parent-child relationship may be rewarding and loving, the child has permitted the stigma to become a source of stress.

Adopted Children

An adopted child is usually told, "You are special. You were chosen." The child becomes very comfortable with these concepts. Children adopted by single parents or homosexual partners have to deal with these aspects of their lives as circumstances dictate. The children learn to appreciate what freedom of choice means, although some may experience stress due to outside judgments or pressures.

Even in the most secure family setting, one question can surface which denotes stress. "Why did my parents give me up?" Young children ask a series of questions such as, "Will *you* give me up, too?" or "Am I loveable?" They seek reassurances from the adoptive parents. Children who have lived in a series of foster homes prior to the adoptive placement are particularly insecure.

If the older child pursues a search for a biological parent, the adoptive parents should be open-minded about it. If the adoptive parents have facts about the natural parent which might be extremely disturbing to the child, they are in a precarious position. They may want to confer with those involved in organizations which help with searches. A reunion may enrich the lives of some. Some reunions are blatantly disappointing. Nevertheless, the persons involved have added dimensions to their lives. A sense of incompleteness prior to the meeting is a stressor. On some levels, the reunion with the biological parent may reduce, or add stress. It can be most threatening to the adoptive parents.

A new concept of adoption attempts to solve many of the old problems and frustrations of traditional adoption procedures. Nowadays, some relinquishing parents select the adoptive parents or communicate with the child whom they relinquished. These contacts range from a single letter to the child to periodic visits and regular letter exchanges. This provides a chance for the child to get answers to questions which have created uncertainty, perhaps stress. The concept is described as successful when handled with limits and facts and does not threaten the bond between the child and the adoptive parents. Contacts with the natural parent must not be allowed to interfere with the in-charge management regime the adoptive parents utilize.

Communal Life

Stress occurs when children perceive their lifestyle as different from others. Although happy, they still want to know how you lived when you were their age. Why are we here now? Why didn't you stay in Shaker

Heights or Dallas? They learn about traditional lifestyles from books, TV, other kids, or movies.

Teenagers may rebel. Their questions may be more profound. Exposure to the media or from outside contacts pose new ideas. They ask each other, "What is ahead for us? Are our parents happy? What else do I want in my life? Do I have an identity beyond being a part of this place?" Some will never question the family commitment to the situation. Others may face a deep struggle in an effort to become independent. They may not want to hurt their parents but, as adolescents, they question almost everything and begin to pull away. "Because my parents made a commitment, does it mean that *I* am committed for the rest of my life? Can I make it on the outside?" It is very difficult to pull away from community living.

Symptoms of Stress

Any parent in any setting can provide warmth and security. The underlying stress for the children stems from identity problems, a sense of incompleteness, or the element of "differentness" in their lifestyle. "There is something missing in my life." "I don't know who I am." "I live in a family set-up different from most." The most commonly observed symptoms, *usually* sporadic, are anxiety, depression, or anger.

Strategies for Support

(1) Be proud of the decisions that you have made. Your attitude influences the well-being of everyone involved.

(2) Be frank about the shortcomings or deficiencies in the lifestyle you have chosen. *All* families, traditional or otherwise, have problems.

(3) Accept your children's feelings.

(4) Reiterate the advantages that your lifestyle presents. In a communal setting, there are numerous ethical and practical considerations which may be beneficial to all.

(5) Open the way for your child to seek some of the answers he or she needs. The attachment between you and your children will not be shredded in the process. Teenagers breaking away from a group-living situation need reassurance that as adults they will have the same right to choose their lifestyle that you enjoy. If they decide to stay with you, be open to these decisions as well.

Alternative lifestyles won't carry negative or critical labels in the future. Already the media present many unbiased facts. Differences may not seem different in the years ahead. Your children benefit by the decisions you have made because they will face the future with broad-minded attitudes.

Sex Stereotyping: An Underlying Source of Stress

Sex stereotyping can undermine any lifestyle. Sexism corrodes relationships because traditional attitudes and expectations are everywhere. The newborn child is greeted with sexist gifts. A mobile for the crib of a boy has plastic boxing gloves, a football, motorcycle, and a Datsun 240Z! In order for a child to acquire healthy self-esteem and a successful coping style, parents must help to understand sex stereotyping and do something about it.

As a parent, you can:

(1) Be informed. Try to assess what influence your parents' attitudes had on you. Were you fortunate enough to have your parents help you become aware of your "masculine" *and* "feminine" characteristics without embarrassment, confusion, or stress? Have you read about studies which establish that there are very few inherent differences between the sexes?

(2) Demonstrate your conviction that you can handle so-called role reversals without being uneasy or defensive. As a dad, how do you answer when asked "You ironing again, Bud? When do you have a chance to go fishing?" Your answers influence the stress level of your kids. Children of either sex will learn caring behavior, usually expected from the mother, and "power" qualities, usually expected from the father, from *anyone* who displays them. Persons of both sexes are sensitive, caring, and strong.

(3) Express your feelings and your attitudes in words kids can understand. Go through magazines and comment about sex stereotyping in the ads. Talk about personal qualities such as love, bravery, power, tenderness, caring, as applicable to both sexes.

(4) Become involved in the schools. The major source of sex stereotyping today is the classroom. Teachers reflect attitudes that they have learned. They are also sometimes very outspoken about homosexuality in a strongly prejudicial way.

(5) Take an active part at home in criticizing sex stereotyping on TV. Make up a game which the children can learn to play. Make some big signs and put them on top of the TV set. One says, "Old-Fashioned Idea about Women," the other says "Old-Fashioned Idea about Men." Flash them when you spot such a role in a story or commercial. Then allow time to talk to the kids. Let them ask questions. Make suggestions on how they may want to solve this problem at the age they are today.

(6) Check out your home responsibilities and home instruction habits. When you bake a cake, are all the children invited into the kitchen to help? When the mower needs new blades, do all the kids get invited to the hardware store and to help you in the backyard, or just the boys? If the girls are not included, why not?

(7) Examine closely the toys that you choose, the books you read to the children, and casual remarks that you make such as, "That's a good girl." The age of the children determines what they believe are "girlish" or "boyish" things to do. This changes. Parents can influence how rigidly these beliefs are held. The same holds true about occupations. Children need continuous reminders that the occupations of the future do not have "for men only" or "for women only" in the job descriptions. Both men and women are involved in space research, electronics, medical research, and service jobs such as police and fire departments and mental health. The taboos of the past—"No women in the mines"—are no longer tolerated.

Benefits of the work that parents do to undo sex stereotyping may be demonstrated in many ways.

- It will be an important quality of family life that builds and maintains mutual respect.
- It will provide acceptance for changes or shifts that a parent may make, without the children feeling embarrassed, uncertain, or unduly critical. It will provide a nonjudgmental base from which the children can make career choices.
- It can prepare the children to help their friends look at their attitudes. For some, this may mean taking an active role in school politics or organizations.
- It is congruent with assertiveness, your right to make decisions without deferring to sex-role stereotypes.
- It can help your children handle intimate relationships because it does away with traditional sex-stereotype expectations. Girls and boys will understand that phrases such as "Men with courage are called brave, women with courage called brazen," cause hard feelings and misunderstandings because they are judgments. In turn judgments negate intimacy and cause stress. Getting rid of the judgments inherent in sex stereotypes helps everyone to stay person focused—focused on Mary, Jim, Helen, Bill, or Ted and his or her uniqueness. Other examples of sex stereotyping: Forgetful men are called absentminded; forgetful women are called scatterbrained. Angry men are called outraged; angry women are called hysterical.
- As you work with the children to overcome or withstand sex stereotyping, your own relationships and self-esteem will be enhanced. As a result, the stress level for all will diminish.
- With a clear picture of what sexist insults are, girls can learn important, essential ways to defend themselves. The woman of today is aware that rape is violence against a woman, a deep-

seated sexist issue. It is not that the rapist merely seeks an outlet for sexual gratification.

Sex stereotyping in America will diminish when everyone understands that people must be free to develop any talents, express any emotions, fill any role, or play any game that they want to, providing no one else is harmed. This understanding must be initiated and supported by everything that you say and do.

46. THE FUTURE AS A SOURCE OF STRESS

When the first *Whole Earth Catalog* appeared in 1968, it was great fun to peruse the descriptions of activities, articles, and ads. The lifestyle of the American family was being challenged to get rid of hypocrisy and to use natural means and modern technical advancements to support warm, human relationships.

At the same time, in other written material, all kinds of new concepts and new words were being introduced. Combinations such as megavitamin, megalopolis, geopolitical, and microelectronics introduced complexities and interdependencies which advised us to be aware that simple matters would never be simple anymore. These interpretations of changes were beacons and announcements. The future cannot step back toward the primitive and unsophisticated. We can never get rid of advancements and technology. We are trapped in webs of conflict from which there may be no escape. Some advances help us and provide a sense of well-being; others do not. No matter how we may struggle or protest, the scientific and technological monster will continue and grow. There is no way to eliminate the stress related to this growth. Stress is the handmaiden of progress. Parents want their children to be prepared for issues that confront society. They want childhood experiences to provide their children with the self-confidence, skills, and assertiveness they will need to cope with a high-tech, high-touch society.

Parents have traditionally talked about jobs and the future with their children. It used to be the responsibility of teachers to introduce discussions about current trends and to help students to delineate problems and talk about solutions. Students were urged to visualize where they would fit into the working world. "Where would you like to be five years, ten years, twenty years from now?" Television has preempted parents and teachers by presenting a vivid assortment of programs, and futuristic possibilities. Curiosity and challenge abound when viewing Disney's nature series, wilderness programs, space exploration, the life of an astronaut, the wonders of medical research, the development of microcomputers, instruments for surgery, communications, and interplanetary messages. Career possibilities in law enforcement, chemistry, public service, teaching, and the media are also portrayed again and again.

Does the future create stress for children?

Some high-achieving elementary-aged children may become preoccupied with the future. Their immediate concern is nuclear war. Uncertainties and too many choices are mentioned frequently. Children who are not high achievers do not seem unduly concerned with futuristic issues. Children from marginal families are much more concerned about the issues of *today*. Will there be enough money to buy new and needed shoes? In general, children do not exhibit symptoms of stress because of undue concern about the future. They do enjoy discussions, books, movies, and classes on futuristic fantasies and ideas.

Unlike elementary-aged students, high school boys and girls repeatedly question what is ahead. They have heard that 50 percent of the jobs that will be available in the year 2000 do not exist today. This discourages some and challenges others. Practical issues such as job availability plus futuristic forecasting add up to pessimism, frustration, and stress.

Symptoms of Stress

Concerned teenagers may:

- Be critical or depressed most of the time.
- Be reckless, give up, adopt a "What's the use" approach to life.
- Deny the problems, pretend that they do not exist.
- Cover up worries by abusing alcohol and/or drugs.
- Become obsessed with issues, lose capacity for fun.
- Abandon any commitments they have such as church ties, adopting an attitude of "I better explore while I can" or "Why get tied down—we may all be torn apart anyhow?"
- Become overly attached to material objects. "At least I can enjoy these now."

Teenagers today face the complexities of the future with more pessimism than ever before. Even college graduates report that their optimism is short-lived. In 1982, 924,000 students received baccalaureate degrees. Good jobs were scarce, except in highly technical areas. Many ended up taking jobs which were for less qualified persons. A Ph.D. pumping gas is not an amusing picture. Non-college persons are even more discouraged about what lies ahead.

Many schools advocate vocational training, which no longer has a negative stigma. Students appreciate that job preparation is an important issue today. The acquisition of diversified skills may reduce stress.

Parents should be supportive when their kids take such programs whether for work preparation or enrichment.

Symptoms of stress may be difficult to spot unless your child talks about concerns for the future. Research tells us that gifted children dwell on doomsday predictions. Some overreact to feelings of helplessness in solving the world's problems and may even threaten or commit suicide. This is unusual. Nevertheless, in any school, children express concern about nuclear war.

Futuristic Issues That May Cause Stress—A Little or a Lot!

Pressure on an individual

Family Life Issues

Single parent adoptions.
Interracial marriages.
Surrogate mothers.
Open marriages, open
  extramarital sex.
Abandoned husbands, wives.
Sex selection of children.

Personal Issues

Premarital sex, the right to be
  a virgin.
The right to abortion.
The right to choose death,
  suicide.
Right to have life-sustaining
  machinery stopped.
Living alone.
Sex preferences.
Drug and alcohol abuse.
Therapies—hypnosis, past
  lives, primal, analysis, group
  therapy.
Religious, spiritual beliefs and
  practices.

Family Social Issues

Children in a homosexual
  family, surrogate mothers,
  artificial insemination.
Right to select sperm.
Genetic engineering.
Right to be a male/female
  prostitute.
Multi-generational families.

Family Legal Issues

Personal marriage contract.
Prenuptial contracts.
Separate property contracts.
Divorce, palimony settlements.
Child custody, custody
  kidnapping.
Mercy killings.

Other Men's/Women's Issues

Job, money discrimination.
Credit problems.

Employment, advancement.
Property ownership.

Non-traditional jobs.
Networks.
Sexual harassment.

Philosophical, Spiritual Issues

Life after Death.
Reincarnation.
Karma.
Previous lives therapy.
Primal therapy.
Cults, movements.

Education

School closing, networks of
    community learning centers.
Computerization of the
    classroom.
Values changes, new issues to
    be confronted: What is the
    responsibility of schools?
    How are they achieved?
Violence, survival, social issues
    and competency skills.
Left Brain—Right Brain
    Research Mainstreaming.
Home learning.

Economics, Politics
Unemployment.
Industrial survival, expansion.
Military matters and costs.
Maintaining public services,
    facilities.
Racial issues.
Immigration, integration.

Military obligations.
Job fields open to women.
Robots on production lines.

Social Issues

Lack of day-care facilities.
Revised criminal code.
Effect of poverty.
Missing children.
Violence, abuse, incest.
Senior citizens.
Political issues and decisions.
Care of needy, ill, handicapped.
Institutions.
Provisions for misfits, mentally
    ill.

Medical Issues
Transplants.
Disease cures, new discoveries.
Geriatrics, longevity.
Life-saving measures, impaired
    lives.
Cost of homes service,
    neighborhood service.
Shortage of trained personnel,
    paraprofessionals.
Research.
Issues around cloning, genetic
    changes, experimentation.
Computer diagnoses.
Holistic health, acupuncture,
    herbs.
Organ donors.

Global Issues
Nuclear war.
Pollution.
Overpopulation.
Political/racial wars and
    conflicts.
Computerization of industry.
Communication, leisure time.

Changing role of the clergy.

Space, interplanetary
  communication,
  transportation.
Food supply.
Violence.
Sex stereotyping

Stress Prevention (Strategies)

What strategies can parents use to help the youth of today confront the issues of tomorrow?

(1) Be an example that you are self-accepting of your own intellectual prowess. The days of the intellectual giants have passed. No one can be a Leonardo da Vinci today. It is no longer possible to "know everything" as he did. The knowledge explosion won't subside in marine biology, ornithology, psychology, psychophysiology, law, electronics, applied chemistry, engineering, politics, medicine, and art. Too many persons, too many tools, too much accumulated data and history amount to overload. Help your child to feel reasonably confident that there are niches to be filled or problems ahead that await his or her solution.

(2) If you feel baffled or overwhelmed, admit it. At the same time, encourage your children to attend workshops, exhibits, displays, classes, and public demonstrations in many fields. For example, numerous Scout troops of ten- to twelve-year-old girls and boys go to health fairs. They see many exhibits of instruments, movies and slides about doctors, nurses, paramedics, nurse practitioners, medicines, rehabilitation therapies and facilities, drug rehabilitation programs, and environmental issues such as pollution and sewer management. They receive interesting booklets and handouts that are explicit enough to provoke questions and possible career selections.

(3) Take the time to tell your children about the work that you do. Explain how your work has changed and what new problems you may be having. Talk about machines, company mergers, company reorganization. Bring up the issues of robots. Have you been replaced? How do you feel about that? There are 80,000 robots (and counting) in U.S. plants today.

(4) Explain what continuing education is. In many states, professionals have to continue to go to school in order to be licensed doctors, lawyers, social workers, nurses, or dentists. Help them accept the concept of lifelong learning. If your child chooses to be a mechanic, this, too, requires continuing schooling when engines are retooled and new electronic devices added, for example. New machines are being introduced into offices, printing plants, and schools.

(5) Be reassuring. Most of us make changes and most of us make decisions we regret. The average person today makes five important job changes in a lifetime. The high cost of college requires many people to hold off or take one or two courses at a time rather than plunge into a four-year or longer program. This means that the job one chooses to earn money and pay tuition may have nothing to do with a choice of career. On the other hand, the job-for-now may become interesting and challenging enough to become the career choice. A boy may mark time as a waiter but then develop a fondness for the food industry that will lead to a managerial or ownership position.

(6) Present a positive attitude about job selections, advancements, and achievements. The children hear about miracles; TV ads tell them that with this product impossible spots will come out, grass will grow, cars will be trouble free. Stress prevention includes learning to ask the right questions, read the right critiques, and take time to be experimental. Test-drive cars, for example. Share your experiences. Tell of your reasons for selecting the products that you do and explain why you have discarded others. Product explosion can create stress in a similar way to the knowledge explosion. We tend to think that everyone has set ideas about what to buy. This isn't true—or so the advertising experts would have us believe.

(7) Your children may insist that you face uncomfortable issues. Sensitive issues do not have to jeopardize family relationships. Together talk over your old attitudes. It takes time to change and shifts may create stress. The acceptance of new values and stress go hand in hand. Values shift because circumstances dictate that they must. If your child is hurt by an ethnic gang, your values may switch from a liberal position to a conservative, prejudicial stance. Perhaps you have expressed opposition to interracial marriages, that you believe mixed marriages are too risky. Then your eighteen-year-old announces that he has chosen a bride from another race. This requires you to look at the values you expressed. Personal and societal values are in flux; flux represents uncertainty and uncertainty may create stress.

Doomsday prophets are popular. Nostrodamus is widely read. You and your children should work hard to maintain a positive, yet realistic attitude about the future. Family discussions must emphasize: (1) how to relate effectively, (2) skills acquisition and training, and (3) problem solving. This amounts to mutual understanding, self-improvement, and goal setting, and it provides ways to cope with personal, interpersonal, and societal issues. It provides each individual with competencies and encouragement to face unknowns ahead.

PART III

The Traumatic Sources of Stress

By definition, trauma implies a shock or intense emotional experience which has a lasting psychic effect. Realistically, what may be an intense experience for one person may not be intense for someone else. Therefore, grouping situations together as traumatic is an arbitrary decision. However, the vast experience of mental health persons supports the grouping. Many children are intensely upset when the parents divorce, a death occurs, the family must move, and when subjected to violence and abuse.

Children do not have to be emotionally crippled as a result of trauma. They do need effective support which may include medical or other therapeutic measures.

Parental care must help children picture the bright side so that they will not distort the pain of today into a prophecy of a defeatist future.

Separation and Divorce

47. PARENTS ARE PARENTS FOREVER

Children frequently resent their parents for deciding to break up the family. They feel it is unfair and unjust. They may also feel a combination of grief, relief, anger, loss, disbelief, shock, and guilt. Such a mixture results in stress. It will take time for them to put all these feelings into perspective. Their trust in adults has diminished. Uncertainties abound.

Realistically, divorce may not be considered an event. It is often the solution to a conflict that has been going on for years. It may take months for the children to accept the decision as final. Working through such a realization is disturbing and for some visibly traumatic.

The Pre-divorce Situation and the Meaning of Ambivalence

It is difficult to be objective about a pre-divorce situation. Mixed memories of good times and bad times are confusing and disturbing. The adjustment of the children requires that they understand ambivalence. Ambivalence is simultaneous, conflicting feelings such as love and hate. The ups and downs of all relationships reflect ambivalence.

Most families are not violent. Prior to the divorce, family life may have been by turns full of anger then free of tension, with occasional displays of displeasure, disappointment, or indifference. There were lots of happy times, too—birthday parties, trips, picnics, and ball games. From the children's point of view, that's the way it is in all families. The parents' decision to get a divorce is hard to understand. Knowing about ambivalence saves them from blaming one parent or the other. In cases where one parent has left due to a fight, the fight can be interpreted as an example of the negative side of the marriage.

Help children understand that relationships change. Do not underestimate what children want to know and what they can understand.

Even the pre-school-aged child is entitled to carefully worded explanations which safeguard respect for all. This is not an easy task.

Keep in mind that the *relationship between the parents does not end and never will.* They will always be the parents of the children and always have that tie. They will always have a relationship with each other whether it is based on anger, support, indifference, or friendship.

How the parents manage their relationship is a vital key to the recovery of the children. Set this goal: *Parents must provide a foundation whereby each child is free to develop a stable and mature relationship with each parent.* That is the fervent desire of all children, whether verbalized or not. It requires the parents to stop any bad-mouthing and belittling.

Parents can alleviate some of the stress by maintaining an accepting attitude toward the divorce and the ex-spouse. The positive aspects of the ambivalent relationship must be acknowledged repeatedly, even if one parent is now feeling rejected or bitter. This positive attitude helps diminish the children's anger and stress. Mention things that are admirable in the former mate: he or she a good provider, has athletic ability, beauty, or talents. Parents *must* temper negative criticism. Even though children may have heard endless derogatory descriptions of a parent, they still harbor thoughts that this parent may change or that the unpleasant things that they have heard about one parent are just a reflection of the unhappiness of the other. Children can be far more charitable than grown-ups and want to be loving to both parents. Even the child who has witnessed violence or has been abused will make an effort to excuse the abusive parent. "He couldn't help it, Mom," the child may explain.

48. THE CHILD'S RECOVERY BEGINS

Premises to Promote Recovery

Everyone's recovery is helped when you reaffirm that:

- Living with one parent is *not* necessarily injurious to a child's development. A harmonious single-parent home has decided advantages. Children in a single-parent home learn responsibilities, become more aware of money matters, and frequently develop a supportive role with the parent which teaches them to be sensitive to the needs of others. A *positive* attitude about single-parent families provides a constructive base for coping, diminishing stress and promoting growth.
- Do not overreact to single-parent bad press. Reports about problem children from single-parent families invariably ignore vital aspects such as income, neighborhood, parent's forced ab-

sence from the home, and the critical attitudes of many outside persons. Stress on a child will reflect maturity and personal circumstances surrounding relationships with each parent, school and social pressures.

- Children want their parents married. Before the divorce, school-aged children may make adjustments in hopes that they can effect parental compatibility. For example, they come home from school on time so that Mom and Dad won't quarrel about their lateness. When separation and divorce occur, children feel incompetent, as if they have failed or perhaps even caused the split. This results in loss of self-esteem, depression, and anger, accompanied by grief and anxiety. Dealing with all of these feelings is part of recovery.
- Expect children to plead for a reconciliation. Make certain that they do not construe reasonable communication between the parents as indications that a reconciliation is imminent. For example, take time to explain that because Daddy is invited to share a holiday does not mean that he will be moving back home. Without such an explanation, some young children may be confused and disappointed. The disappointment may trigger or reactivate certain symptoms of stress that have abated.
- Most children are functioning well by two years after a divorce if their parents are no longer bitter and a visitation program has stabilized. If visitation is out of the question, children may superficially accept the situation even as they harbor grief for the absent parent and bitterly resent the divorce. Explain the situation as clearly as possible. Parents do not make decisions to hurt children. Children can understand this.
- Be assured that all children experience times of frustration, unfulfilled needs, and confusions, yet still manage to feel good about themselves. Even in many situations which are unpleasant, scary, disruptive, and bleak, children will not suffer permanent damage if their parents or others are available as helpers.

Remember that children cannot have an ex-mother or an ex-father. The parent is present in thought, if not in person. Children may make unpleasant, unkind, or callous remarks about the absent parent, knowing that this is what the custodial parent wants to hear. But it may not reflect accurately how the child really feels. Therefore, try to develop a team approach with your ex-spouse. Children need to view their parents as allies, if not as husband and wife.

Symptoms of Stress

Symptoms denote the magnitude of stress that a child experiences. Some are more debilitating than others. At the time of parental separation or divorce, young children may exhibit

- Depression.
- Temper tantrums.
- Anger at both parents.
- Disturbed sleep habits.
- Nervous habits like thumb sucking or bedwetting.
- Unusual pleas for dependency.
- Demands to be held, cuddled, or to sleep with parent.
- Agitation, even pacing.

The age of the children may determine their reactions. For school-aged children this may result in

- Lack of interest in school.
- Bedwetting.
- Inability to concentrate at school.
- Signs of hyperactivity, physical problems.
- Aggressive behavior toward siblings, friends, teachers and the custodial parent.
- Exaggerated grown-up behaviors, bravado.

Middle school children may turn to

- New or intensified interest in drugs, alcohol.
- Sexual experimentation.
- Prolonged visits with friends, grandparents, relatives.
- Being either uncooperative or overly solicitous with the custodial parent.
- Non-custodial parent for comfort-long telephone calls.
- Threats to run away.
- Extended periods of moroseness.

High-school-aged students may show stress by

- An increased need to be part of the gang.
- Quitting school, running away.
- Demanding attention.
- Exaggerated concern for younger siblings.
- Expressed disgust at both parents.
- Exclusive relationship with member of opposite sex.
- Antisocial behaviors.
- Depression, suicidal thoughts.

The Needs of the Child of Divorce

The needs of the child of separation and divorce are basic and yet complicated, and the results of your caretaking may be imperceptible. The basic needs serve as a webbing, the fundamental threads of the parent-child relationship which must be strengthened in times of great stress.

The children need

- Affection and respect.
- Reassurance that the divorce, the decision to separate, was not his or her fault.
- To know his or her legal rights.
- To be consulted regarding custody and visitation, commensurate with understanding. The feelings and wishes of the children are important; however, children must understand that the final decision will be up to the courts. Tell them that judges are professionals who have had a great deal of experience and who make every effort to place the children in the best situation. Children need to understand that shuttling back and forth between parents is inadvisable. They can understand about inconsistent rules, school attendance problems, and the advantages of an equitable visitation plan.
- To be allowed to be a child.
- Encouragement to express feelings. Listen!
- To understand that even though the parents no longer love each other, this does not have to disturb their devotion to the children.
- To have their questions about the non-custodial parent answered. This is congruent with the consideration that children love both their parents. *If a child is not permitted to ask questions about the absent parent, he or she may turn to fantasies that can cause additional adjustment problems.* Concern may be heightened at separation, around holidays, and at other special times.

Needs of Teenagers

It is important to remember that adolescence is a time for self-search, explorative social experiences, and intellectual broadening. These needs can be filled or become debilitating in an emotional climate whether established by one parent or two. The teenagers of divorce need:

- Frequent reminders that school is an important priority.
- To be reminded that dwelling on the divorce can result in loss of interest in friends, school, activities, and learning. A self-pitying attitude can turn away much-needed friends.
- Help in understanding relationships, commitments, and working through conflicts, to understand that parents are not inadequate or bad persons simply because they no longer care for each other. Adolescents tend to make judgments and become closed-minded. They need assistance to learn tolerance or perhaps forgiveness.

- To understand the family's economic situation and to make appropriate adjustments. Some may have been unreasonably demanding and have to curtail requests.
- Peer support, both individually and in groups.
- Role models. This can be one person, such as a counselor or coach with admirable qualities to be observed and emulated, or the child can model different qualities from a number of persons.

Research reports that teenagers are more disturbed by parental divorce than any other age group. Many accounts quote teenagers as complaining about the secrecy that their parents displayed. Surprise announcements made them feel discounted and disrespected.

Strategies for Support

(1) Take charge. Be assertive even though it may be easier to take a passive, "this, too, shall pass" position. When your world seems to be coming apart, it is very hard to find the energy you need to deal with your own problems, much less those of the children. But children cannot cope alone and require parental guidance and strength. The young child who clings or whines or screams is not mature enough to know how much stress adults face. When mother pleads, "Leave me alone!", the child only begs for more attention. The adolescent may appear to be cool or relatively detached from the situation, but this may be only a façade. He may say, "That's Mom's problem, let her deal with it!" but this does not alter the fact that teenagers need attention, too. Remember, the parents feel better when the children cope successfully.

(2) Listen to the children. Children feel unimportant when parents are fighting. They regain a sense of importance when Mom or Dad takes time to listen to what they have to say. They have many questions which need to be answered. They gain a sense of importance when their emotional needs are met. Take the time to figure out what the child may be feeling or needing. Observe moods and demands. Little ones cannot express themselves in words; older ones may be afraid to do so. Some do not know what is worrying them. They need someone to talk to about what is going on.

(3) Be honest with the children. Reaffirm that the basic decisions were *adult* decisions.

(4) Talk about your feelings. This may be very difficult to do, but it is an important dimension of any coping style. You may have some grievances that you want to talk about. You may want to tell the children how much you appreciate their thoughtfulness or that you are aware that you have been irritable, withdrawn, or sulky. Children gain a lot from knowing that parents experience the same feelings that they do. As

mentioned earlier (See Section II, #2, on bonding) trying to relate to a parent who is unreachable or who bounces around emotionally compounds the stress for the child. When you can sit down together and explain your unreachable or bouncing behavior, a sense of tolerance and understanding develops. Children love their parents. Parental power is immeasurable. Your honesty and humility are worthy lessons.

(5) Maintain the approach that a child must know as many of the facts as he or she can understand or handle. Facts give a child a foundation for coping with stress. It enables them to proceed with problem solving. Without facts, the child's anxiety increases immeasurably. Try to share facts in a way that will let the child appreciate the problems and still feel compassionate toward all persons involved. Children do not naturally hate other people. Even if there has been a terrible incident, try to describe what has happened in a way that will give the child some insight into the problems and the pain felt by all.

(6) If possible, negotiate plans and decisions with the child. Take into account age, understanding, how upset the child is, and the realistic options. Do not make suggestions or hint at outcomes that could never happen. During times of turmoil, decision making may be very difficult. Ask the children for suggestions. They will learn that you welcome their input even though the recommendations may not be workable. (See Section XI, #49.)

(7) Ease up on some pressures such as getting good grades or keeping a tidy room. Children need limits and guidelines. However, when a child is feeling overwhelmed, certain pressures should be set aside. Stop nagging and cajoling. And remind teachers that their commitment at this time is to the *total child*, not just to his or her math or writing skills. Such a recess may be of short duration, perhaps two or three weeks at most. Those things tentatively set aside will be placed in proper perspective in a short while.

(8) Seek help; it can be important. In family life, the symptoms are contagious. When adults become withdrawn, depressed, or angry, the children react by feeling rejected or worthless. They become extremely anxious as they try to predict the future or grasp things beyond their understanding. Do not assume that immature and unusual behavior which a child exhibits will be permanent. The children do need help. Some children will ask for it. Seeking help is a healthy way to work through painful, complicated situations and ease their impact. (See Sections V, #14 and XVI, #70.)

- Help can minimize disruption and anxiety for all.
- Help can promote problem solving and stability. It can demonstrate to parents how to communicate with the children.

- Help can produce marked improvements in relationships.
- Help may mean spending time and money that may *prevent* problems from starting or becoming increasingly serious.

Where to find help depends a great deal on where one lives. In some areas, few people have been trained to deal with children under stress. The search itself may create additional stress, but it will be worth the effort.

Often, within an organized group such as Parents Without Partners or a grief group, a member may be instrumental in suggesting an especially caring school social worker, clinician in a nearby hospital, or some other professional to whom to turn. You may discover that some professionals relate effectively to children and are less comfortable with adults, or vice-versa. Nevertheless, goals for adults and children are the same: a repaired, healthy sense of personal worth; effective ways to cope; resulting in the elimination or reduction of the symptoms of stress.

49. VISITATION

Significant stress may arise around visitation. The purpose of visitation is to ensure the child and the non-custodial parent a chance to develop and maintain a stable, caring relationship. There must be a workable plan which takes into account many things. A plan is difficult because it is usually outlined shortly after separation while feelings of both parents are still raw. Even when parents try to be fair, the situation is rife with uncertainty. In such an emotional time, and often under pressure from attorneys, it is not surprising that the plan agreed to does not work. It may start out smoothly but within weeks or months, it must be cancelled or changed. It isn't necessary to figure out who is to blame but rather what can be done to keep the children's stress and disappointments to a minimum.

How to Proceed

(1) Start with what is practical. There are at least three sets of schedules to consider: the children's, the custodial parent's, and the non-custodial parent's. Especially when things at home are shaky, it is important for children to keep up activities such as the Scout troop, athletic team, or Sunday school class. The more a child is included in the planning, the more your relationship with the child is safeguarded. Hurt and distress are diminished.

(2) Be practical about expenses and travel time. Long-distance visitation is costly and often difficult to arrange around school or work schedules. In-town visitation can be expensive if the children demand and

get restaurant meals, tickets to the movie, circus, or ballgame, and so forth. The time together is for sharing, affection, and problem solving, not a can-you-top-this spending orgy.

(3) Establish a pattern or schedule that considers the child's need for proper rest.

(4) Bear in mind that children feel secure when they have structure and predictable and consistent patterns and limits. Inconsistency and too much leniency during visits is confusing and detrimental.

(5) Consider the quality of communication concerning visitation. If visits are seen as a "pay-off" for support payments, their purpose is undermined. If either parent asks inappropriate or endless questions of the child, the visits take on a painful dimension. If the non-custodial parent insists on giving material gifts while the custodial parent is having financial problems, children become confused and sometimes inappropriately demanding. If the visit to the non-custodial parent involves the extended family (grandparents, for instance) who maintain a bitter or critical attitude toward the custodial parent, the children will surely suffer. Such visits should reaffirm to the child that family members beyond the custodial parent love them and have accepted the divorce.

(6) Give the child an opportunity to express feelings. If the non-custodial parent has difficulty adjusting to separation from the nuclear family, children may become overwhelmed with sympathy and take it out in anger toward the custodial parent. Frequently, children react by wanting to move in with the non-custodial parent to be a companion or helper. Such an arrangement may not be feasible or desirable. The child will not understand this without some discussion and explanation.

(7) On long-distance visits, the child on the plane is frequently tense. The time lapse between visits can create all kinds of questions and worries. As the non-custodial parent, be gentle. Don't look for enthusiasm. Anticipate that it may take several days to reestablish patterns of affection and communication. When the children return to the custodial parent, they frequently show grief and conflict.

In my many years as a social worker, I have recommended a visitation plan which has worked well for families where school-aged children have been divided between two households. It is a rotation. (Obviously, with infants this may not be practical at all). Let us assume that David (Child A) lives with Daddy, and Louise (Child B) lives with her mother.

Weekend one: Child A at home (Home X) with father.
              Child B at home (Home Y) with mother.
Weekend two: Child A + Child B (Home X) with father.

Weekend three:	Child A (Home Y).
	Child B (Home X).
Weekend four:	Child A + Child B (Home Y) with mother.

This provides opportunities for parents to have time free of any children. It provides time alone with the child from the other home and times with both children. Weekend one is a continuation of the weekday arrangement; no one is shifted around. Parents are urged to stay with this rotation because it enriches all relationships and maintains communication among all members of the family on a regular basis. It negates the subtle problem of territorial ownership. In time the children may not want to move around so much because they want more unscheduled time. This can be negotiated.

Visitation Changes or Problems

In many situations visits from/to the non-custodial parent become less frequent. It is easy for others to be very critical. Criticisms only add to the stress that the children experience. Let the kids express their disappointment, concerns, or any feelings of detachment which may develop. Teenagers may rebel against any organized visitation plan that takes precedence over their own activities. Both parents should anticipate this.

50. THE FADE-AWAY PARENT

A word or two about the fade-away parent—the situation in which the child no longer sees the absent parent. Perhaps the most poignant questions a child may ask in the aftermath of divorce are: "Will Daddy send me a birthday present?" "Will I see Mom at Christmas?" "Do you think my dad will really write to me?" When confronted with questions like these:

- Never answer in a way that offers false hope.
- Take time to let the child express grief, anger, and despair.
- Point out that the situation is not the child's fault.
- Talk about ambivalence.

It may then be worth elaborating on one or more of the following explanations:

- Occasional visits followed by renewed separations became too painful for the parent to handle.
- The absent parent determined the necessity to start a new life for himself or herself, for reasons which the child may not understand.

- The parent's plans may involve remarriage, precluding involvement with two families at the same time, at least for the present.
- The parent cannot handle the ongoing problems and arguments
  that led to the divorce in the first place, and opted to cut off all
  communication.
- A lawyer or judge may be responsible for the decision to disallow
  visitation, as in a restraining order or contingencies with regard to
  support payments, imprisonment, therapy, or matters related to
  child abuse.

The teenager who has not seen an absent parent for a number of
years may become obsessed with this deprivation. Some run away from
home to try to find the missing parent. These youngsters are not actually
running away but rather running *to* the missing father or mother. Some
organizations are currently developing programs to help children in their
search. Reunions can be highly successful or can leave a child with a
number of problems to resolve. If a child should run away from your home
in order to search, don't feel rejected. See the positive side, even though
you staunchly disagree and fear that a relationship with the long-absent
parent will be unsuccessful. When the child returns, take the time to
assess your relationship. Make the child feel welcome.

51. POSSIBLE BENEFITS OF SEPARATION AND DIVORCE

For children of all ages

(1) The children usually learn to be more self-reliant. When the
custodial parent has overwhelming responsibilities, children learn to fend
for themselves when they are told, "Please do your homework alone
tonight" or, "You don't have to have someone tuck you in every night. I
love you, but I have to finish my work." Children acquire competence and
a degree of independence. For some children, this represents a major
shift from a time when mother may have been too solicitous or
overprotective.

(2) The child may learn a number of self-protective measures to avoid
being scapegoated. "Don't take it out on me because you are mad at
Daddy or because we don't have much money." If a parent becomes too
dependent on the child, it doesn't hurt to hear, "Oh, Mom, go by yourself.
I want to stay home and watch TV."

(3) The child may learn the importance of a sense of humor!

(4) The child may turn to friends, relatives, siblings, or teachers or
to a parent for support. Healthy dependency and communication may
develop that might not otherwise have happened. These relationships
may have been initiated by a friend, parent, or teacher when symptoms of
stress were noticed. Happily, the child was able to accept the help that

was offered. It doesn't matter who took the first step. Benefits include the message, "I have someone to turn to." If a child's sense of trust is damaged when a family breaks up, it can be repaired as he or she turns to others for support.

(5) The child may discover that communication based on honesty and sharing can serve as a springboard for entering and surviving troubled times. Children are forthright and may often be the ones who confront adults who are indirect, dishonest, or unreasonable.

(6) The child learns the importance of expressing emotions and respecting the emotional needs of others. When a child sees a parent cry or watches a sibling in a rage, he or she may be puzzled if this is a new experience. It is good to know that others have strong feelings, too. It is also beneficial to be reminded that we still must control ourselves at such a time even though we may want to hurt others.

(7) The child benefits from knowing that many others have had similar experiences and that things turned out okay. He or she may learn early on that self-pity is hard to stop and friends may get tired of hearing it.

(8) Children may derive a greater appreciation of their parents and greater tolerance for the parents' weaknesses. Children may be aware of the changes that parents make in the same way that adults perceive the changes children make.

(9) The children may learn their legal rights.

(10) Children can benefit from a new understanding of the decision-making process. They become more objective, about the family. They may decide to do better in school. They may decide to stop whining or teasing. Decisions add up to taking responsibility for one's own behavior and that becomes a lifelong benefit.

(11) A sense of loneliness may prove to be a benefit. The child learns that others may not always be there to help. Although uncomfortable, it may be a step toward mature independence. It is not a "poor-me" position.

Inasmuch as teenagers seem to be unusually vulnerable when parents divorce, it is worth noting positive benefits which they may derive. The adolescent of divorce frequently displays more maturity than peers. He or she is aware of this difference. It tends to influence, in a constructive way, choice of friends and career, goal setting, activities, general interests, and use of time and money.

Adolescents can learn to give support to the custodial parent, helping with companionship, transportation, babysitting, home responsibilities, and family income.

The teenager may be designated as the emergency contact for a younger sibling if it is not possible to reach a parent. The adolescent may be an important role model for younger children who emulate their cheerfulness and cooperation rather than continual griping and negativism.

Joint custody offers benefits. Children interpret this to mean, "Both my parents really want me!" It avoids the problem of, "My Daddy (or Mother) didn't want me!" which accompanies some single-parent custody arrangements. Although complicated, especially if a parent remarries, shared custody seems to reduce stress.

The children may move from one home to the other or the children may stay at home in familiar surroundings while the parents take turns in the house. Joint custody implies that there is parental cooperation. This is beneficial and may be a real improvement from the stress of the pre-divorce household.

52.   PARENTAL RECOVERY: DATING, REMARRIAGE, STEP-PARENTING

While each parent develops a new lifestyle, the children are bombarded with different arrangements, values, relationships, and assorted expectations. Some children handle this well. They are excited about new possibilities. Others experience a lot of self-doubt.

If the children go through periods of defiance or unruly acting out, keep in mind the normal rebelliousness of youth. For example, boys fourteen years of age can be argumentative and uncooperative. Do not blame the divorce for that! Talk to parents of other kids the same age to discover the universality of these kinds of behavior. This reduces your stress.

Happy memories, dreams, or sentimental moments do not have to disrupt your recovery. They are indicators of the ambivalence of the marriage. Even though in time positive memories may outnumber unhappy or angry ones, this does not mean that a reconciliation is in order. If you now regret the divorce, force yourself to examine the faults and hurts that led to the separation. When divorced couples remarry each other, more than 90 percent of them divorce again. The ones that last have frequently had joint therapy for many months.

It takes courage to handle a divorce. Take time to be proud of the good decisions that you have made. Stress lays the foundation for insights and growth, painful as it may be. Recovery allows you to acknowledge progress and satisfactions.

The Parent Who Is Dating

When a parent starts to date, the children will have mixed emotions. They may rejoice that Mom or Dad is no longer depressed and withdrawn. Or they regard the dating as an infringement on the parent-child or the parent-ex-spouse relationship. You should make it clear that blanket condemnation of your dating is unfair; you do not need their permission. Let the children learn to appreciate your conflict between time for dates and time with them. Help them understand your need for a loving adult relationship. Both sides must make certain adjustments. Young children can learn to stay with a sitter without fussing, and older boys and girls can stop griping. Children may be angry and push to be included or they may be rude to your dates. Share your feelings and acknowledge theirs. Let them talk about being jealous or ask why you are so nice to your date when you used to be so nasty to your ex-spouse. The basic parent-child relationship is not in jeopardy. Your dating is not a sign of rejection.

Depending upon the age of the children, discuss the situation as candidly as possible. They need to understand that not everyone you meet or whose company you enjoy is a prospective stepparent. Young children may implore you to "bring me a new daddy (or mommy)." In some situations children can cause bitter arguments and hard feelings. Time alone with you may help. It may take months before your children warm up to your friend or lover. Be patient! There are so many understandable reasons why they want to stay at arm's length. Don't take it to mean that they don't want you to be happy. See the hesitations as the scars of earlier wounds that left the children fearful.

Live-in Arrangements

A live-in partner may be the facsimile of a stepparent or merely a visitor. This distinction needs to be made clear. It directly affects the answers to such questions as: How much authority does this person have? Does this person have the right to criticize how the parent handles the children? Are the children obligated to do as this person says? Clear answers reduce stress for all because the children understand the roles and all the agreements. There will be rough times when demands or discipline cause problems, but, roles become the foundation upon which everyone stands. Older boys and girls may rebel against a new authority person in the home. It is suggested that adults take the stand that as long as the child is living at home, the rules apply regardless of which adult may be carrying them out.

Children can become confused if a parade of sex-partners stay in the home, either on a short-term or long-term basis. The confusion has less to do with morals in many instances than with unexpressed questions. Do I make friends or don't I? Do I try to get close, or will I have to say good-bye again? Such questions denote stress. Children are basically me-focused and may be reluctant to reach out if there are no guarantees. In one way, this is self-preservative; in another way, it may obstruct the exchange of positive feelings and cause some misunderstandings. Help children confront this dilemma.

Same-Sex Partners

More single persons are choosing lovers of the same sex. The effect on children is often bewilderment, confusion, embarrassment, and shame. If this is your situation, take time to deal with the prejudices and misconceptions that the children may have. Their friends or members of the extended family or your ex-spouse's family may make disturbing, critical remarks. Your goals should be to help the children: (1) accept the life-style you have selected and (2) become friends with your partner on the merits of the person himself or herself. Some recent publications on sexual preference proclaim the normalcy of same-sex relationships. Some talk shows and articles debate the issue and offer both advantages and disadvantages. Statements frequently deal with the difficulties children may experience when working through their male/female identifications. There are no available statistics to verify such statements.

Your children may benefit from your broad-mindedness. Children of today must be helped to live comfortably in a world of diversified and controversial lifestyles. As they learn to confront the many options in life, the impact of parental honesty and sensitivity may far outweigh the impact of parental sexual habits.

Remarriage

THE CUSTODIAL PARENT REMARRIES

Bearing in mind that the goal for a child of divorce is a stable, mature relationship with each parent, the task becomes more difficult when one of the parents remarries. Former symptoms of stress may surface again. Even though the child may like the future stepparent, parental remarriage represents a return to unknowns. A child may perceive the stepparent as a rival. The child may not understand the bedroom arrangement. The child may not want to face a new disciplinarian. However, if workable patterns to reduce stress during the dating period were successful, the new marriage will enhance the experiences of everyone.

Your role must be to explain to your children that your needs are important and your love for your new spouse does not preclude a love for them. At the same time, do not make promises or paint rosy pictures that may not reflect reality. A child does not have a "new Daddy" but a new person with whom to develop a loving relationship.

THE NON-CUSTODIAL PARENT REMARRIES

When the non-custodial parent remarries, feelings of estrangement may increase, or there may be a strong awareness of a lack of involvement. Familiar and intense symptoms of grief and loss may be forthcoming. Other children may be casual or seem disinterested in the new marriage. This may hurt the parent's and new spouse's feelings. No one is to blame. It may reflect anxiety or loyalty to the custodial parent. It is usually temporary. Children may be expected to move cautiously or to make unexpected demands for attention and closeness. Do not personalize a lack of enthusiasm.

The question of custody is sometimes reopened following remarriage of the non-custodial parent. Such negotiations require the utmost tact and objectivity. When consulted, the very young (under seven years of age) may reason on the basis of something simplistic such as, "I get more candy at Dad's," or, "I get to watch more TV at Mommy's." If the custodial parent has not remarried, the child may say, "But I want to live with two parents. That's why I want to go live with Daddy." It is best not to rush into any change. Let the marriage stabilize. Give new relationships a chance to mature. Confer with professionals if a proposal to change is creating conflict or problems.

Stepparenting

A stepparent, in cooperation with the natural parent, can make the child's adjustment easier by following these suggestions:

- Be honest about feelings.
- Establish a level of communication with the stepchild that includes commendation and praise as well as expressions of disappointment, discouragement, and *worries*. The younger the child, and the more the custodial responsibilities, the easier it may be for some children to let go of a negative, "She's only my stepmother" attitude.
- When replacing a deceased parent, don't deliberately try to be different than you really are, or to emulate the idealized parent you are replacing. Be natural.
- Don't expect stepchildren to love you. Maintain a realistic goal of a warm friendship built on respect. There is no time limit for winning over stepchildren. Most stepparent-stepchild relationships seem to harbor a marked ambivalence that dissipates slowly. Without the biological tie, it is difficult to establish the quality of a relationship that natural parents have.
- Expect complaints, gripes, testing by the child, offhand comparisons with the absent parent, and manipulative behavior intended to separate you from your spouse. Also expect behaviors that signal insecurity and jealousy. Some children may be openly hostile and rejecting. Adolescents may be more accepting, depending on their maturity and understanding of adult needs.

- Be open to being called by your first name or a nickname. "Mom" or "Dad" may or may not be appropriate. So much depends on the child's age and ongoing relationship with the non-custodial parent.
- Come to terms with the child's feeling about the natural parent. Do not overreact to statements that begin "I wish I were with my *real* mother (or father)." Such thoughts may be fleeting or may be a reaction to limits or discipline. If the child persists in this, set aside time to talk together and discuss whether changes in the visitation program, communication, or custody should be considered.
- Remember that the wife-husband relationship is the strongest bond. Children acquire a sense of security from it. Problem-solving methods displayed are important to the children. Confront your feelings if the bond between your spouse and the children usurps your position.

STEPBROTHERS AND STEPSISTERS

When stepbrothers or stepsisters move into the home, there is instant competition. There are an infinite number of adjustments to make. Parents need to be sensitive to the fact that it takes months for some of these differences to work themselves out. There are some strategies you can follow to help the adjustment along.

- Take time to be alone with *your* children. They need this time alone with you. You do not need to be defensive to your spouse or stepchildren about this decision. It is not showing favoritism. It nourishes the natural bonds between you. (You will also spend time with stepchildren alone to build *those* relationships.) This reduces stress, builds security, and minimizes rivalry between natural children and stepchildren.
- Anticipate friction and misunderstandings, and don't overreact. Relationships take time to develop.
- Don't push for your children and the stepchildren to be best friends. It is okay if they do not like each other at all. The intensity of competition is far greater than with a classmate or fellow member of the Boy Scout troop. However, you do have to insist that all children involved are as polite and understanding to each other as they are to their friends, neighbors, and classmates.
- Make certain that house rules are for *all* kids. It sometimes happens that a parent, in welcoming the stepchildren, becomes more strict with his or her own children and seems more flexible with the newcomers. "After all," you may say, "it takes time to get adjusted to a new home." True. But *all* the kids are experiencing stress and having to make adjustments. Sharing toys, a bedroom,

and your mom or dad, is a learning process for all and the rules must be *fair*. Fairness is in the eyes of the beholder! For example, older kids should know that the little ones need special considerations.

The strength of the adult relationship will have a positive effect on all the children in the home and family management based on expressing emotions, maintaining limits, and adults taking an in-charge position will benefit everyone. As adults, discuss the situation, listen to the kids, be realistic and project the pros and cons. Ask again and again, "Are we being manipulated? What is really the best arrangement at this time?" You may decide to try a new arrangement to see if the kids are happier and if they adjust well.

Child support will be introduced again with custody changes. In the majority of cases, informal agreements between ex-spouses work very well and allow for future changes, thereby reducing legal fees.

53. CUSTODY CONSIDERATIONS

Custody Changes

Any child may demand to live with the non-custodial parent. He or she wants a change and may make life miserable for everyone in an effort to make the point that things at home just aren't working. Let's suppose that Helen Blaine has custody of Jeff, who is fifteen years old and Mary Anne, eleven. Jim Blaine lives in the same town and his visits with the children have been regular for more than four years. Both the children adore their father. As Helen struggles to manage with limited funds and juggles her social life and time with the kids, there is more and more friction. The stress level gets higher and higher. The kids spend a lot of time griping about their mother and fantasizing that living with Dad would be great. Helen is distraught. Her stress level is bringing on all kinds of symptoms—headaches, insomnia, crying episodes, and depression. The more she pulls away from the children, the more they scream that they hate her and want to live with Dad. Is this a real demand or just a way of saying that they are unhappy? Sit down and talk about it. The kids may be right. Sometimes a change of custody makes sense.

However, changes may take months in the courts and cost hundreds of dollars.

Custody Kidnapping

It is estimated that 125,000 children are taken by non-custodial parents each year. Some are never heard from again. Sometimes the children are not returned after a routine visit. From the child's vantage point, it is an accelerated custody fight with secretive qualities, fears for themselves and for the parent from whom they have been pulled away. Add loss and the problems inherent in fitting into a new home, and you can picture how much stress they experience.

Realistically, some custody kidnappings result from court decisions which appear to penalize the non-custodial parent, or from problems that stem from an unfair visitation regime or unrecognized changes in circumstances. Sometimes court calendars are so jammed that an important, desirable change of custody is unnecessarily delayed. Regardless of explanations, the child is the victim. A change of custody may be in order, but forced or unexpected kidnappings are traumatic and harmful. It may take months or years before the children understand what happened. Some will have adjusted to the new situation happily; some will not. The deception and ongoing conflict between parents will cause problems for all.

SUMMARY: SEPARATION AND DIVORCE

One of every six persons in the U.S. in 1982 is a step-something— mother, father, sister, or brother. The trend of the future promises more of the same. In order to give children confidence, parents must help children avoid looking for total acceptance or unlimited approval from everyone. *The primary task for parents and stepparents is to help children to become self-accepting.*

In the aftermath of separation and divorce, children can become desperate to be liked by all the people in the family circle or circles. They seek constant attention. This seems to give them a sense of connectedness. But the searching creates a great deal of stress. Urge them to be open-minded and loving, knowing that one gets love in return. Relationships, whether distant or close, provide opportunities for growth and insights into ways to cope.

Death: The Transition from Tears to Tranquility

54. THE REALITY OF DEATH: WORKING TOWARD ACCEPTANCE

When my son arrived back home after his father's funeral, he looked up at his grandfather and asked, "Grandpa, will you show me how to tie a tie?" Douglas was ten. He was making an effort to adjust to a fatherless world. Many people were aware that he would need help on various levels. His school principal and teachers found the time to talk to him, to stay involved in Doug's recovery, to go beyond the cursory comment, "I was sorry to hear about your dad." Doug was lucky. So many children lose a parent and get very little comfort and support. They suffer the loss, hide their feelings, and try to be brave.

Piece by piece, step by step, children can let go of intense grief. Reactions of disbelief and anger take a long while. Many times they want to find someone to blame; too often they blame themselves. Young Paul's mother was killed in a car accident following a family argument about his grades. Paul was convinced that the accident was his fault because Mom was upset. Similarly, Jenny's father was killed instantly when his car skidded on ice. He had stormed out of the house, gone to a bar to cool down from a family fight about the grubby ring in the bathtub. Jenny was the "guilty" one; over and over she said "If only I hadn't been so lazy! If only I had cleaned that tub." Children sometimes see death as punishment or rejection. It is essential for them to work through feelings, which they might otherwise hang on to the rest of their lives.

Although it hurts to see a child suffer, there is no way to protect children all the time. Death is a part of the everyday world. We cannot protect children from death. But we can help them face and accept it.

One of every twenty children will face the death of a parent during his or her childhood. Sometimes there are opportunities to say good-bye;

more often there is a sudden loss. No matter what the circumstances, it represents stress at a peak. The most important question of all is: How does a child learn to accept that someone is really dead? For children, in particular, the reality of death has been confused by TV. They see John Wayne killed on Monday and back up on his horse Tuesday. Unless the reality of death is made clear, children may harbor anxiety for many years. The myth that "Grandma is sleeping," or, "We have lost Mother," no longer satisfies the child of today. The child must know that there is no hope that the dead person will return. A year old child, though nonverbal, is acutely aware of the loss and needs a meaningful explanation. Above that age children express disbelief, anger, fear, or grief in what may appear to be babyish or inappropriate behavior. Adults may be looking for behavior similar to their own, whereas young children express feelings briefly and go on to something else. A child becomes distracted by a butterfly at the cemetery; the parent scowls; the child is bewildered. Expect shifting emotions.

School-age children, as well as teenagers, may turn to their friends. In the book entitled *How It Feels When A Parent Dies* by Jill Krementz, Stephen Jayne, age eleven, is quoted. He said, "It helps if your friends treat you the same way as before your parent died. When they start feeling sorry for you, it makes you feel sorry for yourself and then you start crying." Older kids may want to be surrounded by their friends so they can all cry together. Some children may not cry at all. You may have asked people to stay near or to talk with you through the night. Children don't ask for help. When people offer comfort, they may feel uncomfortable. The children may want to sleep beside you. Some run and hide.

With or Without Words: Adults and Children Show Symptoms of Stress

Observable symptoms dencte that children mirror parental behaviors.

Adults in Grief—Predictable Symptoms

Stage 1	Symptoms	Needs
Numbness	Shock.	To be dependent on
	Sorrow.	others.
	Anger.	To let others do tasks.
	Guilt.	To be permitted to be
	Automatic handling of	self-pitying, remote,
	routines.	not responsible for
	Very focused on	others.
	immediate decisions,	
	such as funeral	
	matters, insurance.	

Stage 2	*Symptoms*	*Needs*
Disorganization.	Need to talk about the deceased at length.	To be intimate with friends, children, family.
	Acute loneliness.	
	Disorganization, irrational thoughts.	To be allowed to be distracted.
	Deep depression.	To express feelings.
	Aimlessness.	
	Apathy	
	Extreme fatigue.	
	Anxiety.	
	Greater anger.	
	Tightness in the throat.	
	Loss of sleep.	
	Clinging to deceased's possessions.	

Stage 3		
Reorganization.	Feelings less intense.	To be encouraged to do things—make new friends, for instance.
	Appetite improves.	
	New interests, energy.	
	Release from anxiety.	
	Greater acceptance of the loss.	To acknowledge the growth that has resulted from the grief.

Children show a similar series of stages. The most recognizable differences are:

- Children may deceptively appear to be less profoundly moved.
- Children may be more open in asking friends to help.
- Children will ask for facts that you already know.
- Children will seek reassurances that important changes will not occur—they won't have to leave the house, change schools, or give away their pets.
- Children want reassurances that they will not have to fill the shoes of the deceased.

Other Symptoms of Stress that a Young Child May Display

- Demanding, attention-getting behavior.
- Outbursts of anger directed toward surviving parent, siblings, friends, or animals.
- Evidence of being distracted or confused; daydreaming.

- Depression, disturbed sleep patterns—too much or too little.
- Signs of school phobia, refusal to go to school.
- Temper tantrums with some bodily harm to self.
- A loss of interest in sports, friends, academics, and other people.
- An attitude of feeling lost or bewildered.
- Irritability.

After one year, most children will have expressed and worked through their grief. A lot will depend on the adjustment of the other members of the family. If the surviving parent is still deeply depressed and maintaining a morose attitude in the home, the child's recovery may be stymied. Or the child may adjust well away from home and continue to have problems while under the influence of the parent. On the other hand, if the parent has progressed to the reorganization phase of recovery, the child may reflect this positive adjustment.

For those who are still having difficulties, these symptoms are common:

- Unexplained mood swings including inappropriate laughter.
- Persistent depression.
- Unusual weight gain or loss.
- Psychosomatic illnesses.
- Feelings of unworthiness, incompleteness.
- Violent or negative responses to changes and surprises.
- Exaggerated fears of desertion.
- A need to cling to material love-objects (blankets, toys) beyond traditional age expectations.

The adolescent and a death in the family

The reactions of a teenager to a death in the family depends on maturity, the relationship with the deceased, the role in the family, understanding of the needs of others and much more. It is fair to ask, "Will the teenager act more like the adults in the family or more like the younger children?" In general, in a crisis the teenager shows maturity, reaches out to others, and puts aside personal needs. He or she may feel intense pain but appear strong and controlled, except around peers.

Support from peers may be openly given and greatly appreciated. Tears of friends seem to validate their grief.

The adolescent has an added dimension to his or her grief. Many were in the process of developing a mutually respectful relationship with the parent who died. The death represents unfinished, interrupted business, with appropriate regrets and a deep sense of loss.

Teen years provide opportunities to scrutinize the behaviors of the like-sex parent as a role model. After the death of that parent, fantasies and halo-effects may evolve which interfere with accurate memories and interpretations of past actions. In time, the fantasies and the halo-effect diminish. The surviving parent need not be overly concerned about the interruption in the role-modeling process. Realistically, young people today emulate one quality from one same-sex adult, such as integrity, and a second quality from another, such as sensitivity or generosity. *The incomplete same-sex role model experience does not forecast problems.*

Teenagers are beginning to understand the need to express their feelings of love and appreciation. The death of a loved one may elicit or inhibit such expression. The pain of grief can stifle emotional expressions. Encourage them to share their feelings because openness is invaluable to lifelong adjustment and healthy communication.

A parent is urged to watch for signs of brooding, distraction, and marked depression. If the boy or girl shuns all your attempts to comfort, don't overreact. Occasional hooky days from school may be in order—an escape from classroom pressure in favor of time spent with you. Consider introducing music lessons, assembling stereo speakers, or constructing intricate models, for example. Some teenagers may be attracted to way-out groups or to unwholesome activities which never appealed to them before. Don't sit by and watch passively. Show that you care by taking charge. You do not want your child to get hooked into strange situations in a time of stress while searching for answers. Some may turn to alcohol or drugs to comfort themselves.

Discuss the details of the funeral before and after the fact. Help children understand and relate phrases, psalms, and the eulogy. They may be confused about what they saw and heard. My fifteen-year-old daughter smiled at some family friends while attending her father's funeral. The friends did not smile back. Sally turned to me and asked, "Aren't you allowed to smile at a funeral?" Patient explanations put her at ease.

An adolescent is still a child. Extend the same considerations to the older child as you do to younger siblings. Be affectionate. Be patient. Be understanding. Be available.

The needs of the bereaved

- To be helped to understand that dying does not mean rejection.
- To be allowed to cry unashamedly. To understand there is no need to be embarrassed.
- To be helped to handle any guilt they may harbor. For example, if a parent or grandparent had been ill and unduly irritable or impatient, the child may have wished he or she would "hurry up and die." Such situations result in guilt.
- To be held; to hold others.

- To be encouraged to be creative.
- To express feelings, thoughts, and questions in any way that they can. To have all questions answered. Details can be filled in gradually. What and how much to tell depends on the child's maturity and the circumstances.
- To feel love around them. If separation from a surviving parent is necessary, the child should be reassured that reunion is imminent. If both parents are deceased, adults in the decision-making capacity should listen to a child's pleas and input. The need for familiar people, pets, and things is important. If possible, the child should remain in the same class at school with a supportive teacher and friends.
- To learn that people handle the subject of death in many ways, to understand that other children may not express sympathy or may show discomfort by giggling or silence. A child can learn that a friend really cares but does not know how to show sympathy.
- To be distracted, even to the point of going to the movies, because intense pain may be alleviated for a short time. This does not mean that experiencing intense pain can be avoided, but some distraction may be beneficial.
- Consider medication if the child cannot sleep or has a history of disturbed sleep. If the child is having nightmares about death, corpses, and such, reassure him or her that this is natural and that these will become less frightening and less frequent.
- Read them books and stories that tell about similar experiences of other boys and girls. They will benefit from knowing that others have gone through what they are going through. (See Bibliography.)

Needs of the Adolescent

- Time to be with friends.
- To be involved in some of the decisions about the funeral and burial, as well as decisions about family management and changes.
- Spiritual guidance.
- A listener—someone to hear regrets, guilty thoughts, memories.
- To be permitted to go through an extended period of wholesome dependency. This may begin months after the loss. It may reverse the movement toward independence which preceded the death.
- Advice—to hear it expressed that one must learn from the past and build and improve relationships *now*, as well as the quality of life.
- Guidance to express emotions, not to bury them in alcohol or drugs.
- Time to adjust to new family responsibilities.

Unlike stress from other sources, there is nothing anyone can do to change the *fact* of a loss. One can only help the bereaved through the transition from tears to tranquility. Children can and do adjust. The stress diminishes and with it a balance between the aliveness of today and the memories of the past is attained.

55. VIOLENT DEATH: ANXIETY FOR ALL

Aside from the natural death of a grandparent, parent, or friend, there are unusual accidents and traumatic events. In late 1980 and into 1981, headlines told of slayings of children in Atlanta, Georgia. The articles described their effects on children in that city. Some children were afraid to leave home, others armed themselves with knives and guns before going to school. Support groups for bereaved parents were founded but there was little mention of work on behalf of bereaved siblings.

Suggestions for helping the child who has lost someone through violent death:

- Let the child ask endless questions. Your answers can be supportive even though you cannot always be reassuring.
- Provide repeated instructions for self-protection.
- Allow opportunities for release of anger as well as anxiety. Respect times for crying, wailing, praying, or silence.
- Specify certain times to attend to tasks at home, school, or elsewhere. Ease up on academic expectations.
- Help children sort out their values; make it important to fill each day with as much love as it can hold.
- Avoid dwelling on gory details that children may not understand or that do not serve a useful purpose.
- Expect night terrors.
- Express your fears, too!

56. PREPARING FOR DEATH: KUBLER-ROSS'S THEORY

A parent wants to do everything possible to prevent children from suffering. When someone is killed or dies suddenly, one has to focus on the crisis and to adjust to the loss. That is after the fact. However, when a child must confront his or her own death or the approaching death of a relative or friend, a parent wants desperately to minimize trauma effectively.

The most constructive way is to understand and experience together the processes described as the five mental stages of the dying person. These were identified by Dr. Elisabeth Kubler-Ross and first published in *On Death and Dying* in 1969. The five stages represent the emotional responses of an individual who faces certain death. They offer insights for use with patients and caring family and friends.

Not every terminally ill person goes through the five stages in the described order, and not every person goes through every stage. Furthermore, some persons return to stages they passed through earlier, such as denial. The family of the dying patient goes through essentially the same stages, though perhaps with more or less intensity. The stages are:

1. Denial

When a person first realizes that he or she has a terminal illness, the reaction is, "No, it can't be! Not me!" This denial can last from a few seconds to a few months and recur again and again.

Denial serves an important purpose. It provides time to sort things out emotionally, to process the possibility that one is going to die. It may be important for the person to deny the seriousness of the situation because those around him or her are not ready to face the truth. They express denial to each other. Or sometimes a dying person is more open to talking about the situation than are relatives, spouses, children, or even nurses and doctors.

2. Anger

After a person has passed through the "No, not me!" stage, feelings of anger are expressed. "Why me? Why not Mack? He's never done anything for anybody. Why not him?" There is no comforting answer to this question.

The patient may be irritable and cantankerous when people come to visit, especially in a hospital. Criticism of doctors, nurses, the food, and the noise are commonplace. The patient seems intent on making well people feel guilty that they are well and he or she is ill. But people do not enjoy visiting with someone who is unpleasant or openly hostile, so the visits may be fewer and the length of each visit noticeably shorter. As a result, the person now experiencing rejection begins to feel sorry for himself or herself.

Sometimes a need to scream and rant and rave becomes imperative. Caretakers should expect this and understand that this is a normal stage the dying person goes through.

Family and friends go through anger, too. "Why my husband (or child or best friend)?" They may curse God or become physically violent.

3. Bargaining

As the person becomes increasingly ill, he or she begins to realize that the rage and the anger do not change things. At this point, bargaining begins. Most patients make a bargain with God, usually in private, a direct plea for more time from God; in return, the patient will dedicate himself or herself to the service of God. Or the person bargains with the doctors, promising to give his body to science or work for funds for the medical school.

The message behind bargaining reads, "Yes, I've been told I'm going to die, but ..." When this frame of mind moves on to, "Yes, me ... period," without a need to bargain, to plea, to deny, the next stage begins.

Meanwhile, during the bargaining stage, the spouse, children, and friends may notice brief times of marked improvement. This may result in false encouragement and bring up feelings of denial again. At some point, however, everyone will head into stage four, depression, though this may not be synchronized between patient and loved ones.

4. Depression

When people die, they lose everyone and everything they have known. Survivors lose one person whom they have loved very much. The dying person is very much alone. Survivors have each other for support. Depression is to be expected. Not only does the person face death, but he or she also must deal with the damaged self-esteem that results from a debilitating condition. Loss of virility, less attractive appearance, unrehearsed dependency, pain, relinquished ability to care for others, and many other factors contribute to depression. For a parent, guilt about child care and the high cost of hospitalization are two other important factors.

Many dying patients change in appearance (skin color or weight loss, for example) or lose mobility or take on an unusual odor. Relatives, finding this all too painful, may turn their backs on the patient. Patients need compassion, and yet it is almost impossible for some relatives or friends to come through. They should make every effort not to reject or desert the dying.

One way to help is to listen, or if that is too painful, to make certain that the dying person has someone to talk to.

A second way to help is to comply with requests a person may have, such as, "Please bring the photograph album so I can finish it," or, "Bring my will for me to change." Kubler-Ross says, "We are always impressed by how quickly a patient's depression is lifted when these vital issues are taken care of."

A third way to help is to *show* your feelings. Cry together. Participate in expressions of regret, sorrow, guilt. Don't be artificially cheerful. Kubler-Ross labels these manifestations of depression as "reactive depression."

She has identified a second phase of depression *preparatory depression* or *preparatory grief*. Now the focus is on grieving over the losses that lie ahead. This is not a time for a lot of words. The patient is letting go of the ties that have been his or her way of life.

5. Acceptance

Kubler-Ross says that when a person contemplates the very end, some expression of grief is expected. Physically, the patient may seem exhausted, dozing a lot and restless or disturbed by too much noise in the room. He or she has given up hope of recovery or even of living a few more weeks or months. Terminal patients who are in great pain, steadily or intermittently, are tired of enduring the pain.

The survivors-to-be need reassurance that the peaceful attitude of the dying person must not be equated with rejection of them. They need to understand that the long fight for life is almost over and peace is at hand.

Children want to be understanding, and too often they are not allowed to be. They are often shut off from this kind of information with the excuse that it would be too painful or that they are too young to understand. There is no age at which a child acquires instant awareness or suddenly becomes capable of understanding death. But the child should be given the benefit of the doubt. Attempting to discuss death with a concerned child is preferable to avoiding the issue. Be sure to use a vocabulary that the child can understand.

57.   HOSPICE—A COMFORTING ALTERNATIVE

Death is a stranger to all of us. It brings fear, sorrow, and uncertainty. There is no denial that the journey is lonely and frightening—for the person who is dying and those who must watch it happen.

Hospice is the name for a national organization which is locally controlled. It is found in the United States and Europe. It was formed to provide support, compassion, and practical assistance to the terminally ill, their families and friends. These may be in-patient facilities in a nursing home or hospital. Most often, it is home care and service. A basic premise is that many dying patients, if given the chance, would rather die in the familiarity of their homes than in institutions. Hospice helps make it possible. Its goal is not cure—it is care of the patient and ministering to the family. Both the medical community and government agencies are supportive. Hospice registered nurses and aides consult with and report to the patient's doctor. Other Hospice personnel are available, if and as needed—be it a chaplain or just a trained and comforting presence. They reassure the patient and prepare the family on what to expect. Support continues after the death of the patient, with call-backs and special programs that help the bereaved resolve their grief.

DEATH AND DYING EPILOGUE

The child who experiences a death in the family learns that grief is an expression of love. It can be translated into "I miss you, Daddy. I wish you were here. I'm sad and I cry a lot, but sometimes I laugh with my friends. I hope it is okay to laugh even though you are dead." "I used to love you a lot, Mom, but now I love my new mommy, too. Thanks, Mom, for teaching me how to love."

Regrets are expressed, too. "I never really had a chance to know my little brother. He was only six months old when he died," or, "We were just beginning to be best friends when he was killed in that crash."

Children may feel guilty because they are not as sad as they think they are supposed to be. Some children can let go of hurtful thoughts without undue sentimentality. Don't push them. Limit your references to a member of the family who has died. Keeping the deceased person's room in order, setting a place for a dead person at the dining room table or not celebrating a holiday because someone has died is maudlin. Children are confused by such acts. Adolescents can be very intolerant of them. If you find it necessary to prolong expressions of grief such as these, talk to a counselor or minister.

Accept the fact that many children want new relationships, a stepparent or a new best friend may be welcome in their lives. These persons are not replacements but reaffirmation to the children that people are important and living and loving must go on.

. . . .

As the Arents drove away from the cemetery, daughter Bonnie said "That was a nice allergy about Daddy, wasn't it?" We all smiled. What a magic elixir for stress!

Violence and Abuse: There Is No More Traumatic Way to Live

When you talk to a mother who has battered a child, you can almost predict the story she will tell. "I was lonely. I felt that everything I did was wrong. No one loves me. I couldn't keep the kids happy. I lost control." Many will admit that they had been severely beaten and sexually abused when they were little. These are not vicious women. Most of them are very depressed or unemotional. Battering dads often report that they were drunk or depressed because they hate themselves. "I just lost it," one man commented with no apparent feeling.

Newspapers abound with gory reports of children who are beaten to death. It is hard to fathom that some adult can wallop a three-year-old child for four hours until he dies. It is hard to relate to that kind of insanity. My own fury is not balanced by clinical explanations. The stories make me sick.

It is a fact that more than one million children in the United States were abused or neglected in 1982. It is reported that more than 2,000 of them died. For those who survived, emotional scars may never heal entirely. Clinicians report that one-third of the group will make it, one-third will never recover, and the other third will require lifelong support.

One cannot ignore the statement that a wife is beaten somewhere in America every sixty-five seconds. Children in one out of ten families hit, beat, stab, or shoot their parents at least once a year. This results in the death of 1,500 to 2,000 persons. These attacking children were subjected to abuse they couldn't take anymore. Legal problems dealing with the issue of the rights of victims to strike out are becoming more difficult and more commonplace.

The important question is: Has violence become the American way of life, or are we dealing with relatively isolated examples where individuals have lost control? Does the fact that there are 55 million hand guns scattered about indicate that everyone has learned to shoot, attack, or prepare to kill? Can we become immune to the suffering that so many face? Everyone must take a position to help on one level or another, to find a way to support individuals or organizations.

58. FAMILY VIOLENCE AND THE INDIVIDUAL CHILD

A child is born without a predisposition to harm others. There are cultures, according to Margaret Mead and other renowned anthropologists, in which anger and aggressive impulses are channeled into a sense of humor and play. Punishment does not have to equate with physical violence. There are many cultures in which hitting a child is unthinkable. Yet violence and abuse are rampant in the United States.

The American child will learn about violence from the family, from the media, and from the lifestyle of the neighborhood, including the school. Parents, in particular, are in great stress and strike out physically when overtaxed and frustrated.

Family violence has the greatest impact. It is immeasurably traumatic to watch someone you love beaten or burned, or to be attacked yourself. *A child cannot experience a more traumatic way of life.* The child who lives with violence is learning hate and fear instead of the more gentle emotion of love. As the National Committee for Prevention of Child Abuse announces, "The worst thing that can happen to some children is their parents." The tragedy is that it is cyclical; most abusing parents were abused children.

Child abuse and battering are not restricted to any one level of economics, geographical location, size of family, or ethnic background. It is important to understand *the battering cycle* recognized by specialists in the field of domestic violence. Briefly, tensions between members of a family build, a battering episode occurs, remorse and regrets are expressed and reconciliation follows—then tensions build again. In spouse-battering, the timing of a violent episode may be somewhat predictable. The power of the regrets with accompanying affection and gifts placates the victim enough to maintain the relationship. Also, the victim may be convinced that he or she is actually at fault. As the tensions build again, everyone in the family is in stress.

Child battering is not so predictable. The causes are very complex, the triggers numerous, the methods unlimited. Cruel treatment or serious neglect may precede an episode that results in bodily injury or death. The violent person may be psychotic, sadistic, under drugs, or have infantile impulse control.

Many parents learned from their parents that if you want a kid to obey, you better beat him. Nevertheless, as the impulse to batter starts building the parent may scream as he or she approaches a lack of control. But the person cannot stop. It may take a tragedy or near-tragedy to compel the parent to seek help.

Most battered children are under the age of five, but reports of abuse, especially sexual molestation with junior-high and high-school students are increasing. Older youngsters are more prone to deny violence upon direct questioning, and they make up excuses for problem behaviors or unusual bruises. Accordingly, abuse and molestation may be difficult to uncover. If a child tells you about a beating or manhandling or asks questions, *listen carefully*. The questions may reveal that the child has known such experiences. It takes much courage to talk about such things. To repeat questions or a story may be impossible. Young children do not make up such content. The child's feelings are all mixed up. There have probably been many threats, such as, "If you tell ..." Oftentimes, a stepparent or a parent's boyfriend or girlfriend is involved and the child may tell about how he or she "hates" him or her, without going into detail. Teenagers may be absent from school a lot or may bolster their spirits with drugs or alcohol. It is not unusual for teenagers to threaten to move away from home or to stay with a friend. This may be a hint that things at home are very frightening. Take time to piece together the things that you observe and hear.

What Do The Children Need?

You may be a Girl Scout leader or Sunday school teacher. You have heard rumors that Lucy is a battered child. You try very hard to get her to respond to you. She remains distant, almost disinterested. Nevertheless, you are intent on befriending her. You wonder how you can help. You are not certain what needs she may have, exclusive of professional help.

Lucy may need:

- To be left alone, not to be touched.
- Time to rest.
- To be believed when she says something is wrong at home.
- To be permitted to defend her parents.
- To have fun.
- Time to express intense feelings when alone with you.
- Help to acknowledge successes and accomplishments and the fact that you care.
- Recognition for being honest.
- Appreciation for trying to help herself and others at home.

I am not asking you to be a therapist. Rather, I am providing guidelines whereby an abused child can feel secure in a situation with you. These children cannot recover alone. Years of therapy may be necessary.

Yet they do join Scouts, go to Sunday school, and so on, where persons such as yourself can be sensitive to their needs. You may be the one person who can guide a Lucy and perhaps others in the family toward professional help. But you must not look for a bond or closeness. This child is impaired; self-esteem is damaged and the ability to trust adults has been smashed.

59. UNDERSTANDING BATTERING PARENTS

Descriptions of violent persons are helpful because they provide information in an unemotional way. It is hard to hear about battering in any of its many forms without feeling angry at the person who was out of control.

Bear in mind:

(1) The parents are emotionally needy and look to their children to fill their needs.

(2) The parent misperceives the child's behaviors. The child may be accused of not loving the parent, of being willfully disrespectful or negligent, or of provoking the parent to hit, beat, or burn.

(3) The relationship between parent and child is characterized by a lack of warmth. Parents may not know how to show love, and children do not learn how to accept it.

(4) The parent's background almost always includes a history of battering. Consequently, the parent has not experienced close relationships or rewarding bonding. Fewer than 10 percent, however, are psychotic or mentally ill, though all have suffered emotional stress or disturbance.

(5) A parent may expect adult behavior from a child, which is impossible at the child's age level. A toddler may be expected to understand and meet the parent's needs in addition to having bowel and bladder control, perfect table manners, and the like. Children experience nonstop criticism no matter how hard they try to please. They end up feeling incompetent and unappreciated. They miss affection and approval.

(6) The parent may confuse discipline with abuse. Physical or emotional neglect (also a form of abuse) may not be deliberate but simply a reflection of inadequacies in the parent's upbringing, outrageous standards or capabilities. Many parents abuse their children during or following a drinking or drug episode, or at a time of significant failure, such as loss of spouse, job, or home.

(7) The parent, especially a stepparent, may be very jealous of other relationships in the family and act out this jealousy by beating the child, wishing to get rid of the rival.

(8) The incestuous parent has many other complicated problems involving sexual issues. Violence, as such, may not be the issue, as it is in rape. Nevertheless, the child is victimized.

(9) Many parents of middle or upper-class background, not just of lower socioeconomic status, display inadequate personalities, addictions, or unusual impulsivity.

(10) Therapy can help parents learn to stop the violence, call for help to prevent a crisis, be more self-accepting, and be more comfortable with the children.

There are some successful programs conducted by professionals in prenatal clinics and mental health centers which identify *potential* batterers. Women are interviewed and their personalities checked out against a list, which includes the items noted above. They are then given help to change attitudes, work through problems with their own parents, and, occasionally, to learn to depend upon a community volunteer as a surrogate, supportive "grandmother."

Neglect

Evidence of battering and abuse are listed at the end of this section. They range from burns, broken bones and bruises, to firesetting, truancy, drug abuse, and sexual acting out. Socially, the children may be passive, afraid, or hyperactive and very aggressive. Some lose touch with reality.

Neglect is a form of abuse. Most parents of neglected children are described as markedly immature and face circumstances which are overwhelming. Many times there are insurmountable money problems or the mother and/or father have always had a marginal way of life. Neglect, unlike violence, does not result from loss of control.

Signs of neglect include filth, abandonment, malnutrition, improper and inadequate clothing, an unsafe or unsanitary home, and emotional deprivation. In many instances, the children are left to raise themselves, even though the parents put a roof over their heads and some food in the house. Parents who actually love their children appear to reject them simply because they cannot cope with all the stressors they face. Affluent parents may neglect children, too. They may not care what the kids say or do. They may not spend time with them from one day to the next. These children ask, "Why am I so unimportant to my mom and dad?" This diminishes self-esteem and becomes a clear source of stress. Children in the slums frequently come closer to understanding the absence of Mom or Dad, or parental depression, than children from "nice" neighborhoods. Abused and neglected children have much in common because their parents have many personal problems.

Unwanted or deficient children seem to bear the brunt of parental frustrations, inadequacies, and rage. Affluent, educated parents may resist any confrontation that points out that their child feels neglected.

60. YOUR AWARENESS IS IMPORTANT

These situations may seem very foreign to you and your lifestyle. The information is important because your children undoubtedly will see and know kids who have suffered abuse and neglect. When you hear shocking or sad stories, you may want to:

- Help your children understand how differently others live, that these are not modern fairy stories nor the product of the imagination of a TV script writer.
- Help your children tell you when they feel left out or put aside. Sometimes the reason is simply because you are busy or they catch you at a bad time. Perhaps they are too demanding. In any event you can work toward better understanding.
- Take time to express yourself if you have been unduly harsh with your kids through unusual punishments, extended grounding, hitting, thrashing, or using abusive, derogatory expressions. You may feel that your behavior is justified. At the same time, you may want to admit that adults get frustrated and angry, and that they sometimes overreact, too. Kids can understand and forgive. Give them credit for that. You can all benefit from such discussions.

No matter what your interest in family violence may be, bear in mind that parents do not abuse their children because they want to. More and more abusive persons are seeking help, and law enforcement agencies and hospital and school personnel are becoming increasingly successful in getting violent persons to accept help.

To Reiterate—Help Is Essential.

- It may save your life or the life of someone you love.
- It may stop the batterer. He or she does not choose to lose control. A batterer is not a batterer on purpose.
- It can be a way for the husband and wife or parents and children to learn how to express anger in an appropriate way.
- It can support a spouse or child in his or her efforts to get out of a situation that has become dangerous and unbearable.
- It can help to alleviate the victim's need to feel guilty. "But I didn't clean the tub the way he wanted, so he beat me up." Added guilt comes from hospital expenses or not being able to protect a child from a battering spouse.

Recovery and changes are very difficult. The patient can move only one step at a time. (See Section XVI, #70.)

61. IDENTIFICATION OF BATTERING AND ABUSE (Any Age)

Physical Indicators

Unexplained bruises and welts, clustered, forming regular patterns, often appearing after the weekend or vacation.

Unexplained burns—immersion burns, patterns like electric range burner, iron, for instance.

Unexplained fractures to skull, nose, facial structure in various stages of healing.

Unexplained lacerations or abrasions.

Sexual

Difficulty in walking or sitting.

Torn, stained, or bloody underclothing.

Pain or itching in genital area.

Bruises or bleeding in genital, vaginal, or anal areas.

Exaggerated use of sexual expressions.

Behavioral Indicators

Wariness of adult contacts.

Apprehension when other children cry.

Extreme aggressiveness or withdrawal.

Failure to grow, prosper.

Inability to have fun.

Fear of parents; fear of going home.

Very infantile behavior.

Excessive daydreaming.

Bizarre, sophisticated, or unusual sexual behavior or knowledge.

Poor peer relationships.

Delinquency or running away.

Reports of sexual assault by caretaker.

Reports of sexual relations that friends are having which are, in fact, reports of own.

Other clues:

- Major problems at school.
- Inability to conform with school regulations and policies.
- Increased amount of daydreaming.
- Obsession to hide in locker rooms, avoid gym classes if changing clothes is required, or failure to keep routine appointments in nurse's office.
- Occasional remarks about the situation at home, which denote unusual anger, fear, or disrespect.
- Reports of conflict with stepparents.
- Unusual emotional outbursts such as crying, laughing.
- Knowledge that mother may be sexually promiscuous.

In Adolescence, Additional Clues are Noteworthy:

- Expressed fear of beating by parents. Refusal to go home. May express wish to beat up parents.
- Truancy.
- Sexual acting out.
- Unexplained anger when adult mentions home situation or parent involvement at school, such as at conferences.
- Reports of exploitation by parents (forced into responsibility at home.)
- Setting fires.
- Obsession with weapons—knives, guns.
- Bravado exclamations about not needing a family anymore, yet appearing babyish or needy.
- Drug, alcohol abuse.

VIOLENCE AND ABUSE EPILOGUE

Alarming as the statistics and stories may be, the problem of violence cannot be eradicated until many of the associated problems are confronted. Humanistic schools, expanded social services, increased job possibilities, and widespread promotion of professional help are all necessary. Federal support may be minimal, but forward momentum must be established and maintained. Elimination of violence on TV is essential. The vast increase in crime in the past ten years has been ascribed to TV. This cannot be ignored.

The family of violence must become better understood. The knowledge must be translated into *prevention* so that children and adults will be rescued before they are harmed, physically or emotionally. The circle of family violence which repeats its pattern generation after generation may be broken when victims get sufficient help. Sexist issues must be openly confronted. When people are made to take responsibility for their behavior, they find nonviolent ways to express anger and frustration.

In the meantime, the media must be encouraged to show empathy and compassion towards abusive persons as well as to report the ugly facts. Let it be pointed out that battering adults are needy. Like children who hurt, the violent adult hurts and cannot recover alone.

Adults who sexually molest children are very ill. Nevertheless, they inflict serious damage and immeasurable pain on their victims. Every parent feels outraged when they read that children are raped, manhandled or sodomized. It is essential that parents express their rage to the judicial system where the ultimate punishment must be pronounced. Molesters must be off the streets.

The Family on the Move: Here Today, Where Tomorrow?

One in every five families in the United States moves every year, whether it's across town or across a continent. For some families it is a matter of putting their few possessions in a truck or a trailer and heading to unfamiliar places, with no guarantees of a job for the parents or a place to live. These disruptions may result in stress for everyone involved. The family unit itself may be the only remaining security. However, a move frequently follows parental separation, a serious quarrel, a loss of employment and relationships are in need of repair. Feelings are raw. Uncertainties are overwhelming and the needs of the children may be overlooked. Reassurances are important. Fears of abandonment are common. Separation from familiar surroundings hurts.

However, not all moves create problems. A move may represent upward mobility, an improved living situation, adventure, and the opportunity for growth. It may be welcomed by everyone. Uncertainties produce excitement rather than anxiety and stress.

Benefits

There may be real *benefits*.

- Family ties are strengthened. "We may be in a new house, but we are still a family."
- The child feels competent. "It was hard to leave, but I've made new friends already."
- The child may have to be more independent. "I used to have to depend on Mom for everything. Here she has to work, so I do more things for myself."
- The child and the whole family may take time to talk about what's most important in their lives, or values. "Living in Denver was neat, but I like this place better because it is so much smaller.

206

People are friendlier," or "We were the only black family in that neighborhood, and occasionally this was hard for us. In this racially diverse area, the kids seem much happier!"

- A chance to see new sights, meet new people, and learn about what's unique. "I never heard of grits before! Since we've been living here, we eat them every day," or, "I'd only seen mountains on TV, and here they are in our own backyard!"
- A move gives parents a clearer picture of the child's personality, coping style, and needs. "In the old house, I was too busy to notice that Alice is afraid of dogs and stays by herself a lot. Now that we have a smaller house and less housework to do, I can spend more time with Alice. This is enjoyable for both of us," or, "I never imagined that Jenny would be so unhappy about moving. At least now we can talk about our feelings."

Moving is a time of separation. Parents' attitudes strongly influence the children's adjustment. When the adults feel harassed, children reflect their insecurities. When adults feel devastated and defeated, the children find it difficult to feel optimistic, much less excited. When adults feel comfortable and have a positive attitude, children are more likely to feel the same way. In general, they accept a move more philosophically than children (except in the case of the military family). The major problem facing most children is fear of the unknown.

Sometimes it is necessary for a child to adapt to a new environment that he or she perceives as cheaper or more rustic than previous surroundings. The majority of moves that result in a lower standard of living are preceded by serious family problems or by a breakdown of the family structure. This means that the child has multiple adjustments to make. Complaining about the move and the new setting may be symptomatic of much more deep-seated conflicts and stress.

With or Without Words the Child Exhibits Stress

Before departure a child may: be irritable, cry, tell stories, daydream, exaggerate dependence on family members by clinging, disobey, show signs of anxiety, anger and discouragement, run away, hang on to pets, hide out, or avoid new and close relationships. These same symptoms may be seen for weeks after the move. (See pages 209-211.)

62. PARENTS CAN HELP

There are many ways grown-ups in a family can help the children accept a move. Even if frequent moves are the lifestyle of a family, they do entail saying good-bye to the familiar and facing the unfamiliar. Some children can handle this more readily than others. Most children will ask a lot of questions which denote both curiosity and concern. The concern can build up to considerable stress.

A child needs:

- To be informed ahead of time. A spur-of-the-moment move, a total surprise, will be very, very upsetting. Some children have come home from school in an afternoon to discover most of the family possessions in a truck ready to pull away. Even though the family may be sticking together, such disruption can hurt badly.
- As much reassurance as possible. Children need help in leaving friends, school, or family members. If the move represents the breakup of a family, the child must be told what the breakup is all about. A child may need to be told repeatedly, "You may still love Daddy very much, even if he lives many miles away." If you know that the move will be a break from someone close, be certain to arrange for ways to keep in touch, such as scheduled long-distance phone calls or giving friends addressed postcards to fill out so that they can write. Older siblings may help in such matters if the parents are too busy or unable to do so.
- To be involved in as many of the decisions as possible. Depending on the age of the children, many can help to pack, or choose what to keep and what to discard, for example.
- Time to say good-bye.
- Adult understanding that a move represents loss—loss of "best friends" and favorite play places. When parents share their own feelings, it helps. However, there may be times when the parents are anxious to get out of "this house" or get out of town and the children do not want to. The decision to move is an adult decision. Again, children need to know what the adults are feeling and vice-versa.
- To be encouraged to express anger, grief and tears. The expression, "Not again!" denotes disbelief and may trigger the symptoms of stress.
- To hang onto security blankets and other items of importance without being chided.
- To be involved in the placement of a pet that will not be taken along, unless this means a heart-breaking trip to a Dumb Friend's League.
- As many reassurances as possible that this move is not a temporary one—that the child will stay long enough to finish the school year (at least), to make friends, feel at home and safe from disruptions.

- To keep family routine as steady as possible during preparation time—bedtimes, chores, church, and sports, for example.

Strategies for Parents

Take time to consider what you will need for your own comfort. This will benefit everyone. Make checklists including medications, books, and other emergency supplies.

For Infants

Babies will be the least affected by a move. It is important to keep them comfortable and maintain their routine as much as possible. If the family is to fly, allow for delays and minimal service. Some infants are very aware of unfamiliar surroundings and need to be held, comforted, and reassured. If the child is greeted by grandparents who are total strangers, do not assume that the child will adjust readily.

Infants may cry a lot, refuse to eat, or require holding as symptoms of the insecurities that they are experiencing.

For Toddlers

Tell the child as many of the plans as he or she can understand. Emphasize that the family will be together (if this is the case).

Keep the child with you as much as possible while preparations for the move are being made. If a child is aware that certain things, even pets, will be left behind, he or she may be fearful of the same fate.

Let the child pack a few of his or her most treasured possessions. Keep some out for the trip, whether it is by car or by plane.

Take time to listen to the child's questions and answer as factually as possible. Don't make any false promises such as, "We'll get a new doggy," if this is not what you plan to do.

Arrange for small children to find time to say good-bye to grandparents, friends, babysitters, and other relatives. You may anticipate expressions of anger, sadness, and bewilderment. The child may not use words, but behavior and facial expressions may reveal feelings. Other symptoms of stress may be bedwetting, thumbsucking, and unexpected or prolonged crying, disturbed sleep, or refusal to go to preschool.

Elementary-School-Aged Children

Some persons state that this age group is particularly vulnerable to the unsettling effects of moving, especially for the first time. The child has made adjustments, established his place with teachers, other families, activities, and church groups outside the home. Many people and places feel familiar. It is difficult to give them up. The children are not mature enough to anticipate readily that in a new place there will be happy times ahead. In anticipation of the break, the children may be angry, uncooperative, and stubborn. Some will pretend to be sick so they don't have to leave the house.

Before moving, the shy children may become even more shy, the aggressive youngsters may signal even more aggressiveness, and you may expect pleas for closeness to you. Younger children may start to shadow older siblings, wanting uncharacteristic physical closeness.

Children may ask many questions, seeking answers that no one may be able to give. If possible, share all the facts that you have, such as a picture of the new house or new school. Where once it was considered advisable to move during the summer after school is out, many today recommend the move while schools are still in session, so that there *are* other children immediately. The child isn't marooned in a new neighborhood and you may predict a lively interest mid-term in "the new kid" in the class.

The Middle-School-Aged Child

The promotion from elementary school to middle or junior high school represents a giant step for many boys and girls even when a move isn't involved. They have graduated from the relatively protected environment of a self-contained classroom to impersonal halls and computerized schedules. They feel more independent, more challenged, and more responsible. This attitude may contribute to a cooperative involvement in a family move.

In a new school, most of them reach out for friends. It is easy to spot the ones who are unhappy or overwhelmed. The child in stress may be quickly identified, as most middle-school-aged youngsters are vivid, active kids.

If your child enters middle school at the beginning of the year, he or she may notice immediately that there seem to be lots of others who get lost or feel strange. This helps to give the feeling of being "just like the other kids."

School entrance at any other time may be somewhat more difficult.

Preteen children are open to meeting new classmates and are usually not as critical and standoffish as many high school students tend to be, but they do form cliques. For the entering student, this means that if he or she is open and friendly, the chances are that adjustments to school will be relatively easy.

As a parent, show your interest in what is happening at school. Take time to ask questions. If your child adjusts well at school, his or her positive attitude may be contagious in the home. If the child has difficulties, take time to go to school and get acquainted with teachers or counselors. The fact that you did go to school, that you took time to meet the teachers, carries an important message to your boy or girl. In spite of the mess at home, Mom or Dad really cares!

The Adolescent in the Family of Mobility

High school days are for exploration and discovery. *But,* students want to be in their own balliwick, protected by the nest called "home."

A move for many high school students represents relinquishment of special friendships, love affairs, special student-teacher relationships, and, for some, the end of special endeavors. They may miss the band concert or won't be able to go to the senior prom. School events may be the *most* important parts of their lives, and being wrenched away from them may be very traumatic.

Teenagers whose families have been mobile as a way of life may, for the first time, express anger and disappointment at having to move again. Or they may be resigned to the pattern of short-term friendships and outwardly accede to the move, vowing inwardly not to get close to anyone because leaving them is too painful. And why bother to study because chances are that school will be interrupted in the middle anyway? The next school will probably be some dumb place where they don't know anything anyway—or so go the sour grapes.

The other side of the coin may be that the adolescent hates the school he or she is attending. It is too large, kids are unfriendly, and the teachers disinterested. A move to another school may be a dream come true!

For a teenager, the move may:

- Expedite self-discovery, present ideas around such questions as "What is most important in my life today?" "How much do I help my parents or my brothers and sisters?"
- Be regarded as a lesson on how to separate from loved ones, as a dress rehearsal for what is ahead at graduation. "Can I manage by myself? I'd better figure out how to keep up communication!"
- Be an opportunity to develop new relationships, again, a dress rehearsal for possible dormitory life or meeting people on a job.
- Be an opportunity to put extra effort into academic achievement, to discover that he or she *can* be successful in *any* school, that skills and talents don't go away just because you have to move! It can also be a time to face up to deficiencies and what to do about them.

That's a big order and parent and teacher support is vital. No matter what patterns your adolescent may display, it is important to remember that teenage years are years of rebellion. Mobility may bind the student into family dependency at a time when he or she has been struggling to be free. Displays of outrage are not unusual, along with accusations that parents are cruel, heartless, selfish, or what-have-you. Parents are still the decision makers and though their reasons may be unacceptable to the teenager, the plans proceed. Try to get your child's understanding and help. "This, too, shall pass," is a handy cliché to remember. Talk about the future. Make plans for friends to come and visit. If possible, offer options. In some instances, the teenager might be better off remaining in the old location with a relative or friend for a prescribed time. This can eliminate the pitfalls resulting from leaving a school, loss of friends, or the negative impact the angry teenager may have on brothers and sisters. By listening to what the adolescent wants and negotiating accordingly, you show respect. When you work together, you make the best of a difficult situation. *Express your thanks and appreciation to teenagers who are cooperative and helpful.*

63. SCHOOL PLACEMENT

It would be wonderful if every school were to possess all the desirable attributes imaginable. Such is not the case. Nevertheless, all schools have caring teachers (some have more than others). And information about a school district and the local school is obtainable. Parents should be made aware of this and proceed to look at:

- Appearance of the building.
- Range of programs (classes for the handicapped, vocational or career guidance, provisions for the gifted and talented, extracurricular activities, outdoor education).
- Class size (twenty-five or under is preferable).
- Services—bus (if needed), breakfast and lunch programs, media center/library, provisions for textbooks and materials, field trips.
- The school's philosophy—open classes, self-contained classes, back-to-basics, individualized learning, methods of discipline, rules, basic attitude. Do the teachers and kids appear happy or dreary?
- Possible dress code.
- Busing considerations (Will the child be bused across town at the same time he or she is trying to adjust to the new house and neighborhood?)

Parents should talk to administrators, other parents, and district personnel regarding school. More than one option may be available, and school is so important that it merits more than cursory attention. Because a smooth school placement diminishes stress, take the following steps.

Before the move.

Try to obtain

- Transfer card or latest report card or transcript.
- Birth certificate.
- Medical records.
- List of textbooks and educational materials used.
- Written descriptions of special programs the child may have been in (such as Title I, remedial math, visual-motor training, gifted and talented program).
- Grading method; statement from teachers describing achievement level and interests.
- Standard test scores and results of any special testing.

When admitting the child to school, the staff should be made aware of past placements and needs. For example, if the child has been in a program for the gifted, a similar type of placement should be requested. Most states have open-record laws guaranteeing parents access to all school records. Don't hesitate to ask. The information can be used to your child's advantage at the time of placement.

The First Day of School

The first day in a new neighborhood, the child should not be forced to go to school. He or she may need time in the house, time with family, or time to rest. One day more or less will not affect learning and may certainly help diminish stress.

On the first day of school, the parent should:

- Accompany the child to school.
- Meet the child's teacher(s).
- Supply the child with basic pencils, papers, and similar items appropriate to his or her grade level.
- Make certain the child knows the way home—what bus to take or what sidewalks lead home. A rehearsal beforehand may be a good idea. Point out landmarks such as "the house with the white fence" or "the store on the corner."
- Remind the kids that few schools are ideal, but there is lots to learn and new friendships to make.

If you should discover that your child is depressed and you believe that this reflects school problems, get in touch with the principal, teacher, or social worker. A teacher may not recognize that the new child is depressed or may have been too busy to notice. He or she may have perceived the child as naturally quiet or withdrawn and will be grateful to you for pointing out the real problem. Teachers work on the premise that it takes about six weeks for some children to adjust or perk up, and may not accurately assess the seriousness of the situation.

Parents are urged to be assertive, introducing themselves and the children to the neighbors. One should not wait for the neighbors to reach out. People are not unfriendly and rejecting, just very, very busy keeping up with the demands of everyday life.

Postscript

Pam, a fifteen-year-old girl, moved to Denver with her mother after a divorce, leaving behind an older brother and her father. Her protests never ended. She showed all the classic symptoms of stress.

Several months later, I ran into Pam in a store. She told me that she had gone back to visit in Columbus. All of a sudden, her friends didn't seem close to her anymore. The reunion was fun but disappointing, she added. Then with a smile, she admitted, "When I got on the plane, I realized I wanted to come home and home, now, is here."

Kids are wonderful, aren't they?

PART IV

Stress Takes Its Toll

When a child must adjust to one stressor after another, or many stressors at one time, it becomes a heavy burden. The child may not be able to withstand the onslaught. He or she may be especially vulnerable to stress for an assortment of reasons—health, temperament, past history, beliefs, or others. No one is to blame. Nevertheless, when the child displays a coping style that is unsuccessful—does not reduce or eliminate stress—it indicates that stress has taken its toll.

Severe symptoms of stress are not incidental. They increase in quantity, magnitude, or frequency until parents and teachers become alarmed. Too often nothing is done until law enforcement persons become involved.

This chapter is concerned with the child who habitually malfunctions.Section XV presents significant examples of unsuccessful coping styles, the habitual liar, the child who steals, the child who has been labeled "emotionally disturbed" and the child addict. The child in crisis—the suicidal child—reveals the ultimate breakdown in control or self-esteem; the child can no longer cope. Section XVI provides important information about professional therapy and resources. Many guidelines and suggestions for parents are offered in order to maintain an optimistic, realistic approach to a child in stress.

Examples of Unsuccessful Coping

64. THE HABITUAL LIAR

Little Cissy comes home from school and tells her mother that her teacher shoved her. Her mother is sympathetic. She is also irate. Cissy explains that Billy was behind her in line and pulled her hair. She jumped out of the line to escape him and her teacher shoved her. A plausible story, it was totally untrue.

Cissy is a habitual liar. She makes up stories on a daily basis. She tells tales about Mom and Dad, too. She is in the fourth grade. Her parents and her teachers have the attitude, "There she goes again," yet they react in protective ways. "That teacher is mean," Dad comments to Mom. "Those mean parents," the teacher remarks to herself. No one confronts Cissy. Cissy is in trouble. Her habitual lying is a sign of severe stress.

Children up to six years of age have wonderful imaginations. They learn the game of, "I can do that, too!" or, "My dad is president of an airline!"—something fantastic or glamorous which has nothing to do with reality. They will tell stories that are real to them, based on dreams, fantasy, or TV. When a parent or an older brother says, "That's baloney," they are bewildered. Yet children as young as five can become habitual liars, fully aware that they *are* lying. They may give any answer that pops into their heads; to them credibility is not an issue. *Or they may have learned to protect themselves or someone else by covering up the truth or denying what has happened.* The habitual liar is displaying marked insecurity.

Telling lies is a bad habit. When the child is prone to blurt out an answer, a defense, with the hope that others will not question the truth, every tale is clouded with uncertainty. This adds stress. He needs to remember what story he told about what situation. In rare instances, the

216

kid really doesn't care, feeling that a reckless answer isn't going to make things better or worse. In his eyes, there is no reason to be honest.

Parents must confront lies. Many will simply say, "Hey, I don't believe you." Others may try to get the child to confess or even make a joke of it. "Better luck next time, Buddy!" They may or may not discipline the child. They may talk about trust and occasionally make threats. The child who has become a habitual liar feels boxed in. "If I lie, I'll be in trouble; if I tell the truth (I did throw the snowball) I'll be in trouble anyway."

Strategies for Parents

- Work with the children on the basis that the truth, even if it hurts, is much better than a lie. Discipline for lying should be more severe than the consequences from telling the truth.
- Do not be manipulated by lies. Make certain there is no pay-off for being a liar. Commend them for confessing to lies. Children must understand that you will question what they say. Work together to establish interactions that can be handled truthfully.
- Don't ask for confessions or explanations about events when you already know the truth. You know that Jim knocked the plant off the table or Helen got in trouble on the school bus. Forget the confession and confront the behavior. Lies denote stress. When a normal child tells a lie, he or she feels scared, concerned only for self-preservation. The pathological liar does not feel scared.
- If you have not found a way to stop the lying, take time to consider:
  —Is the discipline in your house too severe?
  —Does this child feel unloved?
  —Does this child use lies in order to compete with others?
  —Could this child be lying to cover up for someone else?
  —Does this child tell lies to cover up deep feelings of inferiority?

Your answers indicate what changes need to be made. Confer with a professional. Counseling may extend to all members of the family. Realize that it takes time to learn to stop lying. It is necessary to reinforce carefully each truthful statement your child makes.

65. THE CHILD WHO STEALS

Your pre-school child is not doomed to be a lifelong thief if he or she slips a nickel out of your purse. Most children do not distinguish between the nickel on the kitchen table and the cookie on the counter. They are equally available. An older child who steals habitually displays significant symptoms of stress.

You may have tried punishing this child for stealing, to no avail. Perhaps you have made up excuses such as, "He is such a loving child, but he does help himself to things that don't belong to him. I do wish he would just ask." This may sound soft and loving, but this child is a thief and cannot stop by himself.

It is important to notice what the child steals and from whom. A little girl I worked with always took things that were soft—stuffed animals from stores, baby blankets, or wool scarves. She was telling the world, "I need affection, I need to be held and cuddled." Not all children give such clear messages.

Children steal for a variety of complex reasons:

- Poor self-esteem runs their lives.
- They have no regard for the property of others.
- They crave love. Possessions make them feel better, at least temporarily.
- They need food, clothes, money—the things that they steal.
- They want to get caught to get attention or to have someone set limits.
- It is the only thing they do that makes them feel successful.
- They are subject to peer pressure, especially in vandalism.
- They discount social pressures and values.
- They are thrill seekers.
- They need to support a habit such as drugs.
- They want to emulate a hero.

By the time a child becomes a confirmed thief, the problem is beyond parental influence and control. Home punishment has had no long-lasting effect. The child's basic needs are still not being met. The stressors in this child's life force him or her to adopt an unsuccessful, antisocial coping style, one that is potentially self-destructive.

If you see inappropriate behavior, *do something* immediately. To do nothing is to condone. If such incidents happen repeatedly, seek help. Authors in the past have suggested that stealing is a symptom of a character disorder and have been pessimistic about how effective therapy might be. I am convinced that significant therapy plus well-managed behavior modification programs can help some young persons learn, accept, and use socially acceptable ways of asking for love, approval, and acceptance. I realize that few offenders have the opportunity to get intensive help. Many do not come from middle-class or affluent families where costly therapy or admission to residential treatment is possible. (See Section XVI, #70.)

If your child should be apprehended, remember that parental support is essential. You do not condone the behavior when you back your kids. You give them the important message that you care about them.

Both you and your child will be embarrassed and upset. The situation adds to your mutual stress. Your child, as a victim of stress, has behaved in an unacceptable way and needs help—from you first of all.

66.   THE CHILD WHO HAS BEEN LABELED "EMOTIONALLY DISTURBED"

Quite by mistake, some kid bumps into Mark, an eighth grader. Mark drops his books. Then he loses control. He starts screaming, swearing, smashing his fists against his locker. Teachers manage to get him into the counseling office to calm him down.

Mark's outbursts have happened before. His teachers are worried about him; they agree that he is emotionally disturbed. It is apparent that when Mark is out of control, he will strike out against anything or anyone. He is considered a danger to himself and to others. School authorities have recommended that he get help but the parents consider Mark a "kid with a bad temper" and haven't taken any action. Mark cannot find a way to change his behavior by himself. Now the school wants to place him in a class for behavior-disordered students. Mark's parents will have to give their permission. Because it is painful to admit that a son has problems, somebody will have to give Mark's parents understanding and support. (See Section XVI, Therapy Is a Must, #70.)

Symptoms of Stress

Using Mark as an example, here is a partial list of severe symptoms of stress which denote that a child may be emotionally disturbed.

Rage.
Callousness towards other persons.
Self-destructive acts.
Obsessions.
Stealing, lying, destructive behavior.
Inability to concentrate.
Impulsiveness.

Withdrawal.
Uninvolved with persons, things.
Severe depression.
Cruelty.
Uncontrolled hyperactivity.
Out of touch with reality.
Nonstop filthy, vulgar vocabulary.

The child who acts out these symptoms may:

Run away.
Become mentally ill.
Use drugs, including glue sniffing.
Quit school.
Attempt suicide.

Become rapists.
Become prostitutes.
Commit violence, including murders, vandalism, or any behavior that represents a breakdown in control.

There are many reasons why children become extremely upset and lose control. Today the diagnosticians include medical, biochemical, and disabilities data along with the child's history as essentials to understanding a child. The search for such relevant information may seem questionable to you. It is important for parents to have an open mind about new approaches. Your flexibility and cooperation as a parent can help immeasurably in the progress a child makes.

67. THE CHILD ADDICT

Many kids today are hooked on drugs and booze. There are more than 500,000 teenage alcoholics. This is a tragedy. There are no benefits. Unlike so many other reactions to stress, physical, emotional, *and* mental processes are harmed by the use of drugs. More important, few persons can go cold turkey and recover from these habits by themselves. They need to have someone (1) help them accept that they have the problem, and (2) guide them into therapy and (3) stand by them as they go through a difficult recovery regime. They must understand that they are ruining their lives.

Drugs are available in any city. It is more difficult to acquire hard drugs in some rural settings. Nevertheless, alcohol can be found anywhere. Why have these children (and there are now many alcoholics in the fifth and sixth grades) chosen to cope with stress in such a destructive way?

In most cases, they learn from the other kids. Peer persuasion is immeasurable. Parents set an example for others. Physical addiction, thought to be inherited, intensifies the problem. Do these children actually face more stress, or different stressors, than non-addicted peers? It's hard to say. Certainly, many have had to make a series of adjustments and for one reason or another, became vulnerable. They were introduced to drugs as the emotional painkiller. Consider that 25 million children in 1983 live in a stepfamily. One million are added each year, so they are experiencing stress as the family is in the process of breaking up. The stress of adjusting to a new family is then compounded by a second separation because 65 percent of all second marriages fail. By no means will all these kids end up on drugs. The vulnerable youngsters will.

Whether rich or poor, the child addicts are exhibiting a self-defeating coping style. Next to suicide, there is no more dramatic way to exhibit that they are not maturing appropriately and that they are acquiring habits which will only produce more stress. For example, the person in an addiction cannot relate to others with honest feelings. The feelings are distorted; all relationships will be erratic and unsatisfactory. This agenda is inescapable unless the person is off drugs. (See Section VIII, #35.)

Parents hurt when their children hurt. Parents are a child's main defense against the pressures of a drug culture. It is hard to remember that many of them started because they thought it was cool and *not* because their parents had failed.

What can parents do? If uncertain that the problem exists:

(1) Observe your child. Look for changes. Note the hours he or she keeps, attitude about school, appetite, and appearance.

(2) Talk to your child and note if he or she is muddled, inconsistent, unduly irritable, complaining about unhappy relationships.

(3) Express your concern. Tell what you have observed. Don't pretend that you don't notice things or that you will stay with the, "That's just kids (adolescents)" approach. Confront inappropriate behaviors. State your expectations. See if the behaviors improve.

Strategies

When certain that your child is an abuser:

(1) Take action. Consult your physician, the school counselor, or whoever will lead you to the place where your child can get help.

(2) Do not assume that the child will stop of his or her own accord.

(3) Be aware that any limits or punishment you now propose are after the fact. Action must be geared to stopping the habit and promoting emotional and personal recovery.

(4) Remember that you are not helpless. Make certain your child understands this. You are free to talk about your concerns or your willingness to go to law enforcement persons. Do not be persuaded by arguments such as, "Oh, Mom, you know I'd never do that!"

(5) Be a model of responsible behavior. As long as you continue to drink or smoke marijuana, there is no use lecturing the kids or insisting that they get help. If you use pills, such as antidepressants or sleeping pills, be certain you know why. Do your habits with so-called legal drugs (and alcohol is legal) give you credibility?

The child in therapy needs your support. You have identified the problem. You have taken action. You must stay involved.

Recovery from substance abuse is very difficult. *Prevention* is a much better course to take. Prevention must focus on your ability to take an *in-charge* position with your children and stick to it.

68. THE CHILD IN CRISIS

Crisis behavior is a breakdown of a once-successful coping style or a severe reaction to overwhelming stress. The child is terrified. The crisis is a dramatic cry for help; stress has taken its toll. It is unpredictable behavior for this person.

A crisis is stressful for everyone, whether it is an accident or a prolonged, dangerous display of uncontrolled emotions. Many parents witness breakdowns and appear totally surprised. "I never imagined that Dick was so upset," or, "I guess I never noticed that Marie was depressed, and now she's attempted suicide!" Don't blame yourself. Use the crisis as a springboard to repair or start to change what needs to be changed, after the child has been given immediate and significant support.

You may ask, "Did this kid run away or deliberately kill the cat just to get to me?" Perhaps the answer is yes, in part. Whatever the reason behind the crisis episode or event, I implore you to see the child's desperation and show love.

You may rationalize that teenage girls are naturally emotional and impulsive. You consider an episode (such as bursting out of the school building, cursing a teacher, or destroying her notebooks) as something that will pass. Please remember that most girls do not resort to crisis behaviors. This is special, intense, and an indication of overwhelming frustration or defeat.

A crisis may be precipitated by:

- Family problems, such as an announced divorce.
- Termination of a friendship or love affair.
- Death of someone important.
- School stress—exams ahead.
- A humiliating incident, such as a poor athletic performance, or a temper tantrum witnessed by others.
- Anxiety overload—money, illness, family problems, all combined.
- Reaction to drug or alcohol use.
- Peer pressure, gang power, or a breaking away from them.
- Fear of pregnancy, venereal disease, herpes.

Parents will:

- Take care of any emergency.
- Want to discover: Why a crisis now? Is this a plea for help to dry out, go cold turkey, get out of *this* school, confront parent drinking?
- Try to see if this is the child's way of seeking help for others, such as a mother's depression or a father's drinking.
- Consider what recent events or happenings may have caused the child to feel overwhelmed, and determine what support you can give now—even if belated.
- Be open to professional help for all concerned.

- Be willing to take some risks such as demanding that your child be placed with another teacher or in another school.

Listen to what the child has to say. Maybe all the child asks is for someone to take the time to be involved in his or her turmoil. After a crisis is over, make certain that your communication encourages frank sharing in order to prevent further episodes.

69. SUICIDE—THE CHOICE WITH NO RETURN

There is no more dramatic way for a child to show stress than to attempt or commit suicide. Everyone who has known the child feels guilty. The universal questions is "What could I have done?"

Childhood suicide is a rare occurrence, but is becoming more prevalent. In the U.S., more than 200 children under age fifteen committed suicide in 1979; 100,000 persons under age twenty five attempted suicide in 1980, and 200,000 to 300,000 more contemplated it. Nearly 5,000 young people under age twenty-five took their lives in 1981. It is second only to automobile accidents as a cause of death in the seventeen to twenty-five age group. Why the epidemic? What more dramatic, tragic way is there to cope with stress than to attempt to end life? It is the ultimate display of hostility and grief.

Young Children

Many young children who have attempted suicide harbored *chronic* stress.

- Had a history of feeling unwanted.
- Never experienced satisfactory relationships; felt worthless and unloved.
- Recently (within three months) lost someone close, usually by accident or suicide.
- Were school failures.
- Lived in a stress-saturated environment with emotionally unstable parents; often encountered violence at home and had strained relationships.
- Had a history of foster homes or adultless homes, or dependence on immature older siblings for care.
- Were frequently exposed to pills and drugs.
- Intended to die; did not harbor the hope that they would be rescued.
- Planned to commit suicide; gave away toys, pets, made elaborate preparations.

Most children who take their own lives hang themselves or take a drug overdose. Some use guns. The suicides are almost always a total surprise to the family, though afterward the loss of a loved one may be the ascribed reason. Frequently, these children have had a series of losses in their lives—through abandonment, by parental separation and divorce, and the loss of one, two or three subsequent stepparents.

A composite description of other children who killed themselves is very different. Many are seemingly well-adjusted, motivated middle-class youngsters. They may have known family turmoil, but outward appearances indicated that they had made comfortable adjustments.

Suicidal Teenagers

Not all who attempt suicide want to die. Many teenage girls, particularly, take pills in order to manipulate others. The message is, "If someone sees how desperate I am, I will get what I want." This may apply to boy friends, parents, or rules in school. Unfortunately, some of these attempts are fatal or successful. Unlike that of younger children, teenage suicidal behavior is often impulsive, showing up in one-car auto accidents or a drug overdose. Many are high or drunk. Suicide among American Indian youth is a major source of concern to tribal and community personnel. It is frequently blamed on the conflict between tribal and non-tribal lifestyles and the struggle to adjust to two cultures.

The most common reasons for teenage suicidal behaviors are:

- Feelings of inadequacy.
- Feelings of alienation from parents or others; an attitude that "no one cares."
- A divorce in the family.
- Cumulative frustration resulting from neighborhood problems, such as slum conditions.
- A history of learning disabilities (dyslexia, for example).
- A specific emotional blow, such as poor grades in school, loss of a girl friend or boy friend, a minor car accident.
- Too many uncertainties ahead and no sense of confidence that things will work out; a sense of hopelessness.
- Depression following a drug episode.
- The recent loss or death of an important relative, friend, or public hero.
- Lack of an adult model for an appropriate coping style; inappropriate adult models.
- Utter frustration, among the more gifted, at being unable to change depressing world conditions such as starvation or poverty.
- Sexual conflicts and anxiety.

Parents should note:

- Remarks such as, "I wish I were dead."
- Marked personality changes (for example, from outgoing to withdrawn).
- Prolonged depression.
- Inability to sleep, or sleeping too much.
- Marked change in school performance.
- Indications of putting things in order; giving away prized possessions, comments such as, "Take care of my dog."
- Conversation about suicide or death that indicates prolonged interest or overconcern.
- Unresolved grief; frequent visits to a cemetery; repeated expressions of guilt, emptiness.
- Severe reactions to family disruption or a move to a new place; a sense of aloneness or of having no friends.
- Unabated fury about something. "I'll get back at you, just you wait and see!"

Strategies for Parents

Should you observe such symptoms, please:

(1) Listen.

(2) Do not chide, scoff, belittle, or joke about the child's feelings.

(3) Ask direct questions such as, "Are you thinking of hurting yourself?" A child contemplating suicide may get significant relief by having a chance to talk over fears or despair. Rest assured, you are not planting the idea in the mind of a person under severe stress.

(4) If a person is threatening suicide, try to determine whether he or she has a plan. What method is mentioned (pills, gun, car, rope, carbon monoxide)? The more detailed a plan, the higher the risk.

(5) Involve a "significant other" —a friend, teacher, coach, or counselor—but do solicit help. Talk to the person in crisis. Be positive. Find nice things to say.

(6) Use community services, hot lines, and similar programs.

All suicidal persons are ambivalent. Part of them wants to die, but even the most severely depressed persons cling to some hope that things will get better. *This hope must be uncovered and nurtured.* Emphasizing the hope, helping with immediate decisions ("Put the gun down."), involving yourself and others can turn things around. The cry for help has been heeded. The children are not mentally ill, just desperate.

Use Professional Help

70. THERAPY IS A MUST

Therapy is a meaningful way to assist a child. There is nothing to be ashamed of when you go to a counselor, social worker, psychologist, or psychiatrist. You can be proud of yourself when you choose to join a group or an organization in order to help you or a child to cope with stressors successfully. When your car breaks down, you welcome the expertise of the mechanic. Have the same welcoming attitude toward experts in the mental health field.

Your attitude is pivotal to your child's attitude. When stress takes its toll, the time has come for a boost. It is essential if you are to rebuild or remodel the child's coping style and perhaps your own as well. Unpleasant or hostile relationships may improve considerably.

Don't wait for a crisis to consider therapy. Try to assess the seriousness of the symptoms you see. Ask others to assess them too.

Goals of Therapy

Whether in an office, detention center, juvenile hall, drug center, or school for offenders, the therapy must be structured to

(1) Establish or repair at least one important adult-child relationship. The child must be convinced that one person really cares. Without this belief, there will be little motivation to cooperate, change, or grow up.

(2) Help a child get through a severe crisis, a breakdown. Treatment may include medication, hospitalization with twenty-four hour supervision, or temporary placement in a mental health facility or foster home. It may call for advice in solving such problems as an unwanted pregnancy, threats to run away, peer fights, or irrational anger. Parental involvement will vary.

226

(3) Restore a sense of self-discipline and responsibility, a sense of impulse control.

(4) Improve the family system.

(5) Help the child emancipate or change his life circumstances if the family system will not work for him.

Often a parent wants to know what a therapist really does with a child. Therapists work on the theory that what goes on in the office cannot and will not be disclosed. Without violating confidentiality, a therapist may share basic concepts. By being informed of concepts and goals, a parent can relate to how difficult and complex therapy really is. It may also be painful for a child and the parents. The therapist will have to help the child to:

- Trust the therapist. This entails confidentiality, availability, and the freedom to express feelings. This takes time and patience. It will be tested.
- Take responsibility to control himself in the office. "You may not hurt me, you may not hurt yourself."
- Tell the truth. "I do not accept lies in this office."
- Put aside self-pity. Develop a philosophy that almost every child experiences rough times in growing up.
- Come in drug free. "If you are stoned, you are wasting my time and your money." This is essential in order to stay reality-oriented and to control emotions.
- Transfer a lot of anger from the parent to the therapist so that the child can let go of it.
- Accept that he or she can be a fine person, even when at odds with parents. Acknowledge friendships.
- Recognize where fears and feelings originate; view parental attitudes and treatment with objectivity.
- Accept the positive things that parents did on his or her behalf.
- Accept the parents' faults without having to emulate them.
- Set goals for self and be open to suggestions on how to achieve them. "Get a job," "Go get your high school equivalency certificate," or, "Move in with a friend."
- Lean less on parents for support and strive to become independent.
- Accept that perhaps he or she is more mature than one or both parents. This needs careful explanation because it may result in further parent-child distance.

Parent Involvement—Family Therapy

Many children improve and recover because their parents are willing to stay involved. If parents wash their hands of the situation, recovery becomes difficult. The children feel abandoned. In many instances, the child with severe symptoms of stress can be seen as the "token problem kid." This is the one whose behaviors and problems *show* that the family system is in trouble. This provokes anger and embarrassment. When a child cries for help, it is not fair to disclaim responsibility or deny that stress at home may have contributed to the situation. It follows that the recovery of the child will depend, at least in part, on the recovery of the family system. That's what *family therapy* demonstrates.

When parents are involved, certain concepts and goals will predictably be handled. The therapist will want to help:

- Parents and child find places where their relationship and communication can be repaired, to build mutual trust, to learn to reconcile expectations with reality.
- Parents let go of some old thoughts, attitudes, and habits. If necessary, become involved in programs such as Alcoholics Anonymous.
- Parents to change style of parenting, to be more assertive or less punitive, for example.
- Parents and child to express feelings openly, let go of secrecy, confront or list stressors.
- The family learn to stop blaming each other, to understand that all families have times of stress.

When relationships become unbearable, placement may be necessary. A reprieve from certain stressors may allow for repair. Whether on a short-range or long-range basis, both you and your child will adjust to being apart, perhaps far more readily than anyone imagined. The tree tends to grow straight, so they say, and so it is with kids. They can bend when they have to without breaking.

Stress takes its toll in so many ways. The children of the slums may face overwhelming stressors to the point that they feel a deep hatred towards others. They feel unwanted by everyone. Therapy is out of the question. Not so with the middle-class children who identify with their families, believing life holds something good for them; they are able to look ahead. For them, therapy is the boost that they need in order to rebuild damaged self-esteem and a successful coping style.

Therapy can help parents let go of any tendency to self-blame. Take advantage of help that is available. Everyone is capable of change. Impaired relationships can be improved and all members of a family can learn to exchange rewarding and loving expressions.

71. THERAPY RESOURCES

There are many qualified therapists in various settings.

Mental Health Centers

Typical Range of Services	Advantages	Disadvantages
Evaluation.	Inexpensive, based	Variable experience
Medication.	on diverse	of staff.
Family	services, groups,	Programs curtailed
involvement.	individual and	due to budget
Groups.	special concerns	cuts.
Placement.	(such as	
	alcoholism).	

Private Psychiatrists

Typical Range of Services	Advantages	Disadvantages
Evaluation.	Privacy ensured.	Expensive.
Medication.	Extended services.	Some are not
Hospitalization,	Special tests.	directive enough
twenty-four-hour		for the teenager
care.		in crisis.
Long-term therapy,		Some may prefer
personality		adult-only
reconstruction.		practice.
		Once-a-week may be
		too infrequent.
		Few, if any, groups.
		No placement
		service.
		Seldom totally
		family-oriented.

Other private services, including clinical psychologists, social workers, vocational counselors, educational diagnosticians, and learning disability specialists, may or may not have the medical backup required for prescriptions and hospitalizations. Additional resources include church groups and leaders who provide counseling to both individuals and families. The community may offer refuge for battered women and children, Alcoholics Anonymous, and other support resources. These may be very personal and helpful. Church or special-group resources may lack newly-advanced professional skills and input from external sources. They may also have built-in judgmental attitudes, particularly true when abortion and alternative lifestyles need to be addressed. Welfare Departments, another source, offer limited casework service on an ability-to-pay basis. Personnel may be limited and regulations may be a problem. Juvenile services are also available in certain locales, offering some crisis intervention, especially for younger abused children. Public agencies strive to maintain an ethnically balanced staff. However, the delivery of services may be very slow and inefficient as a result of large case loads and sometimes inexperienced staff workers.

The list of services includes special programs for the handicapped, the mentally retarded, and the alcohol or drug addict. Funds are available under certain circumstances for venereal disease or eye clinics as well as placement services.

Finally, the courts can back up a decision from other professionals (such as recommendations for placement, parole, probation). But courts, too, are frequently overloaded and understaffed.

Referral resources such as foster homes, detention centers, safe houses, and clinics are limited in many places.

In your situation, when you need help, you may want to start with someone in the local hospital, school persons, or an understanding member of the police or sheriff's department.

These persons will have varied training and professional experience, but they are all allied to the mental health field. They can help you find someone to become involved with your child. All concerned persons want to contribute to the repair or improvement of problems which have become so stressful.

CONCLUSION

The Benefits of Stress

When I was a little girl, I loved the stories that ended, "And they lived happily ever after." I believed them.

Relationships in my life were complicated and ambivalent. I wouldn't make up stories with happy endings. I got the impression that daydreaming was for happy kids.

Are the kids of today free to daydream? Or do they face too much stress? Have they been robbed of a chance to create their own fairies, goblins, monsters, and princesses?

Help your children handle stress so that they are free to have fun, be creative, and laugh. E.T., the extra-terrestrial movie character, was saved by the love of the children. They were able to bring him back to health and send him home. The magic of that love against the worldly panic of the adults was a touching story.

Real-life situations are touching, too. And children do "get better," thanks to the love and the help that is given to them.

Possible Benefits of Stress

Stress can be beneficial. A list of benefits may ease your anxieties and perhaps free you to have fun, to be creative, to laugh, and to daydream.

- Your child may be more self-reliant and feel more competent. "I can do that," or, "I have had to deal with tougher situations than this!"
- Your child may learn that there is no substitute for the open expression of feelings. "No need to hurt Mom, but she's got to know how I feel!"
- Your child may learn to turn to you or to friends, siblings, teachers, or others for support. Healthy dependency and interactive relationships may develop which otherwise might not have. "It's really neat that when I need help, I know I can get it from my dad (or mom). If I hadn't had this problem, I might never have learned how to ask."
- Your child may discover that honesty and sharing are indispensable in troubled times. "It sure helped when we admitted that we all had the same feelings about the divorce," or, "We were all relieved because the doctor was honest with us about Helen's condition. Sitting around guessing was much worse. Now we know what we have to do."
- Your child may become aware of how he or she makes decisions. One positive decision may be to do better at school. "I realized that I was using Rudy's death as an excuse for letting things slide. I decided I'd better get my act together. I'm still around and my grades are important."
- Your child may learn the importance of a sense of humor! A great joke can break the tensions.
- Your child may benefit from knowing that many others have had similar experiences and have handled them. Many will become aware that self-pity can become overwhelming, even boring, and that friends can be turned off by it.
- Your child may recover from stressful times with an increased understanding or tolerance for you. "Now I know why Mom was so crabby." "I'm sorry that Dad and I had so many fights. I didn't realize that he was having troubles at the office." "It isn't easy to put up with parents who fight a lot, but we can give it a try." "I think Mom tries very hard to be fair."
- Your child may learn that it is important to be independent. Others may not always be there to help. "I hoped I could ask my counselor to talk to my mom, but she was out of town. So I had to

do it myself, and that felt okay." "I guess I've learned that I better quit doing things I'm sorry for, because nobody can take the rap for me."

- Your child may learn a number of ways to be self-protective or to avoid being made a scapegoat. "Hey, Mom, stop screaming at me just because you're mad at Dad!" "I know we don't have much money in this family and I want to help. But let's make a deal so I can keep some of my babysitting money."
- Your child may learn his or her legal rights and ways to use them. Lawyers or accountants can explain about custody, inheritances, and college expenses, for instance.
- Your child may express his feelings about family ties if the family has to move from place to place.
- Your child will have known real experiences—the *real* world.

Stress doesn't have to be lonely. As children learn to cope, they rehearse the give and take of relationships. Stress doesn't have to be destructive. Children use stress to build and grow.

WHAT PARENTS WANT FOR THEIR CHILDREN:

Healthy self-esteem

Relationships that are satisfactory, lots of friends

A successful coping style

An excitement about learning – a positive attitude
about school

A healthy body

Few fears and worries

An appreciation of needs and feelings – their
own and those of others

Enthusiasm and joy about life – a ready smile
a sense of adventure

Rewards that come from attaining goals...
small, large, personal, societal.

A sense of satisfaction when they reach out to others
– close persons, the needy, helpless or distraught.

A sense of comfort when alone.

Pride as a member of the family.

No drug or alcohol dependence.

Self-acceptance – a comfortable acceptance of
limitations.

SELECTED REFERENCES/BIBLIOGRAPHY

INTRODUCTION

Arent , Ruth P. *The Child in Stress: Strategies for Support*, 2120 S. Holly, Denver, CO. 80222, 1980. Self-published.

Erikson, Erik H. *Childhood and Society.* N.Y.: W.W. Norton & Co. 1950.

Garmezy, Norman and Michael Rutter. *Stress, Coping and Development.* N.Y.: McGraw-Hill, 1983.

Goldberger, Leo and Shlomo Boeznitz. *Handbook of Stress; Theoretical and Clinical Aspects.* N.Y.: The Free Press, 1982.

Kuczen, Barbara. *Childhood Stress.* N.Y.: Delacorte Press, 1982.

Medeiros, Donald C., Barbara J. Porter, I. David Welch. *Children Under Stress.* Englewood Cliffs, N.J.: Spectrum Books, 1983.

Miller, Mary S. *Childstress.* Garden City, N.Y.: Doubleday, 1982.

Rhodes, Sonya and Josleen Wilson. *Surviving Family Life.* N.Y.: G.P. Putnam's Sons, 1981.

Selye, Hans. *Stress Without Stress.* N.Y.: Signet Books, 1974.

Wolff, Sula. *Children Under Stress.* N.Y.: Penguin Books, 1973.

SECTION I *WHAT PARENTS WANT FOR THEIR CHILDREN*

SECTION II *WHAT PARENTS NEED TO DO (1–4)*

Alberti, Robert E. and Michael L. Emmons. *Your Perfect Right.* San Luis Obispo, CA.: Impact Publications, Inc., 1970.

Alberti, Robert E. and Michael L. Emmons. *Stand Up, Speak Out, Talk Back.* N.Y.: Pocket Books, 1975.

Baer, Jean. *How to be an Assertive (Not Aggressive) Woman in Life, in Love and on the Job.* N.Y.: Signet Books, 1976.

Fensterheim, Herbert and Jean Baer. *Don't Say Yes When You Want to Say No.* N.Y.: David McKay Co., Inc., 1975.

235

SECTION III *PARENTS AS CARETAKERS* (5–9)

Ginnott, Haim G. *Between Parent and Child*. N.Y.: Avon Books, 1965.

Kennedy, Eugene. *Living With Everyday Problems*. Chicago: Thomas More Press, 1974.

York, Phyllis and David, Ted Wachtel. *Tough Love*. N.Y.: Bantam Books, 1982.

SECTION IV *AGES AND STAGES* (10–13)

Boston Women's Health Book Collective. *Ourselves and Our Children*. N.Y.: Random House, 1978.

Elkind, David. *The Hurried Child*. Reading, Mass.: Addison-Wesley Publishing Co., 1981.

Fraiberg, Selma H. *The Magic Years*. N.Y.: Simon & Shuster, 1973.

Gardner, Richard. *Understanding Children*. N.Y.: Jason Aronson, Inc., 1973.

Gesell, Arnold and Frances L. Ilg. *The Child from Five to Ten*. N.Y.: Harper & Bros., 1946.

Janov, Arthur. *The Feeling Child*. N.Y.: Simon & Schuster, 1973.

Kavanaugh, Dorriet, Ed. *Listen to Us! Children's Express Report*. N.Y.: Workmen's Pub., 1978.

Murphy, Lois Barclay. *The Widening World of Childhood*. N.Y.: Basic Books, 1962.

Spock, Benjamin, M.D. *Baby and Child Care*. N.Y.: Simon and Schuster, 1957.

Freidenberg, Edgar. *The Vanishing Adolescent*. N.Y.: Dell Publishing Co., 1962.

Ginott, Haim G. *Between Parent & Teenager*. N.Y.: Avon, 1969.

Gordon, Sol. *You*. N.Y.: New York Times Book Co., 1975.

Manatt, Marsha. *Parents, Peers and Pot*. Rockville, MD.: National Institute on Drug Abuse, 1982.

Mayer, Michael J. *How to Love, Understand and Cope With Teenagers*. Roslyn Hts., N.Y.: Libra Press, 1979.

SECTION V *THE FAMILY AS A SOURCE OF STRESS* (14–15)

Keniston, Kenneth and the Carnegie Council on Children. *All Our Children*. N.Y.: A Harvest/HBJ Book, 1977.

Coles, Robert and Jane Hallowell Coles. *Women of Crisis*. N.Y.: Delta, 1978.

Howard, Jane. *Families*. N.Y.: Berkley Books, 1980.

Lynn, David B. *The Father: His Role in Child Development*. Monterey, CA.: Brooks-Cole Publg. Co., 1974.

SECTION VI *THE INDIVIDUAL IN THE FAMILY* (16–30)

Arent, Ruth P. *The Gifted Child in Family Turmoil*, 2120 S. Holly, Denver, CO. 80222, 1985. Self-published.

Schnall, Maxine, "Why Young Marriages Break Up," Woman's Day (September 1978) pps. 42-44, 46, 48, 109.

Spock, Dr. Benjamin. *Baby & Child Care*. N.Y.: Pocket Books, 1946.

Arent, Ruth P. *The Gifted Child: Gifted Education at a Glance*. 2120 S. Holly, Denver, CO. 80222, 1978. Self-published.

Ginsberg, Gina and Charles H. Harrison. *How to Help Your Gifted Child*. N.Y.: Simon & Schuster, 1977.

G/C/T Magazine for parents, teachers of gifted, creative and talented children, Mobile, ALA. 36660.

SECTION VII *STRESS FROM PERSONAL PROBLEMS* (31–34)

Bruch, Hilde. *The Golden Cage: The Enigma of Anorexia Nervosa*. N.Y.: Vintage, 1979.

Chernin, Kim. *The Obsession*. N.Y.: Harper & Row, 1981.

Mederios, Donald C. and Barbara J. Porter, I. David Welch. *Children Under Stress*. Englewood Cliffs, N.J.: Prentice-Hall, 1983.

Murphy, Lois Barclay. *The Widening World of Childhood*. N.Y.: Basic Books, 1962.

Wolff, Sula. *Children Under Stress*. N.Y.: Penguin Books, 1973.

Arent, Ruth P. and Cora Ann Berryman. *Spice Chart of Learning Disabilities*. 2120 S. Holly, Denver CO. 80222, 1978. Self-published.

Feingold, Ben. *Why Your Child is Hyperactive*. N.Y.: Random House, 1975.

Gardner, Richard A. *MBD: The Family Book About Minimal Brain Dysfunction*. N.Y.: Jason Aronson, Inc., 1973.

Lewis, Richard, Alfred A. Strauss and Laura E. Lehtinen. *The Other Child The Brain-Injured Child*. N.Y.: Grune and Stratton, 1951.

Osman, Betty B. *Learning Disabilities: A Family Affair*. N.Y.: Random House, 1979.

Siegel, Ernest. *The Exceptional Child Grows Up*. N.Y.: E.P. Dutton, 1975.

LIVING WITH A LIFE-THREATENING ILLNESS

Request brochures from organizations such as: Leukemia Society of America, Cystic Fibrosis Foundation, Multiple Sclerosis Society, American Cancer Society, National Kidney Foundation, Children's Diabetes Foundation.

SECTION VIII　*CHRONIC STRESS AT HOME* (35–41)

Black, Claudia. *It Will Never Happen To Me: Children of Alcoholics.* Denver, CO.: M.A.C. Printing Division, 1981.

Milan, James R. and Katherine Ketcham. *Under the Influence.* Seattle: Madrona Publishing, 1981.

Wegscheider, Sharon. *The Family Trap.* St. Paul: Nurturing Networks, 1979.

Wegscheider. *Another Chance.* Palo Alto, CA.: Science and Behavior Books, 1979.

Herr, J. and J.H. Weakland. *Counseling Elders and Their Families.* N.Y.: Springer Pub. Co., 1979.

Mace, Nancy and Peter V. Rabins. *The 36-Hour Day.* Baltimore: John Hopkins Press, 1981.

Otten, J. and E.D. Shelley. *When Parents Grow Old.* N.Y.: McGraw-Hill, 1974.

Percy, Charles H., Sen. *Growing Old in the Country of the Young.* N.Y.: McGraw-Hill, 1974.

Sheehy, Gail. *Passages.* N.Y.: E.P. Dutton, 1976.

Silverstone, Barbara and Helen K. Hyman. *You and Your Aging Parent.* N.Y.: Pantheon Books, 1975.

Boyd, Dan. *The Three Stages.* National Assn. for Retarded Children Pamphlet, Arlington, TX. 1950.

Boyd, Dan. *The Three Stages.* National Assn. for Retarded Children Pamphlet, N.Y.: 1969.

Cunningham, Cliff and Patricia Sloper. *Helping Your Exceptional Baby.* N.Y.: Random House, 1978.

Isaacson, Robert. *The Retarded Child.* Niles, Ill.: Argus Communications, 1974.

Conway, Flo and Jim Siegelman. *Snapping.* N.Y.: Delta, 1979.

Driekurs, Rudolf. *Children: The Challenge.* N.Y.: Hawthorn Books, Inc., 1964.

James, William. *The Varieties of Religious Experience.* N.Y.: Mentor Books, 1958.

SECTION IX　*STRESS FROM OUTSIDE THE HOME* (42–43)

Fanjo, Mary, Barbara Hayes and Peg Isakson. "TV and Your Kid," *Knowing and Growing,* (March/April 1981), pp. 8-9.

Kuczen, Barbara. *Childhood Stress.* N.Y.: Delacorte Press, 1982.

Musan, Howard. "Teenage Violence and the Telly," Psychology Today, (March 1978), pp. 50-54.

Brown, George Isaac. *Human Teaching for Human Learning.* N.Y.: The Viking Press, 1972.

Glasser, William. *Schools Without Failure.* N.Y.: Harper & Row, 1969.

Henderson, George and Robert F. Bibens. *Teachers Should Care: Social Perspectives of Teaching.* N.Y.: Harper & Row, 1970.

Holt, John. *How Children Fail.* N.Y.: Delta Books, 1964.

Holt, John. *How Children Learn.* N.Y.: Pitman Pub. Co., 1969.

Kirschenbaum, Howard, Sidney B. Simon and Rodney W. Napier. *WAD-JE-GET? The Grading Game in American Education.* N.Y.: Hart Publ. Co., 1971.

NEA (National Education Assn.) Research Report. *Violence Against Teachers:* Washington, D.C., Feb./March 1979.

Robert, Marc. *Loneliness in the Schools.* Niles, Ill.: Argus Communications Press, 1973.

Silberman, Charles E. *Crisis in the Classroom.* N.Y.: Vintage Books, 1971.

SECTION X *SOCIAL PROBLEMS WHICH CREATE FAMILY STRESS (44–46)*

Harrington, Michael. *The Other America: Poverty in the U.S.* Baltimore: Penguin Books, Inc., 1971.

Leiner, Marvin. *Children of the Cities.* N.Y.: Plume Books, 1975.

Leinwand, Gerald. *Poverty and the Poor.* N.Y.: Washington Square Press, 1968.

Nelson, Paula. *The Joy of Money.* N.Y.: Bantam Books, 1977.

Collins, Emily. *The Whole Single Person's Catalog.* N.Y.: Peebles Press, 1979.

Dyer, Wayne W. *Pulling Your Own Strings.* N.Y.: Funk & Wagnalls, 1978.

Dyer, Wayne W. *The Sky's The Limit.* N.Y.: Simon & Schuster, 1980.

Feinberg, Mortimer R., Gloria Feinberg and John T. Tarrant. *Leavetaking: How to Successfully Handle Life's Most Difficult Crises.* N.Y.: Simon & Schuster, 1978.

Ford, Edward E. *Why Marriage?* Niles, Ill.: Argus Communications, 1974.

Guttentag, Marcia and Helen Bray. *Undoing Sex Stereotypes.* N.Y.: McGraw-Hill, 1976.

Halcomb, Ruth. *Women Making It.* N.Y.: Ballantine Books, 1979.

Klein, Carole, *Single Parent Experience.* N.Y.: Avon Books, 1973.

McNamara, Joan. *The Adoption Adviser.* N.Y.: Hawthorne Press, 1975.

Tripp, C.A. *The Homosexual Matrix.* N.Y.: Signet Books, 1975.

Brand, Stuart, Ed. *Whole Earth Catalog.* Sausalito, CA. 1968.

Buzan, Tony. *Use Both Sides of Your Brain.* N.Y.: E.P. Dutton, 1974.

Coons, John E. and Stephen D. Sugarman. *Education by Choice.* Berkeley: University of California Press, 1979.

Ferguson, Marilyn. *The Aquarian Conspiracy.* Los Angeles: J.P. Tarcher, Inc., 1980.

Howard, Ted and Jeremy Rifkin. *Who Should Play God?* N.Y.: Dell Books, 1978.

Martin, Del and Phyllis Lyon. *Lesbian Woman.* N.Y.: Bantam Books, 1972.

Naisbett, John. *Megatrends.* N.Y.: Warner Books, 1982.

Toffler, Alvin. *The Third Wave.* N.Y.: Morrow, 1980.

Tripp, C.A. *The Homosexual Matrix.* N.Y.: Signet Books, 1975.

White, John, Ed. *Frontiers of Consciousness.* N.Y.: Avon Books, 1975.

SECTION XI *SEPARATION AND DIVORCE* (47–53)

Arent, Ruth P. "Understanding the Child From the Single Parent Family," *Counseling and Human Development.* Denver: Love Publishing Co., April 1980.

Atkin, E., and Rubin E. *Part-time Father.* New York: Vanguard Press, 1977.

Blume, J. *It's Not the End of the World.* N.Y.: Bradbury Press, 1972.

Gardner, R.A. *The Boys and Girls Book About Divorce.* N.Y.: Bantam Books, 1970.

Gardner, R.A. *The Parents Book About Divorce.* Garden City, N.Y.: Doubleday & Co., 1977.

Grollman, E. *Explaining Divorce to Children.* N.Y.: Beacon Press, 1968.

Grollman, E. *Talking About Divorce: A Dialogue Between Parent and Child.* N.Y.: Beacon Press, 1975.

Krantzler, M. *Learning to Love Again.* N.Y.: Signet Books, 1976.

Macdonald, D. "The Stunted World of Teen Parents," *Human Behavior.* (January 1979), pp. 53–55.

Maddox, B. *The Half-Parent.* N.Y.: Signet Books, 1976.

Mann, P. *My Dad Lives in a Downtown Hotel.* N.Y.: Avon Books, 1973.

Rand, D. *I'm Going to Visit my Daddy.* San Rafael, CA.: Academic Therapy Publications, 1977.

Rhodes, Sonya and Josleen Wilson. *Surviving Family Life.* N.Y.: G.P. Putnam's Sons, 1981.

Robson, B. *My Parents are Divorced, Too.* N.Y.: Everest House, 1979.

Roosevelt, Ruth and Jeanette Lofas. *Living in Step.* N.Y.: McGraw-Hill, 1976.

Spike, Francine. *What About the Children? The Divorced Family, A Parents' Manual.* N.Y.: Crown Publishing, 1979.

Sullivan, J. *Mama Doesn't Live Here Anymore.* N.Y.: Pyramid Books, 1974.

Turow, R. *Daddy Doesn't Live Here Anymore.* Garden City, N.Y.: Anchor Books, 1978.

SECTION XII *DEATH: THE TRANSITION FROM TEARS TO TRANQUILITY* (54–57)

Berg, D.W., & G.G. Daugherty, "Teaching About Death." *Today's Education.*(1973), 46-47, 63.

Caine, L. *Widow.* N.Y.: Bantam Books, 1974.

Clay, V.A., "Children Deal With Death." *School Counselor.* (1976), 23, 175-184.

Grollman, E.A. *Talking About Death: A Dialogue Between Parent and Child.* Boston: Beacon Press, 1976.

Krementz, Jill. *How It Feels When a Parent Dies.* N.Y.: Alfred A. Knopf, Inc., 1981.

Kubler-Ross, E. *On Death and Dying.* N.Y.: Macmillan Publishing Co., 1969.

LeShan, E. *Learning to Say Goodbye.* N.Y.: Macmillan Publishing Co., 1976.

Mitford, J. *The American Way of Death.* Greenwich, CT.: Fawcett Publishing Co., 1963.

Robinson, C.M. "Developmental Counseling Approach to Death and Dying Education." *Elementary School Guidance and Counseling,* Vol. 12 #3, 178-187. Feb. 1978.

Schiff, H.S. *The Bereaved Parent.* New York: Crown Publishers, 1977.

Stein, S.B. *About Dying: An Open Family Book for Parents and Children Together.* N.Y.: Walker & Co., 1974.

Viorst, J. *The Tenth Good Thing About Barney.* Hartford, CT.: Atheneum, 1971.

Zolotow, C. *My Grandson Lew.* N.Y.: Harper & Row, 1974.

SECTION XIII *VIOLENCE AND ABUSE: THERE IS NO MORE TRAUMATIC WAY TO LIVE* (58–61)

Boyles, Peter. "Running on Empty." *Denver Magazine,* (June 1981), pp. 26-31.

Bush, Sheila. "Child Killers: The Murderer is Often the Mother." *Psychology Today,* (November 1978), p. 28.

Davidson, Terry. *Conjugal Crime: Understanding and Changing the Wifebeating Pattern.* N.Y.: Hawthorn Books, Inc., 1978.

Erickson, Erik. *Gandhi's Truth on the Origins of Militant Nonviolence.* N.Y.: W.W. Norton & Co., 1969.

Fontana, Vincent G. *The Maltreated Child.* Springfield, Ill.: 2nd. ed., Charles C. Thomas, 1971.

Fontana, Vincent G. *Somewhere a Child is Crying.* N.Y.: Macmillan, 1973.

Foote, Carol. "Getting Tough About Rape." *Human Behavior,* (December 1978), pp. 24-26.

Hamill, Pete. "Why More Children Will Be Born to be Brutalized." *Rocky Mountain News*, (Oct. 1981), p. 45.

Helfer, Ray E. and Henry C. Kempe, Ed. *The Battered Child*. Chicago: 2nd Ed., The University of Chicago Press, 1974.

Herbruck, Christine C. *Breaking the Cycle of Child Abuse*. Minneapolis: Winston Press, 1979.

Hotchkiss, Sandy. "The Realities of Rape." *Human Behavior*, (December 1978), pp. 18-23.

Kempe, Henry and Ruth S. *Child Abuse, Developing Child*. Cambridge, Mass.: Harvard University Press, 1978.

Kindley, Mark. "Battered Husbands, The Story Never Told." *Denver Magazine*, (August 1977) pp. 31-33.

Martin, Del. *Battered Wives*. N.Y.: Pocket Books, 1977.

Mead, Margaret and James Baldwin. *A Rap on Race*. N.Y.: Delta Books, 1972.

Muson, Howard. "Teenage Violence and the Telly." *Psychology Today*, (March 1978) pp. 50-53.

Rogers, Dale E. *Hear the Children Crying: The Child Abuse Epidemic*. Charlotte, N.C.: Commission Press, Inc., 1978.

Wertham, F.A. *A Sign for Cain: An Exploration of Human Violence*. N.Y.: Macmillan, 1966.

INCEST/SEXUAL ASSAULT
Adams, Caren and Jennifer Fay. *No More Secrets*. San Luis Obispo, CA.: Impact Pubs., 1981.

Hammer, Signe. *Passionate Attachments: Fathers and Daughters in America Today*. N.Y.: Rawson Assoc., 1982.

Herman, Judith L. *Father-Daughter Incest*. Cambridge, Mass.: Harvard University Press, 1981.

Woodbury, John and Elroy Schwartz. *The Silent Sin*. N.Y.: Signet, 1971.

SECTION XIV *THE FAMILY ON THE MOVE* (62–63)

United Van Lines Pamphlet. *Moving With Children*. 1978.

Shuval, Judith T. *Migration and Stress* (Handbook of Stress) N.Y.: The Free Press, 1982 (pp. 677-91).

SECTION XV *EXAMPLES OF UNSUCCESSFUL COPING* (64–69)

D'Ambrosio, Richard. *No Language But a Cry*. N.Y.: Dell Pub., 1970.

Foy, Jessie Gray. *Gone is Shadow's Child*. N.Y.: Pyramid Books, 1972.

Montarava, A.J. and Arthur Henley. *The Difficult Child*. N.Y.: Stein and Day, 1979.

Redl, Fritz and David Wineman. *Children Who Hate*. N.Y.: Free Press, 1951.

Von Hilsheimer, George. *How to Live With Your Special Child.* Washington, D.C.: Acropolis Books, 1970.

SECTION XVI *USE PROFESSIONAL HELP* (70–71)

Allen, Frederick II. *Psychotherapy With Children.* N.Y.: W.W. Norton Co., 1942.
Barten, Harvey H. and Sybil S. *Children and Their Parents in Brief Therapy.* N.Y.: Behavioral Pub., 1973.

COMMUNITY RESOURCES

ALCOHOLISM

For men and women who share the common problems of alcoholism:
Alcoholics Anonymous
P.O. Box 459
Grand Central Station
New York, N.Y. 10163
Phone 212-686-1100

For relatives and friends of persons with an alcohol problem:
Al-Anon Family Groups, Inc.
P.O. Box 182
Madison Square Station
New York, N.Y. 10159
Phone 212-683-1771

BLINDNESS

For blind persons and their families and friends:
National Federation of the Blind
1800 Johnson St.
Baltimore, MD. 21230
Phone 301-659-9314

CANCER

For persons with cancer and their families:
Make Today Count
P.O. Box 303
Burlington, Iowa 52601
Phone 319-753-6521

For parents of children with cancer:
The Candlelighters Foundation
2025 Eye Street, N.W., Suite 1011
Washington, D.C. 20006
Phone 202-659-5136

For women who have had or are about to have mastectomies:
Reach to Recovery
777 Third Avenue
New York, N.Y. 10017
Phone 212-371-2900

CATASTROPHIC ILLNESS

For patients with cancer, multiple sclerosis, strokes, arthritis, and other
catastrophic illnesses, and their families:
We Can Do
P.O. Box 723
Arcadia, CA. 91006
Phone 818-357-7517

CEREBRAL PALSY

For those with cerebral palsy and their families:
United Cerebral Palsy Association, Inc.
66 East 34th St.
New York, N.Y. 10016
Phone 212-481-6300

CHILDREN'S PROBLEMS

For autistic children and their families:
National Society for Children and Adults with Autism
1234 Massachusetts Ave., N.W., Suite 1017
Washington, D.C. 20005
Phone 202-783-0125

For parents who abuse their children:
Parents Anonymous
22330 Hawthorne
Torrance, CA. 90505
Phone 800-421-0353 (except California: 800-352-0386)

Kempe National Center for the Prevention and Treatment of Child Abuse and Neglect
1205 Oneida St.
Denver, Colo. 80020
Phone 1-800-525-0246

For parents and friends of youth with alcohol or drug dependency or other behavioral problems:
Families Anonymous
P.O. Box 528
Van Nuys, CA. 91408
Phone 818-989-7841

For young diabetics and their parents:
The Juvenile Diàbetes Foundation
60 Madison Avenue
New York, N.Y. 10010
Phone 1-800-223-1138 (in New York: 212-889-7575)

For parents and families of handicapped children:
Closer Look
1201 16th St., N.W.
Washington, D.C. 20036
Phone 202-822-7900

For children and adults with learning disabilities:
Association for Children and Adults with Learning Disabilities
4156 Library Road
Pittsburgh, PA. 15234
Phone 412-341-1515

For adopted children who are trying to locate their birth parents:
Adoptees in Search, Inc.
P.O. Box 41016
Bethesda, MD. 20014
Phone 301-656-8555

For help in finding missing children:
Find-Me, Inc.
P.O. Box 1612
La Grange, GA. 30241
Phone 404-884-7419

Missing Children of America
P.O. Box 10-1938
Anchorage, AK. 99510
Phone 907-243-8484

For children in need of a big brother or big sister relationship:
Big Brothers and Big Sisters League of America
220 Suburban Station Bldg.
Philadelphia, PA. 10103

EMOTIONAL, MENTAL PROBLEMS

For bereaved parents:
The Compassionate Friends
P.O. Box 1347
Oak Brook, ILL. 60521
Phone 312-323-5010

For persons with emotional problems (depression, anxiety, phobias):
Emotions Anonymous
P.O. Box 4245
St. Paul, Minn. 55104
Phone 612-647-9712

For family and friends of the severely mentally ill:
National Alliance for the Mentally Ill
1200 15th St., N.W., Suite 400
Washington, D.C. 20005
Phone 202-833-3530

For mentally retarded children and adults and their families:
National Assn. for Retarded Citizens of the United States
2501 Avenue J
Arlington, TEX. 76011
Phone 817-640-0204

For the mentally and emotionally ill:
Neurotics Anonymous
P.O. Box 4866
Cleveland Park Station
Washington, D.C. 20008
Phone 202-628-4379

National Assn. for Mental Health
1800 N. Kent St.
Arlington, VA. 22209

EPILEPSY

For epileptics and their families:
The Epilepsy Foundation of America
4351 Garden City Drive
Landover, MD. 20785

FAMILY

Planned Parenthood Federation of America
810 7th Ave.
New York, N.Y. 10019
Phone 212-541-7800

American Assn. of Marriage & Family Counselors
225 Yale Ave.
Clairemont, CA. 91711

Parents and Friends of Lesbians and Gays
Box 24565
Los Angeles, CA. 90024
Phone 213-472-8952

HEART PROBLEMS

For persons who have successfully undergone heart surgery and their
families and friends:
Mended Hearts, Inc.
7320 Greenville Ave.
Dallas, TEX. 75231
Phone 214-750-5442

JOINT CUSTODY

The Joint Custody Association
10606 Wilkins Ave.
Los Angeles, CA 90024

MUSCULAR DYSTROPHY

For patients with muscular dystrophy and related disorders, and their
families:
Muscular Dystrophy Association
810 17th Ave.
New York, N.Y. 10019
Phone 212-586-0808

NARCOTICS

For narcotic addicts:
Narcotics Anonymous
16155 Wyandotte St.
Van Nuys, CA. 91406
Phone 818-780-3951

For people concerned about drug abuse:
Nar-Anon Family Group Headquarters, Inc.
P.O. Box 2562
Palos Verdes Peninsula, CA. 90274

National Clearinghouse for Drug Abuse Information
11400 Rockville Pike
Rockville, MD. 20852

PARKINSON'S DISEASE

For Parkinson's patients and their families:
National Parkinson Foundation, Inc.
1501 N.W. Ninth Ave.
Miami, FLA. 33136
Phone 800-327-4545 (except Florida: 800-433-7022)

WEIGHT PROBLEMS

For compulsive overeaters:
Overeaters Anonymous
2190 West 190th St.
Torrance, CA. 90504
Phone 213-320-7941

WIDOWED AND DIVORCED PERSONS

For single parents and their children:
Parents Without Partners
7910 Woodmont Ave.
Bethesda, MD. 20814
Phone 800-638-8078 (except Maryland: 301-654-8850)

For widows and widowers of all ages:
The Widowed Persons Service
1909 K Street, N.W.
Washington, D.C. 20049

For young and middle-aged widows and widowers and their families:
Theos Foundation
12 Federal Dr., Suite 410
Pittsburgh, PA. 15235
Phone 412-243-4299

For widowed or retired persons with a desire to help others:
Retired Senior Volunteer Program
Volunteers of American Nat'l Headquarters
3813 N. Causeway Blvd.
Metairie, LA. 70002
Phone 504-837-2652

For any widowed persons:
Widowed Men and Women of America
Box 1597
Wheatridge, Colo. 80034
Phone 303-458-5447

You can write or phone the national headquarters of the groups listed above, or look in your phone book to see if a local chapter is listed.

For information on self-help groups not listed here, write or call: National Self-Help Clearinghouse, 33 West 42nd Street, Room 1222, New York, New York 10036. Phone 212-840-1259.

Index